The Investor's Self-Teaching Seminars

INVESTING IN
GROWTH

FINDING THE NEXT WINNERS
ON WALL STREET

Philip B. Capelle

PROBUS PUBLISHING COMPANY
Chicago, Illinois
Cambridge, England

ISBN 1-55738-298-0

Printed in the United States of America

IPC

2   3   4   5   6   7   8   9   0

To my late Mother and Father.
Thank you for stressing the value of an education.

CONTENTS

LIST OF FIGURES

LIST OF TABLES

PREFACE

Back in October of 1970, Wal-Mart stores raised a little under $5 million in its initial public offering. At that time, sales for this small growth company totaled a mere $44 million. By the end of the fiscal year 1992 (ending January 31, 1991), sales had grown a thousandfold to over $44 billion; Wal-Mart became America's most successful retailer. From the initial public offering until the end of 1991, $1 invested in Wal-Mart's stock would have soared in value to more than $1,800! This represents an annual compound growth rate of over 42% for more than 21 years. Obviously, finding anything even remotely close to the next Wal-Mart could do wonders for your financial well-being.

This book is designed to show serious investors like yourself how to find the next winners on Wall Street and how to take advantage of America's top-performing investment. By properly allocating a portion of your assets into small stocks, you may be able to earn a return on your money that is well above that offered by more conservative investments. Indeed, a properly run small growth stock investment program can be so crucial to your financial future that this may be one of the most important books you will read on investing.

This book is a step-by-step course on how to maximize your profits in small stocks. It presents a sensible approach that covers the basics as well as the fine points of investing in small stocks. You will be taught how to choose and work with a broker, how to manage your portfolio and control your costs, and of course, how to find the next winners on Wall Street.

In my many years of counseling individual investors, I have seen all too many investors make the same fundamental mistakes which can undermine one's investment performance. Such erroneous decision making is totally unnecessary. As always, there is a right and a wrong way of doing things. By the time that you are done with this book, you will be prepared to embark on a successful long-term investment program.

One of the best ways to learn is by doing. Questions are presented at the end of seven of the chapters to test your knowledge and understanding of the text. Answering them successfully should give a boost to your confidence and prepare you to enter the potentially rewarding arena of small growth stocks. To answer the questions you will need a calculator and some basic knowledge of how returns are compounded. Answers are provided at the end of the book.

One note before you begin. The male pronoun has been used throughout the book strictly for convenience. Readers should recognize he also refers to she, and so forth.

I have had a lot of fun writing this book. I truly hope that you find it to be enjoyable reading and that it helps you to find the next winners on Wall Street.

ACKNOWLEDGMENTS

There are a number of people who have been instrumental in helping me with this book, as well as throughout the years during my career in finance. I would like to especially thank John Valenzuela for his friendship and support over the years and for making several valuable comments on the manuscript. Robert Fukunaga provided me with support and enthusiasm for the project. Fred Kalmus taught me to look for "The Gift" in all of life's adversities. I would like to thank Richard Lingley for the opportunity to work with him in the investment advisory business. It was a pleasure to work with Jean Suits and Bob Goss. Special thanks to Mike Stone for believing in my work and to Rick Reif and Dan Cook at the *Orange County Business Journal*. It has been a pleasure to work with people such as Ed Hafer, Margaret Lukaszewicz, and Len Johnson over the years. I would like to thank the people at Probus for their belief in me and for their enthusiasm for the book and helpful suggestions. It was a pleasure to work with Maria Romano, who edited the text.

I have been lucky to have the support of many fine people at Cruttenden and Company. Kathy McLuckey has been a friend and has been very helpful every step of the way. Denise Petersen has offered constant encouragement for all of my projects. Steve DeLuca provided invaluable suggestions for improving the manuscript and on my regular column on investing. Thanks also to Walter Cruttenden, Brad Weddon, Linda Hunt, Dan Jensen, Tom Stellar, and Don Summerell.

I am especially thankful to Lori Cortez, without whose help this book would not have been possible. Lori enthusiastically typed and corrected the entire manuscript. My thanks and apologies to those I may have inadvertently forgotten who have helped along the way.

Philip B. Capelle
Huntington Beach, CA

Chapter 1

INTRODUCTION TO SMALL COMPANY GROWTH STOCKS

Small company growth stocks have been America's top performing investment over the last 66 years. This record of performance has in turn made them a valuable means of helping individual investors meet their financial goals. Because small growth stocks as a whole are comprised of relatively new businesses, they in turn carry with them a greater degree of risk than is associated with large, well-known blue chip stocks. Many investors, therefore, have stayed away from small growth stocks, despite their potential for increasing one's net worth. The chapters ahead present you with some techniques for investing that should enable you to buy small growth stocks with complete confidence. After you've completed this book and begin to invest for growth, be forewarned that you will make some mistakes. Even the best investors are prone to error. Because of this, this book will also teach you how to build a portfolio of small growth stocks. By diversifying your assets, you will lower your risk and increase your chances for a successful investment program.

1

SMALL GROWTH STOCKS DEFINED

When defining a small growth stock, it is important to first understand that there are no hard and fast rules to the selection process or to determining just what exactly a small company growth stock is. In this age of computerized databases, many analysts have tried to take the easy way out by plugging a few key variables into a computer screen and, presto, out pops a list of potential small growth stock purchase candidates. With this in mind, we'll make a few generalizations about just what is and what isn't a growth stock. But bear in mind that when it comes to stock selection, rules are often made to be broken.

As part of the weeding-out process, you can eliminate stocks in the Dow Industrials, which are mistakenly referred to by many as *the market.* The Dow is comprised of 30 very well-known giants of corporate America. All of these companies once started out as small growth stocks, but after 20 to 50 or more years in business their days of above average growth are largely behind them. This is not to say that some of them won't continue to do well in the years ahead. General Electric, Coca Cola, Philip Morris, and Merck are four names in the Dow that seem to defy the odds while continuing to grow at impressive rates. But on the whole, the case against investing in large capitalization issues is a simple one. It's simply very difficult for them to double sales in five years from a base of $5 billion to $10 billion or $20 billion. In addition, if they introduce a hot new product, it can do little to meaningfully improve sales on a percentage basis. On the other hand, it may not require much for a small growth company with a hot product or two to double sales within just a few years.

The Standard and Poor's 500 is a favorite index of professional money managers. Indeed, for many money managers their livelihood and year-end bonuses depend on beating this benchmark. Although this index obviously contains many stocks smaller than the components of the Dow, most of them are still of a size too great to be considered truly exciting small growth stocks. This does not rule out all S&P 500 issues as potential purchases; it only means that by and large you'll do better looking elsewhere.

At the other end of the spectrum of stocks to largely omit from your small growth stocks portfolio are the so-called penny stocks. Stocks priced below $1 are fraught with risk for a couple of good reasons. First of all, you may be tempted by an unscrupulous broker into investing in a company that's really just part of an elaborate scam. Secondly, you may find yourself involved in a legitimate company that simply can't cut the mustard. If you invest in a $10 stock and you see that things are going wrong, it's not too hard to realize your mistake and sell out at $7 for a 30% loss. By contrast, it's all too easy to buy a stock for 75 cents and watch it go to 0 cents for a 100% loss of your money.

So as a rule of thumb, generally you should consider only those issues above $5 per share as small growth stock candidates. If you do yield to temptation, just make sure that you do all of your homework and then some. Small growth stocks shouldn't be too big or too small. As a broad generalization you can figure that most solid small growth stocks trade between $5 and $30 per share. When a successful company reaches $30 or above they tend to split the shares to attract new investors, which helps to keep the price low. Total annual sales should be in the neighborhood of $10 million to $500 million. And, of course, a small growth stock should be growing sales and earnings at an above average rate.

RETURNS ON SMALL GROWTH STOCKS

Returns on small growth stocks and other investments can vary widely from month to month or year to year. However, over the long haul, expected returns tend to gravitate towards the norm. Ibbotson Associates is a Chicago-based research firm that has calculated the historical returns for a number of financial assets going back to 1926. Their findings verify the superiority of small growth stocks as America's best investment. They also give an idea of what you can reasonably expect to earn from a number of investments over the long run.

One dollar invested in small growth stocks in 1926 would have grown to $1,847 by the end of 1991 (Figure 1-1). (*Note:* In this and the following examples, the Ibbotson study assumes reinvestment of dividends, capital gains, and interest.) In contrast, that original dollar invested in common stocks back in 1926 would have grown to $675 by the end of 1991. In either case, investing in stocks has paid off handsomely over the 66-year test period. Investors who stuck with interest-bearing investments would have been, by comparison, extremely disappointed with their results. Holders of long-term government bonds would now have $21.94 to show for their original dollar. T-Bill investors would have done even worse, as their dollar would have grown to only $11.01. Obviously, taking an ownership position by investing in stocks, and especially small growth stocks, has proven to be by far the best strategy when compared to loaning your money to the government.

Figure 1-1
Wealth Indices of Investments in the U.S. Capital Markets

Value of $1 invested at the end of 1925

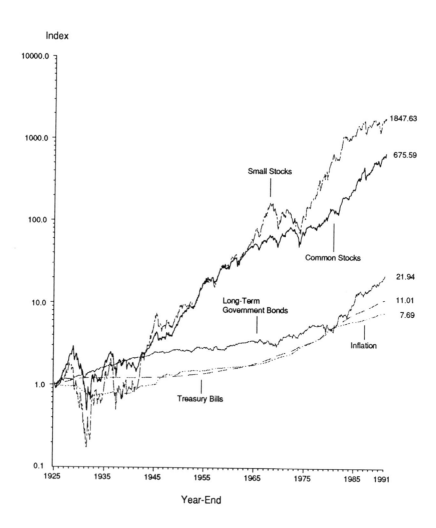

Source: Ibbotson Associates, Chicago.

The results discussed above can be converted into annual percentage gains to give you an idea of how each investment has performed on a yearly basis. These returns are listed in Table 1-1.

One of the most striking points about Table 1-1 is the power of compounding over the long haul. The 10.4% earned by common stocks enabled that original dollar to grow to a rather handsome sum. With the power of compounding at work, the extra 1.7% earned annually by small growth stocks (in excess of common stocks) resulted in a near tripling of the money made in common stocks.

As impressive as the small stock gains are above, it is possible that you could have done even better. The 12.1% annual compound rate earned by small growth stocks is for the average stock within that group. By putting to work the stock picking skills you'll learn in this book, you can quite possibly beat that average by a few percentages each year. Table 1-2 demonstrates how much $10,000 would grow to if you are able to beat the historical small growth stock returns over several different time frames.

Table 1-1
Investment Performance from 1926 to 1991

Compound Rate of Return—$1 Grows To . . . .

Small Growth Stocks	12.1%	$1,847.63
Common Stocks	10.4%	$ 675.59
Long-Term Government Bonds	4.8%	$ 21.94
Treasury Bills	3.7%	$ 11.01
Inflation	3.1%	$ 7.69

Table 1-2
$10,000 Grows to . . . .

	Years	10	15	20	25
Historical Average	12.1%	$31,337	$ 55,473	$ 98,200	$ 173,836
3% Above the Average	15.1%	$40,809	$ 82,438	$166,535	$ 336,421
5% Above the Average	17.1%	$48,481	$106,746	$235,038	$ 517,514
10% Above the Average	22.1%	$73,647	$199,804	$542,392	$1,491,945

As you can see, by exercising your skills and thus beating the averages by a few percentages each year, your money can grow to a substantial sum over the long run. By taking the long-term view toward investing (as demonstrated above), small growth stocks can help you meet your long-term goals of funding your children's education or planning for your retirement.

BEATING THE HISTORICAL AVERAGES

The historical returns discussed are the average returns you can expect over the long haul. However, there are periods when a good thing, such as investing in small growth stocks, gets even better. The market moves in cycles that can last for several years or longer. Sometimes large stocks are in favor. At other times small growth stocks will lead the way.

In its initial stages, the bull market that began in August 1982 was a powerhouse for both big and small stocks. However, as the years passed, the market came to favor the large capitalization issues. Meanwhile, small growth stocks lagged behind. T. Rowe Price and Associates manages a group of mutual funds, including its New Horizon Fund, which invests in small company growth stocks. The fund is compared each quarter to the S&P 500, an index which is dominated by large stocks. When the price to earnings ratio of the New Horizons Fund is twice that of the S&P 500, that's a sign that small company stocks are fully valued. The last time this indicator's reading was above 2.0 was in June 1983 (Figure 1-2). (See Chapter 3 for an in-depth discussion of price to earnings ratio.)

From 1983 until stocks reached an important peak in August 1987, small stocks failed to match the performance of the highly capitalized

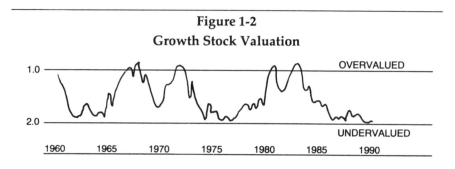

Figure 1-2
Growth Stock Valuation

Credit: T. Rowe Price and Associates.

issues by a wide margin. Then came the crash of 1987, followed by a bear market in 1990. These two market declines brought growth stocks down to their second lowest relative valuation since T. Rowe Price and Associates began keeping the indicator back in 1961. By September of 1991, the indicator stood at .96. With the market, sometimes enough is enough. Small stocks that had suffered for seven years had finally reached an extreme of undervaluation. This lackluster performance has possibly set the stage for a multi-year stretch where small stocks may turn out to be the market's new leaders. When small stocks do return to favor, they are often able to substantially outperform their historical average of 12.1% for several years at a time. Indeed, a good thing can get even better. Following the bear market of 1990, the NASDAQ Composite (a measure of small growth performance) soared 57% in 1991 alone.

THE INDIVIDUAL INVESTOR AND SMALL GROWTH STOCKS

There are basically three groups that make up the bulk of investors in small growth stocks: individuals, corporate insiders, and institutions. The big institutions include pension plans, banks, insurance companies, and mutual funds. Out of necessity, they normally confine their purchases to larger stocks which they can buy and sell with relative ease. However, they will nibble at small growth stocks that they feel have exceptional promise. Corporate insiders may hold large chunks of stocks in the small companies that they work for. They are restricted as to how much stock they can sell at any time. Their buying is much smaller in comparison to their selling. By far, the biggest source of demand for small growth stocks comes from the individual investor.

Individuals can invest in a small growth stock much easier than the big institutions can without disturbing the current price of stock. Perhaps the reason why small stocks turned in such a poor relative performance from June 1983 until October 1991 was that the individual investor largely avoided stocks.

Many potential stock market investors have stayed on the sidelines instead because of the relatively high rates of interest that were available throughout most of the 1980s. Even though rates peaked in 1981, they were still high enough throughout the decade to provide stiff competition for stocks. However, by the end of 1991, short-term interest rates had tumbled to their lowest level since the early 1960s. Those who have been satisfied with the comfort and safety of interest-bearing securities have had to rethink their strategy in light of the new financial reality of low single-digit interest rates. A number of these investors will seek the rewards offered by small growth stocks. This increasing interest in stocks could help fuel a decade-long small stock bull market.

The real estate market has also kept a number of would-be stock investors out of the market. Why, they argue, should you take the risk of owning stocks when real estate is such a sure thing? It certainly seemed that way for a while as the combination of leverage and inflation, along with the proper location, made real estate a bonanza for millions of individual investors throughout the 1970s and 1980s. Unfortunately for the fans of real estate, however, no market stays in an uptrend forever without suffering periodic setbacks along the way. In real estate's case, the setback could very well last for many years, nationally speaking.

There will always be pockets of strength in any market, but on the whole, returns from real estate could be repressed for some time to come. Demographics point toward a lessening of demand for single family housing. Meanwhile, vacancy rates of up to 20% in some cities suggest that it will take years before the excess building in commercial real estate is completely worked off. Therefore, it is reasonable to conclude that a great number of real estate investors may shift over to stocks while their market languishes behind.

Even though many income and real estate investors will convert to stocks, a great many more may continue to fail to benefit from America's top investment. There could be a number of reasons for this, but for the majority who avoid stocks it will be due to the fear of losing money. Hopefully, because you bought this book, you are an eager investor who is ready to work and to take advantage of the opportunity provided by small growth stocks. If you still have your doubts about investing in small growth stocks, try to figure out why they exist and then expel them from your mind.

Unfortunately, all too many investors are still haunted by memories of the crash of 1987 when the Dow Industrials plunged over 20% in one day. They may have sold their stocks and sworn off the market for good. As you will learn later in the book, market declines like the crash of 1987 are opportunities to buy stocks at bargain prices. In fact, as this is being written, the Dow Industrials have risen over 70% from the lows of the crash. In retrospect, the crash and the decline that led up to the crash should be viewed as a very sharp and violent bear market that corrected the excesses of a market that had run from Dow 770 to Dow 2,720 in just five years. Therefore, if the crash is your excuse for not investing in the market, put it in perspective and put it behind you. And remember, this book is all about investing in individual stocks, not the market. As long as you do your homework and buy good solid companies for the long haul, you can be reasonably certain that a good company and, therefore, a good stock, will overcome any short-term deficiencies in the market.

SUMMARY

- Since 1926, small growth stocks have been America's top performing investment.

- Secular trends will every so often especially favor small growth companies.

- T. Rowe Price and Associates' indicator measures relative valuation of small versus large stocks. In September 1990, it reached its second lowest level in 30 years.

- The crash of 1987 proved to be a great buying opportunity—unfortunately some investors developed "CD-itis."

- Your investment returns should cover inflation and taxes plus deliver a positive real rate of return.

- Real estate and other beneficiaries of inflation may take a backseat to stocks in the 1990s; stocks may be the investment of choice for the 1990s and beyond.

- Ibbotson Associates' data show small growth stocks have compounded at 12.1% since 1926.

- The system has been geared to rewarding risk takers and those who assume an ownership position.

- Compounding a few percentages above the average can magnify your returns substantially over time. Skillful investors can and do beat the averages.

- Small growth stocks can be an important part of a sound overall strategy that is designed to meet your long-term objectives.

- You probably won't find small growth stocks in the S&P 500 and definitely not in the Dow Industrials.

- Avoid so-called penny stocks in your quest for small growth stock profits.

- Use a minimum price of $3 to $5 as a rule of thumb for your small stock purchases.
- Small growth stock revenues should be in a range of above $10 million to $500 million.

Chapter 2

INVESTING IN SMALL GROWTH STOCKS

Investing in the small growth stock arena will require that you practice the proper mechanics of investing your money. It also entails opening an account and establishing a relationship with the brokerage that is right for your needs. Knowing the "how to" of placing orders and dealing with brokers will save you from a great deal of frustration. Unfortunately, all too many investors bypass these key ingredients for investment success and survival. Instead, they simply open an account and start buying and selling stock. Little attention is paid to first gaining an understanding of the fine points involved with a successful investment program. The following pages will examine some of the basic fundamentals that should improve your chances for success.

OPENING AN ACCOUNT

Obviously, nothing can happen until you open an account and get ready to do business. This seemingly innocuous step may wind up in the long run to be one of the biggest decisions you will make. Some will head right away to a discounter, thinking that saving on commissions is the most critical factor to making money. Wrong. Others will open an account at a big name brokerage based on an ad they saw on TV. The odds are that they will be siphoned off to the broker of the day, who may be a rookie with very little experience in handling other people's money. Of course, this is no way to treat your financial future. Like anything else, there is a right and a wrong way of doing things. This chapter presents some guidelines to consider before opening your account. If you are already an investor, perhaps these suggestions will help if you find your current brokerage experience to be less than satisfactory.

Over the last five to ten years, there has been a substantial growth in the demand for the services of discount brokerages. Clearly, the do-it-yourself concept of investing has taken hold, especially as information is now more easily and quickly disseminated than ever before. Home computers hooked up to databases allow even novice investors to stay on top of the latest development in stocks. Despite this trend, there still remains a place for full service brokers. If you make proper use of a full service firm, what you may gain in value will be beyond what the higher commissions will cost.

The advice that follows pertains to those investments that are in small growth stocks. The vast majority of investors will probably have additional funds placed in other asset categories. For example, 30% of your money may be in small growth stocks, 40% in blue chips, and 30% in bonds. Some investors may, in all practicality, employ more than one broker. Perhaps the blue chips and bonds are handled at a discounter while the small stock business is done at a full service broker. Each classification of assets should be managed in the most advantageous manner possible. Some of the pros and cons and do's and don'ts of working with a discounter and a full service firm follow.

WORKING WITH A BROKER

The purpose of this book is to help you learn to identify and profit from winning growth stocks. Toward that end, a broker can provide invaluable assistance. To help maximize his efforts on your behalf, you must set the parameters for the relationship. If you are going to make all of the buy/sell decisions, let him know right from the start. In this case, what you want from the broker is service only. The broker serves only as a conduit of information. Should you need a report on a stock, he should be willing to fax or send it to you. If an important development takes place in one of your stocks, you should receive a prompt phone call. Perhaps the company reported earnings well below expectations; that could be the start of a negative trend. This is the type of information that you need to know. However, don't expect a "service only" broker to provide you with daily quotes on your stocks. That's what newspapers are for. The long-term approach presented in this book does not require such close scrutiny of your stocks. Your need for service and the value of the broker's time need to strike a balance so that this kind of relationship works for both of you.

In the next scenario, both you and the broker choose stocks for your portfolio. Let's assume that you've done your homework and that you've put a stock through its paces. When you call to place the order, don't let your broker talk you out of it. After all, you probably know ten times more about the stock than he does. If you don't invest in the stock and it goes straight up afterward, who are you going to blame? Odds are you'll be looking soon for another broker after this happens a couple of times. If you're proficient in your picks, your broker may come to welcome you as a valuable source of new stock ideas.

The other half of the relationship involves the recommendations that you take from a broker. (This advice also applies to the third potential relationship, in which the broker makes all of the stock selections.) When your broker presents a stock to you, don't be bashful about asking him some of the questions you'll learn in this book. Certainly you'll want to know whether or not he's done his homework. Don't necessarily expect an immediate answer to all of your questions. It's not required that you know every last detail to make a wise decision. What you are looking for is the feeling that he knows what he's talking about. Should you need additional data before making a decision, have your broker fax or send you information on the company. After you finish reading this book you'll probably want to apply these criteria to his picks yourself, unless you have a great deal of trust in his judgment.

If you leave the stock picking to the broker, first make sure that this is his area of expertise. Remember also that the final decision to buy or sell is yours, so learn to put a fine filter on the stock ideas he gives you. Just make sure that you don't become such a tough sale that you waste the time of what might be an excellent broker. When working with a broker, don't be pressured into deviating from the path you've chosen. At the same time, a broker who understands what you're trying to accomplish may alert you as to when you've gone astray. Keep an open mind about this. Just like a good coach, he may be able to get you back on track again.

USING A DISCOUNTER

If you are confident of your abilities and feel that you don't need the services of a full service broker, you may choose to use a discount broker. This choice could save you on your commissions. That's the most obvious benefit. In addition, you will not have the input from a broker that in some cases could be unwanted or could cloud your thinking. One of the drawbacks to using a discounter is that you won't be notified during trading hours of any important developments that might take place in one of your positions. In addition, you won't have a broker monitoring your limit orders to buy or sell, or to let you know if an order has been filled, or if the market has moved away from your target price. When choosing between a discounter and a full service brokerage, consider carefully all of the options before making your decision.

WHERE STOCKS TRADE

The vast majority of stock transactions are handled on either the New York Stock Exchange (NYSE), American Stock Exchange (AMEX), or the Over-the-Counter market (OTC). It can be helpful to know the differences in commission structure and how stocks trade between the listed exchanges (NYSE and AMEX) and the OTC market.

Listed stocks are traded in a centralized marketplace. When you place an order for a listed security, your broker then enters the order and it is relayed to a floor broker at the exchange. The floor broker handles the actual execution of the order. Oftentimes he will negotiate with other floor brokers who have an interest in the stock. If he fails to negotiate a transaction with a fellow floor broker, then the order is turned over to what is called a specialist.

Each listed stock has a specialist assigned to it. The specialist's job is to provide a continuous market in his assigned security. In other words, his job is to help keep the spread between the bid (the price where buy orders are at) and the ask (the price at which sell orders are at) reasonably close together. As an example, if a stock were quoted at 45 bid 45 1/4 ask, that would be considered to be a narrow spread. On the other hand, a stock quoted at 45 bid, 46 1/2 ask would have a wide spread. Again, part of the specialist's job is to keep this spread as low as possible. This helps promote liquidity in a stock. Specialists will often buy a stock at a higher price than other existing bids. They will also offer to sell a stock for less than the prevailing ask. In essence, specialists will execute transactions at times between the bid and ask to help maintain a free and continuous market in their stock.

Specialists may act as either brokers or dealers. When acting as a broker, they merely handle orders for the floor brokers. Specialists will also act as dealers, buying and selling for their own account. There has been much said and written concerning the specialist system. Some believe they have an unfair advantage when trading for their own account, because no one is closer to a stock than they are. Specialists make money over the long haul or they wouldn't stay in business. Day in and day out they are able to grind out a fairly decent living. Every now and then, however, they do stand to lose a lot of money rather quickly should they be heavily into their stock and the stock takes off in the opposite direction of their position. When you buy or sell a listed stock, it is considered an agency trade; the brokerage is acting as your agent. A commission is then added (in the case of a buy) or subtracted (in the case of a sell) from the price that the trade is transacted at.

OTC trading is a different matter. When you place an order, your broker then forwards it on to the firm's OTC trading desk. Traders at the desk are called broker/dealers because they can act in either capacity. Acting as a broker, the trader has access by telephone to a network of market makers which may be spread across the country. The trader will check out his electronic display screen and call the market maker offering the best quote. He will then try to get the best price possible.

The bid and ask prices for a stock that are closest to each other are known as the inside market. The smaller order execution system (SOES) guarantees execution, at the inside market, of all orders of 1,000 shares or fewer in National Market System issues. Automatic execution is guaranteed for orders of 500 shares or less on all other NASDAQ securities. The number of market makers in a stock depends on how large the company is and on how frequently it trades. A stock that trades 500,000 shares daily may have 20 to 30 or more market makers. On the other hand, a stock that trades only 3,000 shares a day may only have 5 or 6. Obviously, the higher the volume, the more liquid the stock will be and vice versa. When buying or selling as a broker, the transaction is considered as an agency trade. A commission is then added to or subtracted from the total value of the trade (depending on whether it is a buy or sell order).

A brokerage that maintains a market in a stock is acting as a principal. Traders buying and selling principal stock are then said to be acting as dealers. As a market maker in a given stock, the brokerage stands ready to sell the stock from its own inventory or to buy the stock and take it into inventory. There are limits as to how many shares the market making firm must buy or sell at the prevailing bid/ask quote. Unlike agency trades, there is no set commission added to or subtracted from the trade. Instead, when buying principal stock the price is marked up to arrive at a net price. For example, if a stock is quoted at 10 bid, 10 1/4 ask, and the firm has stock it is willing to sell out of inventory at 10 1/4, a markup of 1/4 would create a net price of 10 1/2. Should the market maker be willing to pay 10 in the event of a sale, the net price to the client after a 1/4 markdown would be 9 3/4. There can be certain advantages to working with a firm that makes a market in a stock. Periodically they will accommodate a large seller of stock by buying a block at the bid. The firm's customers may then be able to purchase the stock (prior to the markup, which acts as a commission) at possibly less than the prevailing ask price.

LIQUIDITY

Large capitalization, highly liquid stocks, usually have a very narrow spread between the bid and ask prices. It's not uncommon to find a stock like General Motors to be selling at 40 bid, 40 1/8 ask. In sharp contrast, you can expect some fairly sizeable gaps between the bid and ask in small growth stocks. That should not necessarily deter you from investing in this segment of the market. Indeed, many of the winners you may discover using the ideas in this book may start out in small, fairly illiquid issues. What you do need to be apprised of is the hidden cost involved in dealing with fairly illiquid issues. To help overcome this cost, you will need to be very selective in your stock purchases.

There are a few tests you can run to determine the liquidity of a stock. The total number of authorized shares that are now in the hands of their owners are called a stock's total shares outstanding. Company officers and directors may hold a substantial number of the shares outstanding, especially in a small growth company. Furthermore, they may be under certain restrictions as to how many shares they can sell at any given time. Stock held by these insiders is commonly deducted from the total shares outstanding. The remaining shares are called the float. Shares that make up the float are those that are easily tradeable. The example below illustrates how you arrive at the float.

Float of XYZ Company

5,000,000	Shares outstanding
-1,500,000	Held by company officers
3,500,000	Float

Liquidity may also be determined by checking the average daily or weekly volume for the stock. Weekly volume can be found in *Barron's Financial Weekly*. Chart services will normally list average daily volume going back a month or two. If you find that a stock trades only a few thousand shares a week, and that often there are days when it doesn't trade at all, you should be exceedingly sure of its long-term potential before considering it for investment.

The bid/ask spread is another key in discovering how easily you can buy or sell a stock. Generally speaking, the wider the spread, the more illiquid the stock is. Spreads should not only be considered in absolutes but also in terms of percentages. For example, ABC Corporation is quoted at 5 bid, 5 1/2 ask while XYZ Corporation is quoted at 10 bid, 10 1/2 ask. Both have a spread of 1/2 between the bid and ask. However, ABC's ask price is 10% away from the bid while XYZ's ask price is only 5% above the bid. A large bid/ask spread can have a profound effect on the profit potential of a stock, especially if you are considering investing for rather modest short-term gains.

The example below illustrates this point. Assume that your goal is to make 50% on a stock that's currently quoted at 4 by 4 1/2 (to simplify matters, commissions are left out). Because you normally must pay the ask, let's say you purchase the stock at 4 1/2. To make your goal of a 50% profit, the bid price of the stock would need to move up 69% (2 3/4 / 4)! Just to get back to even to cover the spread, the bid would need to go from 4 to 4 1/2 (or 12 1/2%). A liquid stock makes it much easier to invest for smaller gains.

The Effect of a Spread on Profits

Buy	4 Bid	4 1/2 Ask	$\frac{6\ 3/4}{4\ 1/2}$	= 1.50 or 50% profit
Sell	6 3/4 Bid	7 1/4 Ask		

Table 2-1
Sample Bid/Ask Spreads*

Company	Number of Market Makers	Bid/Ask	Bid/Ask Percentage Difference
Liberty National Bank	6	8 1/4 – 9 1/2	13.2%
Datron Systems	12	8 1/2 – 9	5.6%
Microsoft	36	117 – 117 1/4	0.2%

*As of 4/2/92.

The following example now assumes that your profit goal is still 50%, but the stock is now trading at 4 by 4 1/8:

Profiting from a Liquid Stock

Buy	4 Bid	4 1/8 Ask	$\dfrac{6\,3/16}{4\,1/8}$ = 1.50 or 50% profit
Sell	6 3/16 Bid	6 3/8 Ask	

Notice that a move on the bid of only 55% (from 4 to 6 3/16) was necessary to create the same 50% gain. As you can see from the examples above, it is difficult to trade illiquid stocks for small gains. However, the focus of this book is to teach you how to invest for the long haul in stocks that can go up several-fold.

When you invest for big gains, liquidity at the start becomes less of an issue. But remember that, to some extent, you can become locked into a stock because of a substantial cost of buying, in terms of the spread plus brokerage commissions. So make doubly sure that when you are buying an infrequently traded issue that it has extraordinary upside potential. If you have any doubts about a thinly traded stock, move on to the next one. Table 2-1 shows you some examples of liquidity in a number of stocks. Notice how the number of market makers increases as liquidity of a stock improves.

HOW TO USE DIFFERENT ORDERS

The returns on your investments can be significantly affected by the choice or orders you use when you go to buy or sell stocks. Factors such as the bid/ask spread and average daily volume, as well as the current price

---

Table 2-2
Commonly Used Orders

The most commonly used orders include the following: market order, limit order, good till canceled order, and a stop order. A discussion of each follows.

Market Order. The most commonly used order that buys or sells a stock as quickly as possible at the best available price.

Limit Order. This order specifies a specific price that a stock will be bought or sold at. Limit orders to buy are always below the market; limit orders to sell are always above the current value.

Good Till Canceled. A type of limit order that remains in effect for up to several months before it needs to be renewed if it hasn't yet been filled.

Stop Order. An order to sell stock that is placed below the prevailing price. It becomes a market order when the stock trades at the stop price. Stop orders are often used to protect profits or to prevent large losses.

---

action of the stock are all important ingredients in helping you to decide which orders are most appropriate for each particular trade.

Market orders are the most commonly used (Table 2-2). With a market order, your buy or sell of stock is quickly executed at the best available price. You can never be sure when you enter a market order what price you will get, because a market order does not specify a price. Let's assume you are trying to buy 1,500 shares of a fairly liquid stock that is quoted at 20 x 20 3/8. Because of the size of the order, you could expect to have it executed at 20 3/8 (unless the quote changes by the time the order is entered). With a market order, the trade or floor broker may even get you a price below the ask (in the case of a buy order).

In sharp contrast to the example above, assume that you are trying to buy 5,000 shares at market of an illiquid stock quoted at 20 x 21 1/4. Chances are you may only get part of your order filled at 21 1/4. You may wind up paying perhaps 21 1/2 or 21 3/4 for additional shares to complete your 5,000 share market order. With small orders of 500 to 1,000 shares, a market order should most likely be executed within the prevailing quote. However, if you wish to buy large quantities of an illiquid stock on the listed exchanges and definitely on the NASDAQ, don't be too surprised if you wind up paying more for the stock than the prevailing quote when using a market order. Of course, the opposite of the above holds true for sell orders. If you attempt to sell a few thousand shares of an illiquid stock at the market, you may in fact depress the price of the stock.

The main advantage of a market order is that it gives you, in almost all cases, the fastest possible execution of your order. In highly liquid markets, it is generally the best way to go. For example, if a stock is trading at 30 x 30 1/8 and it is trading 500,000 to 1,000,000 shares daily, you shouldn't have too much trouble selling even a few thousand shares at the bid with a market order.

Oftentimes you will find that you wish to buy a fast-moving stock. Rather than chancing that you'll miss buying the stock altogether (by using a preset price), you might be best off using a market order and not worrying that you had to pay an extra 1/4 or 1/2 more. If your fast mover has run up from 10 to 10 1/4, to 11, and your research tells you it could be a 30 stock in two years, don't quibble over small change. Buy at the market. Conversely, if you are in a disaster that is going downhill fast and only appears to be getting worse, don't mess around trying for an extra 3/8 on the sale. Put in a market order, get out, and move on to something more promising.

The main disadvantages to market orders are that you can never be sure exactly what price you will get when you enter your order. This problem can be solved by the proper use of a limit order. A limit order allows you to specify the exact price that you will buy or sell a stock. For example, ABC Corporation is a fairly illiquid stock that is quoted at 12 x 12 1/2. If you placed a market order for 4,000 shares, your average purchase price could wind up being more than the current ask of 12 1/2. However, with a limit order, you can set your price at 12 1/2 and be sure that you will not pay more than that for the stock.

Limit orders can help keep your buy or sell within prescribed boundaries, which can help in orders of illiquid stocks. If you find that a stock is not moving, or is trading within a very narrow range, a limit order can help you save an 1/8 or 1/2 here or there. Just remember when using limit orders not to be penny wise, pound foolish. As in the previous example, you do not want to save a 1/4 at the expense of missing a 10 or 20 point move in a stock. Now of course, there's nothing to say you can't buy a stock at 12 when you missed it by an 1/8 at 10. But many investors find this a difficult thing to do. They will, especially in the case of a potentially rewarding stock, figure they missed this one and will drop it from consideration, even though the majority of the stock's move still lies ahead. In sum, a limit price guarantees you won't buy or sell stock for anything beyond your prescribed price. The risk you run is that your order may lie dormant while the stock moves away from your price.

A further variation of a limit order is a good till canceled order, GTC. This order is used when the current quote for a stock may be some distance from where you would like to buy or sell and, therefore, you don't expect the order to be executed on the day that it is entered or even possibly for a few weeks thereafter. For example, let's say that you really like XYZ Corporation, but you feel that at 10 it is priced too high. However, if XYZ were to pull back to 8, you would want to be a buyer. You would then place a GTC order at 8, and when and if XYZ does decline, you may very well get it at the price you want (depending on whether or not there are any buy orders ahead of you at 8). This tactic can be especially useful if you are very busy, or perhaps on vacation and can't monitor the stock constantly.

One drawback to GTC orders like this is that the stock could pull back to only 8 1/4, bottom out, and head back up. Again, you may miss out on a bargain because you wanted to save an extra 1/4. Another negative is that by the time the stock trades at 8 and your buy order has been executed, the outlook for the company may have changed. Your bargain purchase at 8 may be on its way to 5. By the same token, a limit order to sell and lock in a profit a few points above the current ask price could short-circuit your potential for a truly big gain in a top stock that is just gaining momentum.

Stop orders are another type of order that has gained in popularity over the last several years. Stops are available for listed stocks (NYSE and AMEX) and, depending on the firm, for some OTC stocks. Stop orders are typically used for selling stock.

The stop is placed below the current quote. For example, ABC Corporation is currently trading at 15 x 15 1/4. You might place a stop at 13. Should ABC decline to 13, your stop would then be triggered. The stop then converts into a market order and the stock is sold at the best available price (just like with a regular market order). You could conceivably sell for less than 13 in the example with a stop at 13.

Stop orders are used to prevent losses and to lock in profits. Let's say you bought a stock at 20 and then placed your protective stop at 16. The advantage here is that you limited your losses, which is inherently a good thing to do. However, with a mechanical approach like this, you could very well wind up selling your stock when it has suffered through a normal correction in price. If your fundamental analysis was correct and the company is a winner, you should probably be buying more shares at 16 at just the time you're getting stopped out. Traders generally employ close stops (perhaps 7% to 10%). On the other hand, long-term investors (which hopefully you'll become after reading this book) are better served by using much wider stops (15% to 20%+) or foregoing this type of order altogether.

Stop orders are also used to lock in profits. For example, XYZ Corporation has rallied from your purchase price of 10 to 35. By placing a stop at 30, you can lock in a gain of about 20 points (200%) should the stock decline from its current price. If the stock continues to move higher, you may wish to increase the price of the stop periodically to help lock in an even bigger profit.

As stated earlier, in the majority of cases you may wish to simply enter a market order when you wish to buy or sell a stock. However, there are times when other types of orders can enhance your results. Be aware of the different orders and use the one that is most fitting to the particular stock in question at that time.

SUMMARY

- Consider the advantages and disadvantages of working with a full service firm and a discounter.

- Set the parameters for your relationship with a full service broker. Get the service you need and, if you wish, stock ideas.

- If your broker makes small growth stock selections, make sure he's very knowledgeable or even a specialist in this area.

- Make sure that the relationship with your broker is mutually beneficial. Don't expect too much, and don't accept too little service.

- If your broker starts to step consistently out of the boundaries of your implicit relationship, find another broker to work with.

- Put your broker's recommendations to the test to make sure he's done his homework.

- If you are confident of your abilities and don't need the service or input from a broker, consider using a discounter.

- Listed stocks (NYSE and AMEX) use a specialist system; his job is to maintain an orderly market in his assigned stock's area.

- The bid is the price you can generally expect to sell a stock at. The ask is the price you generally can expect to pay for a stock.

- OTC trading is handled by a network of market makers.

- The small order execution system guarantees execution of small trades at the inside market.

- Firms that make a market in a particular stock can sometimes get you a better price than the prevailing quote.

- Largely capitalized stocks usually have a narrow bid/ask spread while smaller OTC issues may have a wide spread. Generally, you should only invest for long-term profits if you are in a stock that has a wide spread.

- A stock's liquidity can be determined by the following: float, bid/ask spread, and average daily volume.

- Choose the orders you use very carefully. They can significantly impact your results if used incorrectly.

- Market orders guarantee fast execution at the best available price. These orders are especially valuable in fast-moving markets when you don't want to "miss the market."

- Limit orders specify a price you want to buy or sell at. Good till cancel orders will keep your limit order open until it is executed (or needs to be renewed). Limit orders can help you get the price you want in illiquid stocks.

- Stop orders are set under the current quote. They can protect a gain or prevent a loss from becoming too large. If you use stops, make sure to give your stocks enough room to accommodate normal market fluctuations.

QUESTIONS

1. If you decide to work with a broker on your small stock investments, what's the first thing that you should do?

2. What services should you expect from a full service broker?

3. When you've done your homework and decide to buy a stock, what should you avoid or let happen to you when you call your broker?

4. On the listed exchanges, what is the main job of the specialist?

5. A stock is trading at 16 1/8 by 16 1/2. You purchase shares at the ask price with a markup of 3/8. What's your total cost per share?

6. You've found a company that you like. Its stock is quoted at 6-6 3/4. Should you buy it for a stock-term trade or a long-term investment?

7. What are three tests you can run to determine the liquidity of a stock?

8. How do a stock's total shares outstanding differ from shares in the float?

9. A stock is quoted at 7 x 7 3/4 and you bought at the ask. How much would the bid have to go up for you to sell at a 100% profit (assuming that you sell at the bid)? How much would the bid have to go up in percentages for you to break even?

10. You bought 500 shares of a stock midway between the bid/ask of 9 1/4 x 10 and sold it for a loss at the bid when the stock was quoted at 6 7/8 x 7 1/4. What was your loss in dollars and in percentages?

11. You've been working with a broker for a while and his stock selections have been mediocre while yours have done well. You've just called to place an order and he wants you to buy one of his latest picks instead. What should you do?

12. You own several thousand shares of XYZ Corporation. They've just announced very poor results for the latest quarter, and the stock is starting to drop quickly. You remain unaware of these developments until later in the day after the market is closed. Up to this point you've only used a discount broker. Should this prompt you to change to a full service broker?

Chapter 3

HOW TO FIND THE NEXT WINNERS ON WALL STREET

When you begin your search for the ideal growth stocks for your portfolio remember this: There are literally thousands of publicly traded companies to choose from. To be successful, you need only to find perhaps 10 to 12 stocks that exhibit outstanding potential. In other words, you can afford to be very choosy. Select only the cream of the crop for your portfolio.

Selecting top growth companies to invest in requires some work on your part, but the rewards can be well worth it. If you are successful in picking just one or two big winners, the effect on your portfolio's results can be rather astounding. For example, let's say you invested $10,000 equally in ten stocks and they all gained at an average compounded rate of 15%. After five years, your portfolio would have grown to a little over $201,000. Now, assume that one of the ten stocks turned out to be a super-star and registered a gain of 900% (a tenfold increase in value). Your holdings would have grown to $280,022 instead, or a compound growth rate of 23%!

Now that you're convinced that good growth stocks can do wonders for your portfolio, please keep in mind that in almost all cases it takes time for stocks to pay off in a big way. For instance, a stock that compounds at 25% for five years will enable $1 to grow to $3.05. This may not seem like a spectacular return, and yet a 25% growth rate is well in excess of the historical norm for small growth stocks. It takes time for even the best of small stocks to grow tall, so learn to be patient. Because you're going to have to do your homework to arrive at your portfolio of top stocks, make sure that it pays off for you. To get the rewards you deserve for sound stock selection, be prepared to hold your stocks for several years (providing the fundamentals remain solid). The techniques discussed in the following chapters are designed to help you identify stocks that can be held for years as investments, as opposed to those that only offer opportunities for short-term profits.

Like the TV detective Columbo, you will need to learn all of the appropriate facts to arrive at an intelligent decision to purchase a stock. Oftentimes a stock will appear to have unlimited potential, only to turn out to become a complete bust. What went wrong? What piece of the puzzle in your analysis was missing? What key question about the company prior to your purchase was left unanswered? The more you play the devil's advocate and the more you look at each candidate for membership in your portfolio with a discerning eye, the more you will stack the odds of investment success in your favor. Quite often you may get a positive response to every question on a company but one, which you may choose to gloss over. That one negative may be enough to derail the company. Perhaps ABC Computers is great in every way, except for the fact that they're in an industry that's easy to enter and where the competition will ultimately prove to be their undoing. On the other hand, XYZ Waste Services may have access to the only dump site for 500 miles which gives them a virtual monopoly. They could afford to be weak in some areas where ABC Computer is strong and still be successful.

What you need to realize is that the questions you will learn to ask are tools to help you in your analysis. Very few stocks will register a perfect score in all categories. So you must learn to develop an intuition, a sixth sense if you will, about what's important to know, pro or con, in each company you review. Above all else, don't let yourself succumb to paralysis by analysis. Some would-be investors, with the best of intentions, never seem to be able to pull the trigger or to make a decision. Don't let that happen to you. When you're satisfied that you know what's important to be known about a company and the results of your analysis say buy, by all means step to the plate, give your broker a call with confidence, and buy 1,000 shares of the next Wal-Mart. After all, the purpose of this book is to help you make money—it is not intended to be strictly an academic exercise.

THE BUSINESS

Before including any growth stock in your portfolio, it must first pass a number of screens for suitability. The first test is a highly subjective evaluation of the business the company is involved in. If a stock fails to pass this initial examination, then there is really no need to move forward with the other criteria presented in this and the following chapters. Because the growth stocks you want to invest in will be held for several years, you should only invest in companies that you're comfortable with. Therefore, your initial feeling about a stock, your gut reaction, should be given substantial weight in the selection process. After all, do you really want to put your money in something that doesn't seem quite right to you from the start? You're certainly not going to feel very good about taking a loss in that kind of situation when your instincts told you from the start that it could be a loser. In essence, your first criterion for successfully picking winning growth stocks is the development of a sixth sense—the ability to size up the merits or drawbacks of a business using a conceptual approach.

You will need to ask yourself a few basic questions. Just what does the business do? Does the concept make sense? Do they have an unusual and valuable new product that's in demand? Are they providing a medical service that saves lives? Are they riding with or against the prevailing megatrends of the business world? In short, does what this company do make sense to you, and can you summarize their modus operandi in a sentence or two? (Chapter 6 lists a number of good sources to investigate, including a company's annual report.)

To give you an idea of some concepts that have worked, let's look at some success stories on Wall Street. The following is a capsule look at some companies that have been consistent gainers in revenues, earnings, and stock price over the last few years. Some have products with real sizzle, while others provide services that have gained great customer acceptance.

Because the stocks listed below have gained so dramatically in recent years, it is possible that their rate of ascent will slow down. However, most of them may continue to do well in the years ahead. If you weren't in these stocks as they shot up in value, take heart. There will always be other emerging stars in the years ahead. It's up to you to find them.

- Buffets, Inc.—Restaurants. Company restaurants offer a wide variety of foods in sizeable restaurants. Customers pay one price that

includes everything.
Stock: Low in 1988 $4 7/8—close December 31, 1991, $32

- Cambex—Computer products. Manufactures high quality enhancements for IBM computers at very competitive prices—small, fast growing company in a huge market.
Stock: Low in 1990, $3 1/8—December 31, $31 1/2

- Costco Wholesale—Retail. Company operates wholesale membership warehouses featuring a wide variety of well-known merchandise priced below traditional wholesalers. Company took advantage of trend toward discounting.
Stock: Low following crash of 1987, $2 13/16—December 31, 1991, $55 3/4

- Cracker Barrel Old Country—Restaurant and gift shop combination. Owns and operates a chain of stores featuring home style country home cooking located near well-traveled highways.
Stock: Low in 1987, $3 5/8—December 31, 1991, $46

- Microsoft—Software for microcomputers. Wide line of systems and applications including MS-DOS operating systems helping computers become more productive.
Stock: Low in 1986, 3 1/2—December 31, 1991, $111 1/4

- Novell—Computer networking. Company's proprietary NetWare local area network operating system is the industry standard. Products allow PCs to work together.
Stock: Under $1 (adjusting for splits) in 1985—December 31, 1991, $60

- St. Jude Medical—Medical devices. Company is the world's leading producer of mechanical heart valves.
Stock: Low in 1985, $1—December 31, 1991, $55 1/2

- T2 Medical—Medical services. Taking advantage of trend toward reducing medical costs. Company is the leading developer and manager of home infusion therapy centers; it saves money versus costs of hospital treatment.
Stock: Low in 1988, $4—December 31, 1991, $57 3/4

Many opportunities for growth today are coming from emerging new technologies and from creative new services. New technologies are breeding new mini-industries seemingly overnight. It is possible that a company with a new product and a proprietary niche can dominate its industry if its products are unique and the best. For example, radio frequency identification allows objects to be scanned in a way that's similar to bar coding. The big difference is that you don't need to have a light shine directly on the object being scanned. The beauty of the new technology is that it has now become feasible to scan objects with a simplicity and accuracy that would have previously been unthinkable. As this is being written, Amtech Corporation is the leading player in this fledgling industry. Its RFID Systems routinely scan objects such as box cars and cars on turnpikes.

Rainbow Technologies is a small but rapidly growing young company whose stock gained over 257% in 1991. Rainbow's products provide a very simple and low-cost solution to software piracy. They also protect software licensed to networks of computers so that software users can keep their costs down. Rainbow is featured later in this chapter. Amtech Corporation and Rainbow are just two of the hundreds of small but fast growing companies that have latched onto an exciting and valuable new technology.

Both individuals and businesses are always receptive to a new service that can make life easier and perhaps more profitable. It's quite possible that a young company could come in as a "Me Too" service business and be successful. However, your odds are greatly enhanced if the company you are considering provides a whole new service or can greatly improve, if not revolutionize, an existing service.

Rather than reinvent the wheel, many aspiring entrepreneurs will quickly move in to copy a successful young growing business. Therefore, you'll want to make sure that the company you are looking at has a competitive advantage, or that there are considerable barriers to entering their business. A product-oriented company may possess certain patents that protect it from potential competitors. If the product is similar to others on the market, perhaps its status, according to things like industry trade publications, may help to give it a competitive advantage. These third-party endorsements can give instant respectability to a growing company's line of products, although it still takes years to gain the brand loyalty of a company such as Coca Cola.

Service businesses generally have less to protect them, at least formally (such as patents), than do product companies. To lock out the competition, a service business needs to provide something unique or needs to do their job so well that customers wouldn't think of jumping ship. Even though price is a consideration, most consumers of service businesses will remain loyal to a company as long as they are not given a good reason to change. Just ask yourself how often you go looking for a new barber or hair salon just to save a couple of bucks if you are satisfied with where you've been doing business.

As part of your initial sorting process you will want to keep a number of existing industries in mind, while remaining open to the emerging industries that keep bursting on the scene. In addition, for purposes of prudent diversification, you should have stocks from a number of unrelated industries. (This will be discussed further in Chapter 8.) Listed below are a number of fast-growing industries that should provide abundant opportunities in the years ahead. This list may prove useful in guiding you to companies that offer the greatest potential for superior returns.

Growth Industries

Advanced Materials
Aerospace
Audio/Video Products
BioEngineering
BioTechnology
Business Employment Services
Cellular Telephones
Communications
Computers - Equipment
Computers - Services
Computers - Software
Drugs
Engineering and Construction
Engineering - Research and
 Development Services
Electronics
Entertainment
Financial Services
Food
Health Care
Health Care Facilities

Health Care Outpatients
Health Care Services
Home Entertainment
Hotel - Motel
Laser Systems
Leisure and Recreation
Manufacturing and Production
Medical Devices
Medical Equipment and Supplies
Office Automation
Office Equipment and Supplies
Pollution Control
Protection Systems and Equipment
Restaurants and Lodging
Retail-Discount
Retail-Specialty
Telecommunications-Systems-
 Equipment
Transportation
Travel
Waste Disposal

Now assume that your potential big winner has passed your first hurdle and that the foundation for the company's future success seems to make sense to you. The next step is to consider its recent earnings, potential for future profit, and qualifications for living up to Wall Street's number one fundamental criterion—earnings per share.

EARNINGS PER SHARE

When evaluating any company, especially a growth stock, Wall Street is most concerned with the bottom line. How much are you making? What are your earnings per share (EPS)? A company can be doing a lot of things right, but if their earnings don't reflect this, in most cases Wall Street says, "Too bad, the money's going to other more profitable stocks." Of course there are exceptions to this basic rule. Perhaps the best example in recent years is the Biotech stocks that have been bid to the moon in anticipation of future profits. But for all practical purposes, these stocks are exceptions to the norm.

If you do choose to go for stocks that are in their early stages and are losing money, you have the potential to get in on the ground floor of what may prove to be a big winner. However, for every stock you invest in that is in this stage of the development cycle that works out, you'll probably have to suffer with 10 to 20 duds that wind up costing you money. In the long run, you'll be better off selecting stocks that have been around long enough to show some profitability but still have their peak growth years ahead of them.

Because there are so many stocks to choose from, often a company can report a number of good years of rising earnings before finally becoming noticed. This can give a growth stock investor a big advantage. The trick is to pick a stock with a few good years behind it that has gone unnoticed.

To be confident that your potential growth stock is a possible big winner, you should look for a positive trend in the growth of its earnings over at least a three- to five-year time frame. Obviously, if you choose a stock with three rather than five years of impressive growth, for example, that stock will have to have more going for it in other areas.

Several growth stocks and their earnings trends over the last seven years are listed below. These will help you to determine what an ideal pattern of growth looks like. All are expressed in earnings per share.

Earnings Progression Comparison

	Year	1	2	3	4	5	6	7
Stock	A	(.42)	(.23)	(.10)	(.01)	.03	(.14)	(.05)
	B	(.25)	(.27)	.00	.20	.25	(.03)	(.10)
	C	(.50)	(.20)	(.16)	(.08)	.17	.35	.55
	D	(.22)	(.05)	.14	.25	.42	.66	.92

Note: Figures in parentheses indicate loss per share.

Earnings per share are calculated by dividing a company's net income by the total shares of common stock outstanding. Suppose a company had a net income of $500,000 and there were 3,000,000 shares outstanding. The formula for computing the company's earnings per share would be as follows:

$$\frac{\$500,000 \text{ Earnings}}{3,000,000 \text{ Shares}} = 16.7 \text{ cents per share}$$

In the example, Stock A has only had one marginally profitable year. The rest of the time it has been bleeding red ink. This type of pattern is common among stocks like those in biotechnology. Here you must be willing to wait for years hoping that your stock finally pans out. Stocks with this kind of earnings history should be largely avoided. Stock B showed a nice progression to profitability but has since traced out an erratic pattern and looks too unpredictable. Stock C has a few years of making money behind it, but the trend is very positive all along. This is the kind of stock you can invest in if the rest of its fundamentals prove to be equally compelling. Out of this group, Stock D clearly demonstrates a consistent and impressive rate of growth to warrant serious consideration for your portfolio. Many great growth stocks in fact start out with a pattern of earnings growth very similar to that of Stock D.

Table 3-1 lists some stocks discussed earlier that have been big winners. Notice the steady upward pattern of earnings growth in each one of them.

Table 3-1
Earnings Progression - Top Winners

	1986	1987	1988	1989	1990	1991	Fiscal Year Ends
Buffets, Inc.	.11	.21	.28	.39	.55	.76	December
Cracker Barrel Old Country	.20	.26	.39	.57	.71	1.00	July
Costco Wholesale	.08	.07	.23	.49	.70	1.11	August
Cambex	(.80)	.11	.29	.52	.89	1.40	August
Novell	.12	.20	.28	.37	.68	1.10	October
Microsoft	.26	.43	.74	1.01	1.56	2.47	June
St. Jude Medical	.30	.41	.71	1.07	1.35	1.75	December
T2 Medical	.12	.27	.33	.40	.57	1.02	September

Note: Figure in parentheses indicates loss per share.

An ideal growth stock should show a consistent and above-average rate of growth. A rate of 15% would definitely be on the low end of the spectrum. Earnings growth of 20% or more is desirable. However, you should be a little suspicious if a company's earnings are growing at, perhaps, 50% or greater annually. At 50%, a company's earnings would more than triple every three years. That kind of growth is usually not sustainable for a very long period of time. What often happens to stocks whose earnings are growing that rapidly is that their shares get bid up to astronomical levels. In addition, they are very susceptible to a serious decline should the company's growth begin to slow noticeably.

The following example gives some rules of thumb to remember when examining a small company's growth rates:

Small Company Growth Rates—Rules of Thumb

15-20%	Absolute lowest for a true growth stock.
20-25%	Excellent return if it is consistent over a number of years.
25-35%	Hot growth stocks can maintain this for several years and can produce big winners.
35-50%	A great rate to compound at, but be ready for a slowdown.
50%+	Generally an unsustainable rate; hold stocks for all their worth, but be ready for a serious pullback.

Quarterly Results

Corporate earnings are reported every quarter. For smaller growth companies that have fewer analysts following them, and which are inherently less predictable, this can be a time of both crisis and opportunity. In this day and age of instant gratification, many investors will jump ship when an otherwise good quality stock stumbles and reports an off quarter. Sometimes their action is justified as the company may be giving off the first signs of a loss of momentum. Perhaps if it is a service business they may have gotten complacent and lost a key client. In the case of a product-oriented business, possibly a new product failed to live up to customer expectations as a result of incomplete research into the customers' needs.

On the other hand, a bad quarter may be caused by a number of things that will have little effect on the company's long-run prosperity. In cases like this, a sell-off due to a negative earnings report in the short run can create an opportunity to acquire shares at a bargain price. The lesson to be learned here is: If you know a company well and believe strongly in its long-term growth potential, then be ready to seize the opportunity to buy the stock should uninformed investors bail out because of a temporary setback.

Quarterly results often have a seasonality to them. Therefore, when you compare quarterly results, in most cases it is more relevant to compare earnings to the same quarter of a year ago. In other words, if you are looking to evaluate earnings for the three months ending in September 1992, then you should compare them to those of the September quarter of 1991. Table 3-2 is an example of a company with a positive annual progression of earnings growth. Note how each quarter compares to the one immediately before it, as well as how it compares to the same quarter from a year ago. This business is demonstrating seasonality.

ABC Corporation shows very healthy annual earnings growth. All quarterly comparisons versus the same quarter of a year ago are favorable. Note also that the December and March quarters are consistently weaker than those of June and September. Top growth companies that have virtually no seasonal effects to their business, however, will demonstrate the characteristics of XYZ Corporation presented in Table 3-3. This stock was able to have its quarterly earnings grow quarter after quarter for the period shown.

On top of seasonality factors, quarterly earnings can be distorted in a given year for nonrecurring charges or even gains. For example, if one quarter's earnings are abnormally large, perhaps it is because they sold off an asset at a substantial profit. On the other hand, a particularly bad quarter may be explained by a large one-time expense that was lumped into that one quarter. These expenses could include the cost for expensive

---

Table 3-2

Earnings Progression—ABC Corporation—A Seasonal Business

Quarter	March	June	September	December	Annual	Percentage Increase
1987	.10	.15	.20	.12	.57	—
1988	.12	.20	.26	.15	.73	+28.1%
1989	.14	.27	.32	.20	.93	+27.4%
1990	.18	.34	.45	.31	1.28	+37.6%

Table 3-3

Earnings Progression—XYZ Corporation—No Seasonality

Quarter	March	June	September	December	Annual	Percentage Change
1987	.10	.11	.13	.15	.49	—
1988	.16	.18	.20	.21	.75	+53.1%
1989	.22	.24	.25	.29	1.00	+33.3%
1990	.32	.35	.39	.41	1.47	+47.0%

new machinery, the opening of new offices, or possibly a restructuring charge. Any reasons that have caused a company's earnings to fluctuate wildly in a single quarter should be dismissed in light of the company's longer-term growth potential.

Finally, some solid smaller growth companies' earnings may vary greatly from quarter to quarter simply because of the nature of the business. Companies that fall in this category often sell a few big ticket items whose sale may fall unpredictably in any given quarter. Also in this group are businesses that manufacture products that involve large contracts that can be awarded or postponed at any given time. Unless you have a strong stomach for wider than normal fluctuations in stock prices, you'll be better off sticking to businesses with more readily identifiable sales cycles.

Components of a Company's Earnings

The components of a company's earnings can be broken into different categories. What you want to see is the majority of a stock's earnings coming from continuing operations, from the sale of products, or the performance of their services. Sometimes, however, a company will have a rather substantial cash position that creates an inordinate amount of interest income. A good growth company should be able to invest large cash balances to create even greater profits than they would get simply by earning interest on these funds. In addition, by subtracting out interest income, you may discover that profits from a company's ongoing operations may not be nearly as impressive.

While some companies can't adequately use all of their available cash, others will actively seek out new funds periodically to help finance additional growth. One source of additional capital is the issuance of additional shares of stock. If you notice that your prospect has done this in the past, were they able to profitably put this new money to use? Should they be planning another stock offering, it is important to know what the new money is going to be used for. Ideally, it will be used for sensible new ventures such as research for a new product, additional plant and equipment, or expansion into desirable overseas markets. All of these are signs of a growing and prosperous young business. Beware that when additional shares are issued, they will dilute the earnings of the company and, therefore, those of the current shareholders.

Lets say, for example, that Company XYZ had a net income in the first quarter of $100,000 and there were 1,000,000 shares outstanding. This would result in earnings per share of 10 cents. During the second quarter the company issued 500,000 shares to fund some new equipment and XYZ had a net profit of $120,000. This represented a gain of 20% over the first quarter. However, because of the additional new shares, per share earnings fell to 8 cents.

First Quarter - Before Dilution

$$\frac{\text{Net Income}}{\text{Shares Outstanding}} \quad \frac{\$100,000}{1,000,000} = 10 \text{ cents per share earnings}$$

Second Quarter - After Dilution

$$\frac{\text{Net Income}}{\text{Shares Outstanding}} \quad \frac{\$120,000}{1,500,000} = 8 \text{ cents per share earnings}$$

In the short run, the side effects of dilution on earnings per share should not be taken too seriously, provided the company's business is expanding rapidly and the new money will quickly be put to good use. However, if you're not impressed by what they are doing with the new money (such as voting the officers and directors huge salary increases), then this stock should best be avoided.

Because Wall Street seems to have a fetish over quarterly earnings, many businesses seem to have a preoccupation with having their quarterly numbers look good. Although substantial quarterly fluctuations can create sell-offs in a stock, and thus bargains for the savvy investor, the annual numbers are by far the most important. The overwhelming majority of successful businesses have a strategy that is geared to long-term results. Accordingly, they manage their business for the long haul while letting the short-term cards fall where they may. And remember, this book is about helping you find stocks that you can invest in for several years to make several fold gains. It is not about trying to time quarterly earnings reports for a 20% to 30% potential gain.

A trend of steadily if not spectacularly rising earnings is the hallmark of a desirable growth stock. Still, you don't want to pay any price for a stock just because its concept seems good to you and its earnings growth pattern is positive. There must be some way to correlate the value between a stock's past, present, and future earnings and the price investors are willing to pay for its shares.

PRICE TO EARNINGS (P/E) RATIO

A stock's price to earnings ratio, more commonly known as its P/E, is one of the most widely used tools on Wall Street for evaluating a stock's current value. P/E ratios are the result of a very simple calculation: divide the stock's price by its latest 12 months' earnings. As an example, if Stock ABC has earned 60 cents over the last 12 months and its stock is trading at $9 per share, ABC's P/E ratio is 15. Investors are willing to pay $15 for every $1 that ABC earns.

P/E Ratio of Company ABC

$$\frac{\text{Stock Price}}{\text{Annual Earnings}} = \text{P/E Ratio} \qquad \frac{\$9.00}{\$0.60} = 15\,\text{P/E}$$

Generally speaking, the faster a company is growing, the more investors are willing to pay for the stock and the higher its P/E will be. The reason for this is that if a growth company's earnings are compounding at an accelerated rate, they will, within a few years' time, catch up to and pass those of a slower growing company. Investors highly value a company whose earnings are consistently and rapidly increasing year after year. If a stock has several years of great earnings but also suffers through an occasional year or two of subpar earnings, its stock price will suffer accordingly.

Table 3-4 demonstrates this point. Companies A, B, and C all earned the same amount over the last 12 months. In fact, A and B both earned more money in total over the last five years. However, the market has placed a different current value on each company's stock because of the varying progression of their annual earnings.

Table 3-4
Contrast in Earnings Progression

Year	1	2	3	4	5	Total 5 Years	Current Stock Price	P/E
A	1.75	1.90	2.06	2.44	2.44	10.39	24 3/8	10
B	3.10	1.10	4.30	.55	2.44	11.49	17	7
C	1.00	1.25	1.56	1.95	2.44	8.20	61	25

Stock A might resemble a utility stock in a good growth area of the country. Earnings are growing at a slow but steady pace and, thus, the market values it at a rather modest P/E of 10. Stock B has earned the most money of the three over the last five years, but its record is very erratic. Because investors don't know what to expect next, the stock is now trading at a very low P/E of just seven times its last 12 months' earnings. The kind of company you should be looking for is Stock C. Although its five-year earnings are the lowest, it commands the highest P/E and the highest price because of the rapid and consistent growth in earnings over the last several years.

As stated earlier, P/Es are typically calculated based on a company's latest 12 months or trailing earnings. However, it is also common for P/Es to be calculated on expected earnings one or even two years out. When this is done, often a stock with a lofty P/E and a high growth rate does not look so overpriced after all. This is especially true if there is a very high likelihood that the predicted earnings will actually be realized. Table 3-5 illustrates how this works:

Table 3-5
P/Es for a Top Growth Stock

Year	1	2	3
Current Stock Price	$30	$30	$30
Earnings	$1	$1.30 (EST)	$1.69 (EST)
P/E Ratio	30	23.1	17.8

In the example, the stock's earnings are compounding at 30% per year. With a P/E ratio of 30, based on current earnings of $1, the stock looks somewhat expensive. But when you factor in its superior earnings growth rate, the stock's P/E of 17.8 based on the estimated profits two years out makes it appear more reasonably priced. Again, the faster a company's earnings are growing, the higher its P/E is likely to be. But remember, when the growth rate is abnormally high and the P/E is high, the stock carries great expectations. The potential then exists for serious disappointment should actual future earnings slip even slightly from their projected fast-track growth.

Investors will look ahead, as stated above, to future earnings growth and a more reasonable P/E for their stock. Companies with a proven record of earnings growth may also witness an expansion of their stock's P/E multiple. This can happen even if the earnings growth rate remains fairly stable but is growing at an above-average rate. What makes this P/E multiple expansion possible, and hence the increase in a stock's price, is the investment community's realization that a gem of a growth stock is lying in the weeds, as yet undiscovered. Because there are a great number of good quality growth stocks, often many get overlooked for inappropriately long periods of time considering their investment merits. However, when a stock like this is discovered by perhaps an analyst or two at a regional or national brokerage, the stock may then shoot up dramatically. So often, when you have an undiscovered jewel, it pays to get in ahead of the crowd and then wait for Wall Street to jump on board. Table 3-6 shows what the power of multiple expansion may do to a stock's value.

In Years 2 and 3, XYZ's earnings grew 30% and so did its stock price. Despite this growth, the stock went unnoticed and carried a rather low P/E of 10. During the fourth year, earnings once again grew at 30%. However, the stock had a fantastic year with an advance of 226%! This was possible because investors finally woke up to XYZ's growth record

Table 3-6
P/E Multiple Expansion - Effect on Stock Price

Year	1	2	3	4
Stock Price	10	13	16 7/8	55
Earnings per Share	$1	$1.30	$1.69	$2.20
P/E	10	10	10	25

and rewarded its 30% earnings growth record with a more realistic P/E of 25. Indeed, the combination of rising earnings and a rising P/E can do wonders for a stock's price. It is also not uncommon for a stock's P/E to increase gradually over the years as investors become increasingly confident in a company's past and future performance (Table 3-7).

In the example, earnings grew at a 25% compound rate each year. In four years earnings increased 144%. But because of the stock's expanding P/E multiple, the price of the stock grew by over 400%. In sum, you can make big money by either investing in an undiscovered stock with a low P/E or by jumping on board one whose P/E is expanding year after year.

Two other measurements are important in gauging a stock's relative value. One approach is to contrast your prospect's P/E to that of the overall market as measured by an indicator such as the S&P 500. Stocks in the S&P are generally the largest and most well-known in America. Because of their size, they also, taken as a group, cannot grow nearly as fast as a good growth company can. Therefore, if the P/E for the S&P 500 is 18 and your hot growth stock is selling at 12 times its earnings, it is said to be selling at a discount to the market. On this basis alone, the stock's price may be subject to an upward revision. A stock with a P/E of 30, on the other hand, would be said to be selling at a premium to the markets multiple. As pointed out, if the stock with a P/E of 30 is experiencing rapid growth of earnings, this premium multiple may easily be justified.

P/E Multiples and the Market

12 P/E	Discount to the market
18 P/E	Standard & Poor's 500
30 P/E	Premium to the market

Table 3-7
P/E Multiple Consistently Expanding

Year	1	2	3	4	5
Stock Price	10	15	22 1/2	33 3/4	50 1/2
Earnings per Share	$1.00	$1.25	$1.56	$1.95	$2.44
P/E	10	12	14.4	17.3	20.7

Similarly, you can gain some measure of a growth stock's value by comparing it to other companies within the same industry. If two stocks both demonstrate fairly similar characteristics and growth rates, you may be able to spot a real bargain if one has a P/E considerably lower than the other. Just make sure before you invest in the obvious bargain that there isn't some overriding consideration that is holding down the price of the possibly undervalued stock.

MANAGEMENT

Managing a growing business so that you produce consistently better results year after year is not necessarily the easiest thing to do. And yet that is exactly what is called for from the top executives of a growth stock if its shares are going to experience the kind of growth you are looking for. Consistency and a high level of achievement are most desirable. If the management of a growth company is unable to smoothly and skillfully handle the growing pains they will almost certainly experience, the stock may suffer some nasty setbacks from time to time. These shakeouts can be unsettling to most investors. They may also cause you to abandon a company that truly has exceptional long-term promise. The key is to be able to tell what is a reasonable setback and one that won't kill the stock price. This must be contrasted to the kind of bumbling by management that could easily have been avoided by sharper minds. Perhaps a weak economy really could be put to blame for a temporary slowdown of a company's business.

What you don't want is excessive excuse making for management's mistakes. A good place to look for clues as to the quality of management is the company's annual and quarterly reports. These are available from the company for the price of a phone call. If possible, you may wish to get hold of annual reports going back at least a couple of years. What you would like to see while perusing these documents is statements from the chief executive officer regarding what the company is trying to achieve. What are their goals? What are their plans? How do they propose to overcome any obstacles in their way? How are they going to continue to make the company grow and produce superior financial results? Answers to questions like these will give you some idea of the thought processes of those in charge of making your growth stock successful.

When reviewing a company's annual and quarterly messages, the comments you read will usually break down into basically financial and nonfinancial information. Ideally, what you'd like to see is a blend of positive statements and results on both. For example, if you get a lot of flowery prose about what the company is planning to do, as well as excuses why things haven't worked out quite as well as planned, then chances are this is a stock to be avoided. Management has probably blown it in the past and is hoping that the shareholders believe that things will be getting better soon. All of this is quite possible, but don't forget that what you are looking for is superior growth stocks that have done the job well in recent years with every indication that this favorable trend will continue.

You may be equally concerned if management dwells almost exclusively on financial results, on the numbers alone. Certainly, they have a right to be proud of how recent annual and quarterly results have met and/or beat the expectations of management and shareholders alike. In the real world of business, and especially with a growth company, it is not only important what you have done for me lately, but what is going to happen next. Are new competitors coming into your market that will need to be dealt with? Have any new products been developed lately to foster future growth? If a CEO dwells on past performance but has little to say of a nonfinancial nature about how the company is going to continue to grow and handle obstacles along the way, look out. This leader may have hit the wall and now is stumped as to how to manage the business successfully from here on out.

The nature of a company's business will also dictate how successful management will be. Some businesses are easy to run and can be handled well by a management team that may not be the most talented, as long as they stay focused on the job at hand. At the other end of the spectrum, some businesses are so challenging that even the best of executive talent may find themselves running uphill constantly just to stay a few steps ahead of the competition. So when you are evaluating a growth company's management talent, assess the degree of difficulty factor in the business they are running.

The company proxy statement (also obtainable with a phone call) can provide you with additional information on the skills of management. This handy document will give you a biography of the key people in top management. Here you will learn their previous successes in other business, their education, and possibly how well-connected they are in this particular business. Be sure to emphasize their previous experience as it relates to the business that they are now in change of. Pay close attention to how long they have been with the company. This will tell you if they are responsible for your hot growth company's outstanding recent history. If it is a young company, there's an excellent chance that the current management team may well be the founders of the company.

Management that's highly motivated to produce top results is what you want in a growth company. To optimize its returns, a growth company must be operating on all cylinders. Therefore, employees must be motivated by management to do the best job possible. Management sets the tone here with incentives for performance such as stock options. In addition, because money isn't the only motivating force, they must create a climate where workers want to do the best job possible. Without customers there would be no business, so their needs must always be given top priority. And then there are the company's stockholders who expect their investment to be given maximum consideration. Because management is so crucial to a successful growth company, they also must be highly motivated. So what you have are employees, customers, stockholders, and management all wanting good things to happen to the company.

Unfortunately, however, management sometimes places their own profit objectives ahead of the common good of the stockholders of the company. There's a very simple test you can perform to see whether management is motivated more by their own pocketbook, or whether their rewards come only when all prosper. Simply page through the proxy statement until you come up with the number of shares management owns, as well as their most recent annual salaries. If the CEO and his cronies are drawing down salaries well into the six-figure range and own very little or none of the company's stock, watch out! They may be lining their pockets at the expense of the company's bottom-line profits and the shareholders as well. Ideally, what you want to see are modest or reasonable salaries combined with substantial positions in the company's stock. When a company's top management does best, i.e., their stock goes up, you as a shareholder also make out best.

Let's look at an example to see how this works. At the ABC Company, the first CEO, John Smith, makes $1 million in salary during 1990, regardless of what the stock does. Of course he doesn't want the stock to collapse or he might be out of a job. But as long as he does okay, he pockets a cool million. In contrast, let's observe the compensation for the second CEO, George Jones. If the stock stays flat for the year, he stands to earn $300,000.

Salaries in ABC Company

- 10 million shares outstanding
- January 1, 1990, to December 31, 1990 - Stock rallies from $10 to $15.
- CEO, John Smith, has a $1-million salary, but no stock.

- CEO, George Jones, has a $300,000 salary and 500,000 shares of stock.

For George Jones, if the stock had declined even one point, his loss of $500,000 on the value of his 500,000 shares theoretically would have more than wiped out his salary. On the other hand, because ABC rallied from $10 to $15 in 1990, he made an additional $2.5 million on top of his salary. Key executives like Mr. Jones do have certain restrictions on selling their shares so that it's highly unlikely that he would sell all of his stock and realize this kind of profit at year's end. Nevertheless, even key management types such as Mr. Jones will, especially if the company's stock has rallied significantly, diversify their assets by selling some shares. This is a prudent move and should not be looked at as a negative unless their sale of stock eventually reduces their holding to a small and insignificant amount.

Big companies with 50 to 100 or more people in management may sometimes get away with having executives of less than the best caliber. This luxury cannot be afforded by your potential small growth stock purchase. You will therefore want to make sure you are satisfied with the motivational level and competency of the company's leaders of the stock that you are considering for investment.

SERVICE

In today's highly competitive world, a young growth company with an exciting new product or innovative service must not forget to offer the best possible service. Remember that quality service is the key to any successful business. That first sale is only the tip of the iceberg. It also means providing top-notch service after the sale, following up with new and existing customers to make certain they are well satisfied with your company and its offerings. Because customers are not won in today's environment without a struggle, a company must do everything within reason and within its power not to lose business from existing customers. After all it's no secret that the true test of success for any business is repeat business.

During the 1980s providing top-quality service became almost an obsession with corporate America. Several fine books have been written that deal exclusively with this subject alone, such as *The Service Edge* and *Service America*. Companies are now more than ever aware of the need to provide quality service. Customers are increasingly flocking to those companies that provide good service and are more than ever, thanks to today's advanced communications, aware of when they are getting it and when they are not. When evaluating your potential purchase, make sure you give it a big plus if your impression of its service is favorable. If their service is sloppy, however, they better have a lot else going for them, such as having a patent on a product that's in great demand and is virtually indispensable. Otherwise, if your prospect company offers poor service, drop it from your potential buy list like a hot potato.

There are a number of ways for you, the investor, to test the quality of service at a company you are investigating. For starters, simply give the company a call and note the friendliness, responsiveness, knowledge, and willingness of the receptionist in giving you information and/or properly directing your call. If the receptionist hasn't been trained to get you where you want to go, already you are going to start wondering what kind of operation you are dealing with. One of the wonders of today's high-tech world are these systems that initially greet you with a recording that plays a number of potential options in trying to help direct your call. You are then supposed to hit the appropriate buttons on your touch-tone phone. Be alert to those systems that make it easy for you to get your call routed in the right direction. At the same time, if they read off a host of options that only leave you confused, and then you have to wait endlessly for a live voice at the other end of the phone, beware! If this initial impression of a company is upsetting to you, imagine how much the company's customers must like it.

Your initial foray via the phone into company headquarters will probably take you, the inquisitive investor, to investor relations. The job of these folks is to answer your questions on the company in a cheerful and friendly manner and to promptly send you the literature you request on the company. Check to see how knowledgeable they are on the company. When you get your literature, look at the postmark to see if it was mailed within a day of when you asked for it.

Once you know enough about a company to ask some really tough, penetrating questions, the type that will set you apart as an investor, give the investor relations department another call. If they are really sharp, they will have the answers. However, there's a good chance that you will stump them on a number of key points. Stress to them that you are very interested in their company and that you're considering making a sizeable investment in it. You don't need to discuss the amount. Sizeable to you may be 100 shares or 10,000. So what? It's your money and you want it only in the best possible stocks. Proceed onward. Ask to speak to a corporate officer who can give you the information you need before you invest your cold hard cash. This approach will more often than not, at least in smaller growth companies, buy you an audience with the chief financial officer or maybe the CEO.

When you get a key executive on the line, don't be shy. Ask the questions you need answers to. Test their knowledge. Do they seem to have a handle on things? Are they believable? And of course, do they make you feel wanted as an investor? Is their attitude one of friendliness, or does your call seem to be an intrusion? In all fairness to these executives, don't plan on grilling them for an hour or two, because they're more than likely very busy. Plan instead to spend five to ten minutes asking the key questions, and do be impressed that they took the time to talk to you. If the company you are calling is rather small, there is a possibility that you'll reach an officer on your first call, as they may not yet have budgeted for an investor relations department.

The company's customers and suppliers are another good source of information on the quality of their service. What do their suppliers have to say about XYZ? Do they like doing business with them? Are they easy to work with? Perhaps you can question some of their customers to find out their level of satisfaction with the company's product or service. Best of all, you may even have the opportunity to be a customer of the company whose stock you are considering for purchase. A friend traveling through the south phoned me and mentioned the popularity and quality of the Cracker Barrel Old Country restaurants. I'd wished he'd made the trip a few months earlier as the stock had already tripled in price. This kind of grass roots analysis may help you spot a winning stock. If you experience for yourself, or hear from a friend, of a company that provides a quality service, or if a company sells a product and provides top service before and after the sale, open your eyes to the possibility of a potential winning stock.

SPONSORSHIP

Top growth stocks do not exist in a vacuum, at least not the ones whose shares are happily trending upward. On the contrary, the future winners should be in the earlier stages of developing sponsorship, of acquiring a following. This can be evidenced by analysts who begin to write research reports on the company as well as by positions taken by big-money institutions. There are several means available to you to test a company's sponsorship.

In the beginning most small growth companies may be written up by only one analyst, perhaps the one at the firm that brought the company public. Some small stocks have even failed to garner one such report. What an initial research report says about a company is that there is at least one analyst who is willing to step forward, to put his name on a report and in essence tell those who read it that he believes it is a good investment. He could, obviously, be right or wrong, but at least he's willing to put his professional judgment on the line and say this one is worth buying. That is a start toward sponsorship. But as stated earlier, you can make a lot of mistakes this early in the game. You'll improve your odds tremendously by seeing additional confirmation in the form of other analysts' favorable reports on the stock.

In the early stages, brokerage reports will most likely be issued by a small local brokerage that's probably located somewhat near the company in question. The stock may then gain coverage from a regional brokerage which will provide additional clout in marketing the company's shares. Let's say that hot Stock ABC has just been written up by a regional brokerage with 200 brokers. They all then receive a copy of the report and 50 of the brokers then decide to offer the stock to their clients. This can create a snowball effect on the stock as eager investors clamor to get on board their brokerage's next big winner. This kind of move in a stock may be absent when the first or second report is written at the local level. Carrying this a step further, when one or a number of national brokerages start following and recommending the stock, look out! Now you've got national attention working for you and the power of thousands of brokers phoning their customers to pitch the stock all over the country! When sponsorship rises to this level and you were in the stock ahead of the crowd, you are in the enviable position of watching latecomers turn your stock into one of the darlings of Wall Street. By now the stock could be on several prominent analysts' buy lists and you are now merely along for the ride.

There are a number of sources you can pursue to find out just how widely your hot prospect is now being followed. The investor relations department may be willing to inform you of who has written on the company. However, not all are willing to send you copies of the analyst's reports. You may have to then call the brokerage that put out the analyst's report to receive a copy. *Barron's Financial Weekly* lists a number of new reports that have just been issued.

Institutional Ownership

For the most part, the big institutions such as mutual funds, insurance companies, banks, and pension plans invest primarily in large capitalization stocks. They must follow this approach because they have huge amounts of money to invest. Of necessity, they need to buy and sell stocks that have liquidity, stocks where they can take a meaningful position or that they can sell without substantially disturbing the current price. Let's say Joe Fund Manager has $200 million to invest in 50 stocks. That would work out to $4 million per stock, although in actuality most all positions will be much larger or smaller than this average. If Joe puts $1,000,000 (only .50% of the fund) into a small stock at $10 a share, that's equal to a 100,000-share buy order. To purchase this many shares at the prevailing price might take days or weeks. To buy it all at once could drive the stock up several points. By now you probably get the picture. Institutions face a big problem in buying and selling small growth stocks. But that's not to say they don't enter this segment of the market. When institutional investors do invest in small growth stocks it usually represents a serious, long-term commitment on their part. They can't easily buy and sell 300 or 1,000 shares near or at the current quote like you, the individual investor can. This of course gives you a big advantage due to your superior liquidity.

The ideal situation is to find stocks whose institutional ownership has begun, but is still in its early stages. As a rule of thumb, you would like to see institutional ownership of 10% to 20% of the stock. This percentage indicates that the big-money boys have enough faith in your prospect to invest a large sum for long haul. That's not to say they won't sell out and drive the company's shares lower if things turn for the worse; they probably will. But from their perspective they wouldn't have made a commitment in an illiquid stock in the first place if they didn't believe it would be a winner for years to come. They can't play hopscotch with stocks like this the way they can with GM, ATT, or IBM. These behemoths, by the way, are typically 50% to 80% owned by the institutions.

Now as the stock gains in prominence over months and years and its liquidity improves through a higher stock price and as additional shares are issued, other big institutions will follow with a herdlike instinct to the next favorite of Wall Street. This increasing demand for the shares of your stock can help catapult it skyward.

You can find out the current level of institutional ownership from a number of sources. Each month Standard and Poor's publishes its *Stock Guide,* which contains current data on about 5,000 publicly traded companies. The listing includes each company's total shares outstanding and those held by institutions. If XYZ Corporation has 12,000,000 shares outstanding and institutions own 1,440,000 shares, that would figure out to be 12% of the total. By subscribing to the *Stock Guide*, you can compare current ownership figures to those of the previous month to determine if the institutions are net buyers or sellers of the stock in question.

$$\frac{\text{Shares Held by Institutions}}{\text{Shares Outstanding}} = \text{Percentage Owned by Institutions}$$

Table 3-8 shows changes in institutional ownership for a number of leading growth stocks. During 1991, institutional ownership rose significantly, as did each company's stock price.

William O'Neil in Los Angeles publishes charts on thousands of small growth companies. The service is expensive, but it covers a wealth of data. The charts show institutional ownership and they go a couple of steps further by breaking it down into categories, such as banks or mutual funds. They also list each institution that owns the stock and how many shares they have. If you really want to get fanatical in your analysis, you can check out these names to see if any well-known and prestigious institutions with good track records own shares of your stock.

To a lesser, but still sometimes meaningful degree, sponsorship for a stock can come from some additional sources. Growing in popularity are a number of small growth stock conferences held throughout the country. These meetings allow presenting companies to tell their story to hundreds of interested investors, both individual and institutional, in one setting. It is not uncommon for a top-quality growth stock to stand out from the

---

Table 3-8
Institutional Buying

	End of 1990		End of 1991		
	Number of Institutions	Ownership Percentage	Number of Institutions	Ownership Percentage	Stock Gain 1991
Cambex	5	3.9%	19	18.7%	+293.8%
Immune Response	14	8.2%	64	45.2%	+1265.2%
Mail Boxes, Etc.	30	16.3%	35	30.5%	+136.5%
T2 Medical	66	35.2%	116	49.3%	+301.7%
Tokos Medical	35	27.0%	107	60.2%	+252.9%
Vencor	14	9.8%	77	39.2%	+306.7%
Rainbow Technologies	13	16.6%	31	30.5%	+257.7%

crowd at one of these meetings and gain an influential following. There's an old saying, if you've got it, flaunt it. With this in mind, it is desirable for a quality growth company to have an active public relations department or to hire a firm to do it for them. Getting the word out on new contracts, new products, positive financial results, and so forth on a consistent basis can eventually work to build investor interest. You should consider it as a negative if a company is doing great things, but management fails to let the investment community know what is happening.

In sum, what you are looking for is attention. You want the world to know about your hot growth stock, to get excited about it, to buy shares in it and send its price skyward. All of the sponsorship items mentioned above will help to achieve this goal.

SALES GROWTH

Sales of a growth company, by definition, must be expanding at a rapid rate. The company's product or service should not only be in great demand now, but it should show characteristics that would lead you to believe that demand will continue for several years or more to come. Companies that sell faddish products like Hoola Hoops or Cabbage Patch dolls aren't interesting. Instead, the company's goods or services should be in line with the macro trends in the economy that may last for possibly ten years or longer. You may have witnessed what has happened to stocks that rode the major trends in the environment, medical services, and software industries, to name a few. These trends more than likely will continue to grow in the years ahead, and other macro trends will also develop. What you are looking for from a company's sales is a record of impressive growth, the likelihood that the record will continue, and the proof that the sales effort is a profitable one.

Ideally, recent quarterly and annual sales figures will demonstrate impressive double growth. As a rule of thumb, you should expect a growth rate of at least 20%. It's not uncommon to find a small growth company with sales growth of 50% to 100% or more. These astronomical rates normally don't last too long because they are for the most part unsustainable. Nevertheless, a company that is growing at 75% may be a good investment, because nobody realistically expects that kind of growth to last too long. Most growth stock investors are quite pleased with sales that grow from 20% to 30% annually, year after year.

If sales growth has accelerated lately at an above-average pace, it's worth finding out why. Perhaps a company may have just released a new product that's selling like gangbusters. Maybe some large customers have just signed up for their service. An acceleration in sales for those reasons can be the start of an exciting growth phase for the stock of the company in question. Pharmaceutical stocks can jump five to ten points in a day when the FDA. approves a new drug. Although not as dramatic, the same thing happens with small growth stocks that add a new product or service to their existing line.

You should study the quarterly figures to make sure each quarter is progressing favorably versus the same quarter of a year or two ago. Growth companies that are ramping up should have very few, if any, quarterly results that don't meet and beat the same quarter of a year ago. If you do discover a quarter that's not too impressive, try to find out the reason for the less than robust results. There could be a legitimate reason such as a slowdown in the economy or a delay in bringing a new product to market. Quarterly figures are also subject to seasonal tendencies depending on the business. Although quarterly results are important, at least because Wall Street thinks so, you should really place your emphasis on annual results. Twelve-month sales figures have a way of smoothing out the twists and turns of the quarterly data. If the annual comparisons don't stack up, move on to the next stock. In today's dynamic economy there are numerous companies with businesses that are expanding rapidly, so you need only settle for the best, for those that demonstrate consistently high growth.

Sales figures can be broken down in several ways to give you additional insights as to how a business is doing and how it is growing. In the annual report, you'll find a consolidated statement of income. This will break revenues down into various categories. Each segment may be broken down even further in the footnotes that follow the financial statements. A business that sells just one product may list sales of that product and interest income from corporate investments. Obviously, you need look no further in this case.

More complex businesses may list several sources of revenue. Here you should be looking for signs of some positive trends in the most significant as well as developing sources of revenue. For instance, assume that the company's core business, which represents 65% of revenues, is growing at 30%, but that rate of growth has been slowing somewhat. On the other hand, a segment that represents only 30% of the business is expanding at a rate of 75% annually. At these rates of growth, within a few years the smaller segment may now become the company's most important source of income. Examples of this can be found in companies that have relied heavily on work for the defense department, but because of the cold war's ending are now shifting over to civilian work. There's nothing necessarily wrong with a company whose emphasis is changing. Just be sure to take note of where its income is coming from. Do you still want to own the company if its primary business looks like it is heading toward widgets and away from buggy whips?

Although not all segments of a company's business will grow at exactly the same rate, perhaps you will find that no one area is necessarily outpacing any other to a great degree. In this case, the company's balance of revenue may be unchanged for some years to come. In other words, what you see now is what you get.

Businesses that go global are in line with one of the megatrends that shows no signs of abating. You should consider it a real plus if your company has successfully undertaken an international sales effort. In the footnotes you will often find reference to the last few years' growth in nondomestic sales. Because this figure probably represents far less than half of sales of a small company, in many cases you should expect to find international sales growing at a very rapid clip. Companies with an international focus, as evidenced by a rapidly growing presence overseas, are demonstrating an opportunistic approach that will only serve to help in their efforts to grow the business.

Generally speaking, businesses either provide a service or manufacture and sell products. There is, of course, a great deal of overlap between these two categories. For instance, companies that sell products may also be heavily involved in servicing those goods. Nevertheless, this discussion focuses on the concept of a company either providing a service or producing and selling a product.

In today's highly competitive world, service companies must either perform an existing service with a high degree of excellence or help meet a customer's needs with a new approach if they wish to stay in business long, much less prosper. Service companies that exploit new high technology to more effectively get a job done or bring goods to market at cheaper prices are rapidly establishing footholds for themselves. Examples of this are the increasing demand for home health care and the explosion in the growth of retail outlets with huge discount superstores. Some of the ideas presented in this chapter have applicability to some, but not all, of a variety of service industries, including heath care, retail, restaurants, cable television, and financial services.

You should also determine why customers are flocking to a company's service. Are sales growing because they provide equal or better service at a lower cost? Is the growth in sales being fueled by the opening of new outlets? Are same store sales growing impressively? What about the closure rate? Try to find out if additional services are being added to the current channels of distribution. Have you noticed how some convenience stores now sell burgers and lotto tickets? Franchises can bring in revenue from a variety of sources, including licensing fees, royalties, and the sales of products to the franchisees.

If a service company is growing fast, you will want to know their current level of market penetration. Are they just beginning to tap a large market, or has their growth just about topped out? H & R Block has a base of potential demand of millions of American taxpayers. This has enabled the company to grow steadily over the years as it continues to carve out a larger share of the market. Sales grew from about $319 million to well over $1 billion from 1981 to 1990. This service-based franchise business has recently added electronic filing, which has been a real boost to their business as it is preferred by both taxpayers and the IRS.

Office Depot has taken advantage of the desire by businesses to save on costs wherever possible. This chain of discount office supply superstores has grown from a startup in 1986 to the largest service of its kind. In 1991, sales were way over the $1 billion mark. As you might expect, the shares of both of these companies have appreciated impressively over the last few years. In 1991 alone, H & R Block was up 73% while Office Depot gained 223%.

With companies that manufacture and sell products, you will need to find out why their product is a hot seller and why this demand should continue to grow over the years ahead. What problem does their product solve? How does it make life easier? What is the major benefit to purchasing their product? Does it do something new or is it cheaper and/or more useful than a competitor's product? The answers to questions like these will give you a good idea of a company's potential for sustained growth over a period of several years. What you want to avoid are businesses whose flame burns brightly for a short period of time and then goes out quickly. These burnouts can occur quickly, especially as technology continues to evolve. So be careful to make sure your product-oriented selections have staying power. Try to find product businesses that operate in a niche market.

It was easy to classify industries in the past. You had the following industries: autos, steels, papers, utilities, and so on. The technological explosion has spawned substantial growth and an explosion in a number of industries now in existence. Indeed, many small companies can lay claim to being the originator and leading player in a highly specialized niche/mini-industry. Indeed, their position can often be very secure due to their ownership of a proprietary product. Because customer demands for products can change quickly, you will want to know what's being done to upgrade the company's products. Find out what's being spent on research and development and how effective these expenditures have been in the past. You need more than research and development dollars; your company needs results.

Trade journals can also serve as a useful guide in indicating the status of a company's offerings within its industry. Obviously, you will want to see your purchase candidate near or at the top of the standings. These surveys are often very valuable clues as to just how much acceptance a product has when in the hands of the customers that they need to satisfy.

Software companies provide a product that is relatively inexpensive to manufacture. On the other hand, some product companies may have a substantial investment in their manufacturing facility. If their plant is only being used at 40% of its capacity, they have room to grow before adding another plant. Unit sales, as opposed to dollar sales, could grow at a 30% compounded rate for over three years before a new plant would be needed. Should their current plant be running at or near capacity, you will need to know what their expansion plans are. The company should not lose future sales because it hasn't geared up for increased demand. In addition, you may not want to be in the stock if the expansion is going to be costly and create a drag on its earnings for several quarters.

From December 31, 1989, to December 31, 1991, shares of Novell, Inc., shot up over 674%. Fueling this growth was the company's proprietary (a key word) line of products that allows PCs to communicate with others in the same network. Novell's local area networks have captured over half the market with sales in excess of $600 million in 1991. That's not too bad considering they were only $33.6 million back in 1985. Novell is a prime example of what can happen to a company that provides a new and needed product.

PROFIT MARGINS

Rapidly escalating revenues from providing a service or selling a product are not enough alone to make a company's stock a winner. These operations must be carried on profitably, or all is for naught. Earnings per share was identified as the number-one fundamental in the eyes of Wall Street. What helps create a rapid growth of earnings in excess of sales is an expansion of a company's profit margin.

Profit margins are calculated both before and after taxes. Because many businesses within an industry have differing tax rates, many analysts choose to use pretax earnings. This calculation allows a company to be easily compared with its peers to find out which one is getting the best return from its sales efforts, irrespective of taxes. Companies with significantly higher margins than their competitors often have more leeway in using pricing strategies to grab market share from their competitors. They also have more flexibility and a greater degree of safety in meeting downturns in the economy should a general slowdown in business push industry prices lower. However, this discussion focuses on after-tax margins, or net-profit margins. As mentioned earlier, many successful young companies are doing well because they sell a unique product or provide a service differently than it has been done before. Therefore, industry classification does not carry as much relevance, especially when you are doing something by yourself or with only one or two competitors.

$$\text{Net Profit Margin} = \frac{\text{Net Income}}{\text{Total Revenues}}$$

Profit margins come as the result of a very simple calculation. Just divide net income by total revenues. If a company earned $1 million after taxes and its revenues were $5 million, its net profit margin would be 20%. As with the other key measures of financial performance, what you are looking for is a positive trend. Margins that are growing at what may be a slight percentage each year can have an explosive effect on earnings. A growing business should experience a number of years of margin expansion as economies of scale and increasing efficiencies by management in running the business take hold. A franchise company, for example, may advertise in a large metropolitan area. While its advertising cost remains the same, it may now cover 50 fast-food stores versus 20 previously. Without adding to capacity, a manufacturing company whose sales are growing may gain a greater return from its investment in a plant that was sitting still a large part of the time when the business was just getting going.

Ideally, the stock you're evaluating will have both increasing sales and margins. There is, however, a time when only so much in profits can be squeezed out of a sales dollar. When margins do level off, hopefully it will be at a high and sustainable rate. In the meantime, while your potential winner is in its explosive growth phase, it is best to have some margin expansion taking place. Because you are investing for the long term, don't be overly concerned if margins flatten or even decline slightly for a few quarters or a year. There could be a very good reason for this. However, you will want to see no more than perhaps a 12-month interruption within an overall positive trend.

Consider the following examples which show you what expanding margins can do for earnings. Table 3-9 shows margins and sales growth for two companies—ABC Corporation and XYZ Corporation. ABC Corporation is experiencing steady growth in sales of 20% annually. Meanwhile, its net profit margin remains stable at 10%. After four years, sales have grown from $1 million to $2.07 million. During this time, earnings have increased exactly the same (in terms of percentages) from $100,000 to $207,360. ABC's performance is certainly nothing to sneeze at. But remember, if margin expansion tops out at a relatively low rate, it may eventually give way and start receding. The impact on earnings and the price of a stock undergoing margin contraction can often be disastrous. (This will be covered in more detail in Chapter 7.)

The second company, XYZ Corporation, also has sales that are growing at 20% annually. In sharp contrast to ABC, however, are XYZ's margins,

Table 3-9
Profit Margin Comparison

ABC Corporation - Margins Stable - 20% Sales Growth

Year	Base Year	1	2	3	4
Sales	$1,000,000	$1,200,000	$1,440,000	$1,728,000	$2,073,600
Net Profit Margin	10%	10%	10%	10%	10%
Earnings	$100,000	$120,000	$144,000	$172,800	$207,360
% Earnings Growth	—	20%	20%	20%	20%

XYZ Corporation - Margins Expanding - 20% Sales Growth

Year	Base Year	1	2	3	4
Sales	$1,000,000	$1,200,000	$1,440,000	$1,728,000	$2,073,600
Net Profit Margin	10%	11%	12%	13%	14%
Earnings	$100,000	$133,000	$172,800	$244,640	$290,304
% Earnings Growth	—	32%	30.9%	30.0%	29.2%

which are expanding each year. Note what this seemingly small annual 1% increase in margins has done for earnings. After the fourth year, XYZ's net income is $290,304 versus $207,360 for ABC. Also observe the increase in the annual percentage growth of earnings.

Clearly, a company whose net profit margin is on the rise and whose revenues are growing at a rapid clip is poised to produce some impressive results in the years ahead, providing that these trends continue. But that's not all! There's a third factor that can cause a stock to go into orbit—multiple expansion. A stock with the characteristics of XYZ will be awarded a correspondingly higher P/E ratio as investors gain confidence in the company's ability to perform year in and year out. Table 3-10 shows how XYZ's P/E and stock price might have grown over the years in concert with sales, margins, and earnings.

At the start, XYZ is trading at a rather modest multiple of 20. One year later, Wall Street is impressed enough to push XYZ's multiple to 24. With the higher EPS, XYZ's stock has gained 56% (from 2 to 3 1/8). However, the best is yet to come. As the years go by, the triple-barreled combination of increasing sales, expanding margins, and an upward revision in the stock's multiple combine to catapult the stock's price even higher. Table 3-11 summarizes the results of XYZ's growth. Growth of 20% annually enabled sales to more than double in four years. Margin expansion helped push earnings even higher as they nearly tripled during the same time.

Table 3-10
XYZ Corporation — Triple-Barreled Growth

Year	Base Year	1	2	3	4
Sales	$1,000,000	$1,200,000	$1,440,000	$1,728,000	$2,073,600
Net Profit Margin	10%	11%	12%	13%	14%
Earnings	$100,000	$132,000	$172,800	$224,640	$290,304
Earnings per Share	10 cents	13 cents	17 cents	22 cents	29 cents
P/E	20	24	28	31	35
Stock Price	$2	$3 1/8	$4 3/4	$6 7/8	$10 1/8

Please note: Due to rounding, earnings per share reported in cents per share may be slightly more or less than the actual number. Assume that XYZ's shares outstanding remain at $1 million. Earnings per share and stock prices are rounded off to conform with normal financial reporting.

Table 3-11
XYZ Corporation's Four-Year Growth

	Beginning	4 Years Later	% Growth	Compound % Growth Rate
Sales	$1,000,000	$2,073,600	207%	20.0%
Earnings	$100,000	$290,304	290%	30.5%
Stock	$2	$10 1/8	406%	42.0%

Finally, XYZ's stock soared over 400% as a result of increasing sales, margins, and a rising P/E.

Figure 3-1 gives another perception of how this combination of events can serve to help shoot a stock's price through the roof. In fact, this figure alone may be the most important one in the book. Keep it in mind as you are searching for the next winners on Wall Street.

In Figure 3-1, Line 1 shows what you may expect from a stock if sales grow steadily but with no margin or P/E expansion. Sales growth combined with margin expansion serves to create a steeper ascent in a stock's price as evidenced by Line 2 in Figure 3-1. When Wall Street wakes up to the fact that this stock is a winner, its P/E multiple will expand accordingly, creating an even steeper ascent in a stock's price, shown in Figure 3-1 by Line 3.

Happily enough, in the real world of investing, stocks actually do perform in a similar fashion to the hypothetical stock XYZ. Biomet, Inc., a maker of a variety of medical products, is a great example of what can happen when the forces making up the "triple play" are in operation (Table 3-12). As you can see, Biomet's sales and earnings grew extremely fast over this five-year period. But look what happened to the price of Biomet's shares! If you can find the ideal combination of sales, margin, and P/E growth before everyone else on Wall Street, you just might have found yourself a stock that could perform like Biomet and possibly match its meteoric rise.

RETURN ON EQUITY

The shareholder of a small growth company must place a great deal of faith in management's ability to increase the value of their investment. This is especially so in small growth companies, because they pay little, or

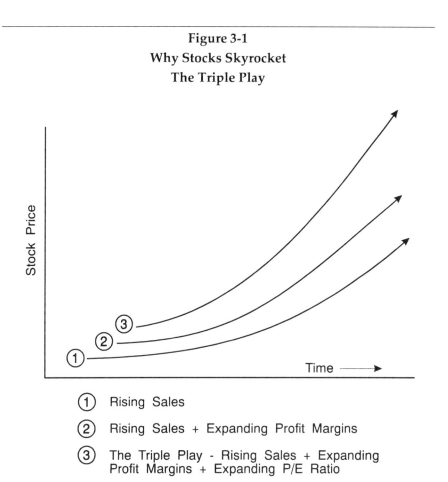

Figure 3-1
Why Stocks Skyrocket
The Triple Play

① Rising Sales

② Rising Sales + Expanding Profit Margins

③ The Triple Play - Rising Sales + Expanding
   Profit Margins + Expanding P/E Ratio

in most cases, no dividends. Instead, virtually all earnings are retained by the company with the intent that they be used to foster future growth. The extent to which management can earn an above-average return on these reinvested funds is a measure of their talent, as well as the quality of the business itself.

There is an easy calculation you can perform which reveals the return that retained profits are earning. By subtracting a company's liabilities from its assets you will get its net worth. This is commonly referred to as stockholders' equity. Should you wish to carry this a step further, you can divide the net worth of the business by the total number of shares outstanding to arrive at the company's book value.

Table 3-12
Biomet's Triple Play
1986 - 1991

	1986	1991	% Gain
Sales	$44.1 million	$209.7 million	376%
Net Profit Margin	11.8%	18.8%	—
EPS	6 cents	36 cents	500%
P/E	35.4	85.4	—
Stock	2 1/8*	30 3/4	1,347%

Note: All figures are for Biomet's fiscal year, which ends on May 31.
*Stock price adjusted for all splits.

Shareholders' Equity = Total Assets – Total Liabilities

The rate of return that management is able to earn on the funds under its management is called return on equity (ROE). This is calculated by dividing a company's net income by stockholders' equity (net worth). The easy way is to use the year-end figure for stockholders' equity. However, if you wish to be more precise, you should add the beginning and end of the year figures together and divide them by two. Divide this figure into net income and you have the average ROE earned by the company. The rationale for this extra step is that the net income was earned throughout the year. In either case, you are looking for a rather attractive return to adequately compensate you for the risk of investing in a growth stock, and for the fact that you continue to trust management with all (or nearly all if it pays a small dividend) of the company's earnings. ROE is also important because it is a measure of how fast the company can grow without raising additional sources of capital, such as long-term debt which increases risk, or new offerings of equity which may dilute earnings. As a guideline, you should drop any small growth company with an ROE under 15% to 20% from your consideration. Many new, fast-growing companies may have an ROE in excess of 40% to 50%. However, you should not expect a company earning this rate of return on its stockholders' equity to do so for more than a few years, so don't be too alarmed when ROE slows down to a much more realistic figure.

$$\text{Return on Equity} = \frac{\text{Net Income}}{\text{Stockholders' Equity}}$$

The purpose of the business (from the shareholder's viewpoint) is to build the net worth of the business and for it to continue to be a highly profitable enterprise. By plowing profit back into the business each year, you create a continuous compounding of the company's net worth.

Because net worth keeps expanding rapidly in a small growth company, that's one of the reasons why shares of its stock often sell at a substantial premium to the current book value (net worth per share). The following example compares a company's current valuation to that of an interest-bearing account. Let's assume you invest $10,000 in a CD paying 7% for five years. After five years is up (with reinvestment of interest at 7%) you would then have $13,026. Now consider a stock investor who buys $10,000 worth of stock in a company. His share of stockholders' equity might be only $4,000. In other words, the company's stock is selling for 2.5 times the book value. You might ask why anyone would pay 2.5 times more than the current net worth for shares in a business. There are several reasons. Part of the answer comes from the annual compounding of the company's net worth, as well as its future earnings potential. In the example, assume that stockholders' equity is compounding at 35% annually and that the company pays no dividends. Within three years, book value has nearly caught up to the amount of the original investment. In five years the investor's share of the stockholders' equity would have gone from $4,000 to $17,936! That's more than the return generated from the CD. In addition, the stock remains an investment whose intrinsic net worth is growing by 35% annually.

So don't be overly concerned if you discover that the price of the stock you are evaluating is running well ahead of its book value. A consistently high ROE will, in a few years, build book value to a point where it may exceed your original cost of investment. Don't forget that there are a number of other things to consider in valuing a business that make its true value often well in excess of its net worth at any given time.

DIVIDENDS

Growth companies typically pay little or no dividends. In management's view, the company's profits are best put to work by being reinvested back into the business. There is nothing wrong with that. After all, the purpose of investing in an emerging growth stock is for capital appreciation, not income. Investors who need both income and growth would be best served by a quality utility stock or blue chip stocks. As an added bonus, funds that are reinvested into the business (rather than being paid as dividends) can theoretically continue to compound for you without current taxation. After a few years of successful operations, your small growth stock may declare its first dividend. When this happens the stock may gain in appeal to a number of investors, especially the big institutions, who view a first dividend announcement as a sign that a stock has arrived. In fact, many institutions and individual investors will not consider buying a stock unless it pays a dividend. With these investors, the size of the dividend is not nearly as important as the fact that the company now is paying a dividend, period. An initial dividend, therefore, may create additional demand for a stock. It also signals that the company is moving along the growth curve toward maturity and may soon be no longer considered a small growth stock.

Should your target company pay a dividend, you should expect to see it grow at a rapid rate. The annual percentage increase may mirror the growth rate of the company's net income. A small but rapidly rising dividend is a clear sign given by management of their continuing belief in the profitability of the business. Indeed, investors come to expect sizeable annual percentage hikes in the company's dividend. You should consider it to be a negative if a company fails to raise its dividend after several years of increases in its payout. Worse yet, if the dividend is cut or omitted, you may, by the time that happens, want to have been out of the stock for quite some time.

Although a small dividend, taken as a percentage of your original investment, may not seem like much, it could develop into a meaningful source of income given enough time. For example, assume you invest $10,000 in a company and that investment pays you an annual income of $100 (or 1%). Let's figure that the dividend grew at a compound rate of 20% over the next ten years. After ten years is up, your annual dividend would have grown to $619! That represents better than a 6% annual yield based on your original investment of $10,000!

Small dividends that don't seem like much may wind up being a fairly sizeable percentage of a company's net income. For example, ABC Corporation's stock sells for $10 per share. The current dividend of ten cents (or 1% based on the current stock price) appears to be rather insignificant. However, ABC is a reasonably fast-growing company that sells at a P/E of 25. That means that ABC's net income is 40 cents per share. The ten cent dividend, therefore, represents a 25% payout of the company's net income. Most small companies in their dynamic growth phase should be able to find a use for that ten cents, rather than distributing it as income.

The criteria just discussed on selecting potentially rewarding small growth stocks will hopefully help you to find some of the future winners on Wall Street. To further your understanding of these concepts, we'll take a detailed look at two small growth companies that have turned in very credible performances over the last several years. The two companies are Rainbow Technologies, a product company, and Mail Boxes, Etc., a service business. Both of the companies continue to exhibit some of the ideal characteristics of a solid long-term growth stock. However, please be advised that the future of any company is never guaranteed. When reading the case study below, try to imagine yourself analyzing other stocks of interest to you. This will help you to turn theory into practice.

CASE STUDY:
RAINBOW TECHNOLOGIES—PRODUCT COMPANY

The Business. Rainbow Technologies designs, manufactures, and markets a complete line of products that help software publishers to protect their programs from piracy. Since going public in September 1987, through December 31, 1991, Rainbow's stock has gained 830%. According to the December 12, 1991, edition of the *Computer Dealer News*, a study by the Software Publishers Association estimates that publishers lost $2.4 billion in revenues alone in 1990 to piracy. These estimates are believed to be conservative. In essence, Rainbow is the leading player in a small but rapidly growing industry that is helping to solve a big problem.

Earnings per Share. As you recall, earnings per share is Wall Street's number-one fundamental for a small growth company. Except for the second half of 1990, Rainbow has turned in an excellent performance since going public in September of 1987 (Table 3-13). (A discussion of Rainbow's performance during the second half of 1990 appears later in this chapter.) From the end of 1987 to the end of 1991, earnings per share compounded at 55% annually.

Management. Rainbow's CEO and co-founder, Walter Straub, has instilled a profitability culture at the company. Top management places a high emphasis on product development to maintain its leadership position in the industry. They also stress customer service. Management has extensive experience in finance and the computer industry. Management

Table 3-13
Rainbow's Earnings per Share Percentage Growth

Year	EPS	% Growth from Previous Year
1986	.07	
1987	.14	100.0%
1988	.27	92.9%
1989	.45	66.7%
1990	.49	8.9%
1991	.80	63.3%

appears to be more motivated by the performance of the company than by high salaries. As an example, after its initial public offering in 1987, Mr. Straub's shares in Rainbow were valued at $1.26 million. At the end of 1991, his company holdings were valued at $10.06 million. In contrast, his salary in 1990 was $190,000. He stands to benefit primarily by the stock going up in value.

Service. Although Rainbow is a product company, it nevertheless emphasizes customer service. Repeat business makes up a substantial portion of revenues, and new customers come largely from referrals. A quarterly newsletter is sent to all of the company's customers. Visits and phone calls to the company have proven that employees are very courteous and responsive to inquiries.

Sponsorship. Although it has been a highly successful company to date, Rainbow has remained relatively under-followed by the brokerage community because of its size. At the end of 1991, only three firms were following and writing reports on the company. Institutional ownership was relatively light at the end of 1990, as it stood at 16.6% of total shares outstanding. By the end of 1991, institutions increasingly became believers in Rainbow as their position increased to 30.5%.

Sales Growth. Rainbow is well positioned for the long term as it is a beneficiary of the ever increasing worldwide demand for software. As mentioned earlier, their products help prevent piracy of software. New products from the company's ongoing research and development effort are helping to build sales in new markets. Their Net Sentinel provides revenue protection and license control for site-licensed software programs used on local area networks. This is accomplished via a special key which is attached to a file server or designated work station. Research and development spending also brings existing products up to date. International sales as a percentage of total sales are growing rapidly, which demonstrates the company's aggressiveness. Rainbow's impressive revenue growth record is detailed in Table 3-14.

Net Profit Margin. Rainbow's net profit margin grew rapidly for a few years before sliding to 13.8% in 1990. It grew from 10.0% to 15.5% from 1986 to 1988. This decline was caused by the recession as sales growth slowed while expenses incurred for the company's move to new headquarters, proposed acquisition costs, and expenses for a German subsidiary all ate into margins. In 1991, Rainbow was back on track as net margins swelled to 18.1%. This margin expansion was part of the triple play (along with growing sales and an expanding P/E) that helped Rainbow's stock to a gain of 258% in 1991 (Table 3-15).

As you can see, a nice revenue gain combined with improving margins served to create an even better increase in EPS. This in turn led to an expansion in Rainbow's P/E, which all translated into the substantial gain in the company's stock. Ideally, the triple play is what you should be looking for from your candidates for purchase.

Return on Equity. Shareholders in Rainbow have been very pleased by what the company has been able to earn on its net equity. Over the last five years, ROE has ranged between about 25% in 1990, the year of the slowdown, and over 50% in 1991. Because of its high ROE, Rainbow has remained debt free while being able to meet its growth objectives.

Table 3-14
Rainbow's Revenue Growth Record

Year	Revenues (000)	% Change	International Sales
1986	$1,127	—	—
1987	$2,757	144.6%	10%
1988	$6,153	123.2%	11%
1989	$11,473	86.5%	28%
1990	$13,945	21.5%	30%
1991	$18,945	35.9%	N/A

	1990	1991	Percent Change
	Table 3-15		
	Rainbow's Triple Play		
Revenues	$13,945,000	$18,945,000	36%
Net Profit Margin	13.8%	18.1%	—
EPS	.49	.80	63%
P/E	13.3	29.4	—
Stock	6 1/2	23 1/4	258%

Stockholders' equity has grown rapidly over the last several years from $3.5 million in 1987 to an estimated $12 million at the end of 1991.

Dividends. The company has no plans to pay dividends in the immediate future as it prefers to invest profits back into the business.

Conclusion. Rainbow Technologies has been an excellent example of what you should be looking for in a small growth company stock. Indeed, it meets most all of the criteria precisely. You could have bought Rainbow at any time prior to its banner year in 1991, and at the end of 1991 you would have had a substantial profit. However, sometimes a good company becomes a great bargain in the stock market. Those investors who reacted negatively to the recession and the subsequent two-quarter slow-down in Rainbow's business in late 1990, failed to keep their focus on the long-term potential of this solid little company. Their selling created a great bargain for investors who upon weighing the long-term pluses could see that Rainbow's detour was temporary (Figure 3-2). This is demonstrated by the arrow in Figure 3-2, indicating the price lows in late 1990.

INTERVIEW WITH A CEO

The following is an excerpt from an interview with CEO and co-founder Walter Straub of Rainbow Technologies.

Capelle: What got you started in the software protection business?

Straub: We were looking to get into the computer industry in the early 1980s. We found a potential customer with a need to

Figure 3-2

Buying Opportunities in Rainbow Technologies

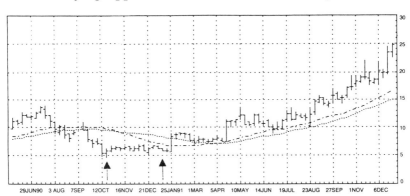

Source: Bloomberg Financial Services.

protect information. The customer had a revenue problem. He'd make one copy and it would then spread all over. He asked us (the founders of Rainbow), "What can you guys do for us?" We knew there were solutions to keeping software from being copied. But we also wanted to keep software from running unless it was an authorized and paid-for copy. So we felt there was a market for our kind of product.

Capelle: You went public in 1987, right before the crash. How did the crash affect your company?

Straub: In the middle of September 1987 we went public and raised about $3 million. We were going like crazy and then the next month the market crashes and our stock drops to 2 1/2 (from the initial public offering price of $5, (the stock has since split 2-1) but business was great. I told my people not to let the psychology of the market impact our goals and vision for the business. The economy and the software business hadn't changed as a result of the stock market.

Capelle: Rainbow has been profitable every year since you went public. What do you attribute that to?

Straub: The fundamental thing I've tried to do with Rainbow is instill this profitability culture with everybody who works here. We've set high expectations for our shareholders. I want everybody to think bottom line in this company, no matter what we do.

Capelle: Despite this emphasis on profitability, I understand that you use fairly conservative methods of accounting.

Straub: We're a very conservative company. We've never amortized for the balance sheet any kind of software development. We expense all our software right away. We balance sheet very little things. We don't do any revenue recognition tricks.

Capelle: As far as your technology goes, would you feel comfortable in saying that you are the industry leader?

Straub: We've always taken that position. We have the predominant share of the market. The technology of our software and hardware is, we feel, equal to or better than our competitors. To maintain our leadership we spend about 10% of sales on research and development. You just can't get away from that. Beyond product, a big part of this business is the fact that we give good ongoing service to the customer.

Capelle: What specifically do you do in the area of servicing the customers?

Straub: Let's say that Microsoft has introduced a new version of Windows. We're an advanced developer for Microsoft. We make sure that our products are compatible with what's coming out before it is actually out on the marketplace. So we are always upgrading our software and our hardware. It's an ongoing effort.

Capelle: In 1991, margins and profits went up sharply. Can you explain further?

Straub: At Rainbow we've placed a big emphasis on total quality commitment. When a customer places an order we make sure that it's delivered on time, that the order is correct in product and quantity. Improperly handling orders is just one of those things that costs you money. We've made a commitment throughout the organization for quality improvements. Quality service, in conjunction with product improvements from a cost standpoint, drive our margins higher.

Capelle: Many companies have had problems dealing with the recession. Perhaps your slowdown in 1990 could be attributed to the weak economy. Yet at the same time your market seems to be relatively recession-resistant.

Straub: The recession was responsible for our slowdown in the second half of 1990. Even so, certain industries have done well in the recession. The software industry in general worldwide, as shown by the results provided by such organizations as the Software Publishers Association, all demonstrate good year to year growth in the software industry. So because we are part of that economy our market is certainly not saturated, so we're penetrating a very large market. So even if that market is in a slowdown, if we're penetrating that's going to help us.

Capelle: What is your marketing strategy? You have a very large customer base (numbering in the thousands). How do you go about getting all of those new customers?

Straub: Right now, after years of missionary marketing, our number-one source is referrals, but besides that we participate in about 12 industry shows a year in the U.S. plus three or four in Europe. We rely heavily on those shows. We advertise in certain trade magazines every month. We know who the top 100 publishers are, so we go after them. We have some people who sell over the phone, and we send people out to call on the big guys. But again, a good source of leads for us right now is referrals. We just have a lot of keys (Rainbow's product) out there.

Capelle: Is there any chance that any of the top two or three customers in terms of size would ever go to another product or develop this kind of product on their own?

Straub: We hope not. But we're close enough to them that we're providing the service to them, and we believe that we've done everything so they don't even think about that option. This product looks so simple, but we have many, many years of programming behind this little thing so that it doesn't make it that easy for them to come up with something like it. If they tried to make their own, they'd run into a lot of difficulties that we've run into over the years.

Capelle: International business is really helping you to grow. You've recently announced an acquisition of a French software protection company, Microphar, based in Paris, partly for stock and partly for cash. Are you using the proceeds from your second offering of stock in 1991 for this purchase?

Straub: We're using the proceeds from the recent stock offering to fund most of that. That was the purpose of the offering, to look at synergistic-type acquisitions. Obviously, Microphar is a company in our industry. We know that industry. They're the leader in France, Italy, and Spain. So it was an ideal fit for us. It's not like venturing into a new marketplace like PC board replacements.

Capelle: Looking ahead, where do you see the company in another five to ten years?

Straub: We continue to see ourselves focusing on the area of information software and information control and distribution. We want our products to control the developer's revenue and how that revenue is managed, as well as the information that's distributed for use on the personal computer. We will continue to stress maintaining margins and profitability. We want to grow at a manageable rate—we are not doubling or anything like that, but we are growing at 35% to 40% annually and managing the bottom line. That's the focus of Rainbow.

CASE STUDY: MAIL BOXES, ETC.—SERVICE BUSINESS

The Business. Founder and CEO, Anthony W. (Tony) DeSio, started Mail Boxes, Etc. (MAIL) based on the belief that a lot of people were dissatisfied with the postal service. What MAIL does is provide a convenient alternative to the post office by providing private mailbox service, stamps, packaging, and much more. MAIL also emphasizes service for the small business owner. Since going public in 1986, MAIL franchises have grown from 255 to nearly 1,600 as of December 31, 1991. From an offering price of 5.09 (adjusted for stock splits) in June 1986, MAIL's stock has risen to 34 as of December 31, 1991. The total gain of 568% represents a compounded annual return of about 41% since going public.

Earnings per Share. MAIL's earnings were hurt in 1990 and 1991 by the settlement of a lawsuit and losses incurred in a start-up by MBE Service Corporation, MAIL's electronic tax-filing subsidiary. Table 3-16 shows MAIL's earning with and without these charges. Excluding these nonrecurring events, MAIL's earnings have shown a steady pattern of growth.

Management. Management has set some lofty goals for MAIL. They want to become the dominant factor in the industry and plan to have 5,000 franchises open by the year 2000. CEO DeSio believes that MAIL's foreign business can be even bigger than its domestic business. Management's strategy of decentralization has helped MAIL to become a presence in over 100 metropolitan areas. Over 150 area developers are licensed to sell franchises across the country. The company's mission statement includes a commitment to provide top quality service. Management does an excellent job of getting the word out on MAIL's successes. Articles on MAIL have appeared in several publications including: *Success, Entrepreneur,*

Table 3-16

MAIL's Earnings per Share Percentage Growth

Year	EPS	% Growth	EPS (With Charges)
1986	.24	100.0%	.24
1987	.29	20.8%	.29
1988	.36	24.1%	.36
1989	.47	30.6%	.47
1990	.64	36.2%	.30
1991	.81	26.6%	.74

Inc., Forbes, and *BusinessWeek.* DeSio's cash compensation for fiscal year 1991 was $269,337. In sharp contrast, his ownership position in the company, as of April 30, 1991, was at 887,594 shares, valued at 19 1/4 each.

Service. MAIL has succeeded by providing quality service in an area where it was deficient. In addition to postal services, MAIL also offers its customers U.P.S., photocopies, secretarial services, finger printing, and on and on. MAIL's stores are well laid out and positioned in handy locations.

Sponsorship. Institutional interest in MAIL has increased steadily over the last few years and then rose sharply in calendar year 1991. From December 31, 1990, to December 31, 1991, institutional ownership increased from 16.3% to 30.5% as the stock continued to be discovered. In 1991, MAIL's stock gained 136.5%. Brokerage coverage continues to widen as some large and prestigious firms are now following the stock. Figure 3-3 is a weekly price chart of the stock. Arrows are shown to represent when each firm listed began to officially cover the stock and at what price. MAIL is a classic example of how a solid small growth company begins to attract a following after demonstrating positive results for several years running.

Sales Growth. Thanks largely to the widespread use of computers, a major trend has resulted in more business being conducted in the home. More and more small business people will need the type of services offered by MAIL. Royalty and advertisement fees are making this a fast growing segment of MAIL's business and a recurring source of revenue. Same store sales grew 15% in 1990 and 14% in 1991 as MAIL continues to add more services to each location. Table 3-17 summarizes MAIL's reve-

Table 3-17
MAIL's Revenue Growth Record

Year	Revenues (000)	Percent Increase	Royalty and Advertisement Fees (000)	Percent Increase
1986	$ 4,947	105.8%	$ 935	79.5%
1987	$ 9,431	90.6%	$ 1,876	100.6%
1988	$12,503	32.6%	$ 3,030	61.5%
1989	$19,377	55.0%	$ 4,725	55.9%
1990	$25,724	32.8%	$ 7,127	50.8%
1991	$30,303	17.8%	$10,083	41.5%

Figure 3-3
Weekly Price Chart of MAIL BOXES, ETC.

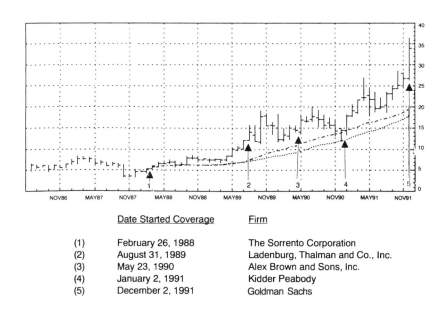

	Date Started Coverage	Firm
(1)	February 26, 1988	The Sorrento Corporation
(2)	August 31, 1989	Ladenburg, Thalman and Co., Inc.
(3)	May 23, 1990	Alex Brown and Sons, Inc.
(4)	January 2, 1991	Kidder Peabody
(5)	December 2, 1991	Goldman Sachs

Source: Bloomberg Financial Services.

nue growth, including a recap of the growth in royalty and advertisement income. Growing from a small base, revenues shot up quickly in the first few years. Although they have slowed in recent years in percentages, they are still growing at a good clip.

Net Profit Margin. MAIL's net profit margin has been fairly consistent over the last several years except for 1990, which was impacted by an expensive lawsuit. The last few years' net margins were as follows:

Year	Net Profit Margin
1988	14.9
1989	12.4
1990	5.9
1991	13.3

It would, of course, be a more favorable sign if these were in a steadily rising trend. However, it's not always possible to have everything fit precisely into the selection criteria presented and sometimes not necessary in order to achieve superior results.

Return on Equity. The net return on average shareholders' equity has been running at a healthy rate of nearly 20% for the last several years with the exception of 1990 (again, the year of the lawsuit). The last several years returns are as follows:

Year	Return
1991	19.1%
1990	11.9%
1989	22.2%
1988	20.8%

Dividends. All income is being reinvested into the company to help fund future growth.

Conclusion. Mail Boxes, Etc., has done an excellent job of providing an attractive alternative to the post office and of addressing the need of the small business consumer. By providing top quality service, MAIL has in turn proven to be an excellent selection for long-term investors. After declining sharply because of the crash of 1987, MAIL's shares have steadily worked their way higher, allowing for periodic and normal corrections along the way. It will be interesting to see if MAIL can reach its goal of becoming the McDonald's of its industry within a few years.

SUMMARY

- There are thousands of companies to choose from, so be selective.
- Be patient; it takes time for small growth stocks to gain several-fold.

- Do your homework so you can stack the odds in your favor.
- Learn to ask the make-or-break questions about a company to develop a sixth sense.
- When you find a company you like and it's priced right, don't hesitate to buy it.

The Business

- Invest in companies whose business you feel good about.
- What does the company do? Does its concept make sense to you?
- What's the company's mission statement?
- Find out if the company has a proprietary product that's in demand or if it provides a needed service in a new or better way.
- Keep in mind some industries you'd like to be in.
- Be on the lookout for some exciting new industries.

Earnings per Share/P/E Ratio

- Remember: Earnings are Wall Street's number-one fundamental concern.
- By and large avoid companies early in their development cycle; go for those with a few years of proven success behind them.
- Try to find companies with good track records of several years that have gone unnoticed.
- Earnings should be in a positive trend for at least three to five years, unless there's a good reason for an off year.
- Look for consistency and an above-average rate of growth (15% - 20%).
- Don't expect super-high EPS growth to continue for long.
- Watch for buying opportunities in a good company that reports an off quarter that is a one-time occurrence.
- Be aware of a company's seasonal tendencies to avoid disappointment in the short run.
- Distinguish between businesses with consistent and irregular sources of income.

- Watch for companies with big cash balances that derive a large portion of revenue from interest income.
- Find out how profitably funds have been put to work from previous stock offerings, if a new one is planned. Discover what the additional funds will be used for.
- Understand the effects of dilution on earnings.
- Place more emphasis on annual rather than quarterly earnings growth.
- Price to earnings ratio (P/E) correlates a stock's current price to its annual earnings per share. Fast-growing stocks have higher P/Es than moderate or slow growers.
- Stocks with consistently high earnings growth command high P/Es.
- Be careful when buying stocks with super-high P/E's - earnings disappointments can torpedo stocks with high multiples.
- Growth stocks with expanding P/E multiples can result in big stock gains.
- Identify stocks with excellent EPS growth whose P/Es have failed to grow.
- Compare a stock's P/E to the market and other stocks within its industry for signs of over- or undervaluation.

Management

- Quality management is especially important in small growth companies.
- Watch for excessive excuse making by management for poor results.
- Read the CEO's message in the annual report. What's the company's mission? What are they trying to accomplish and how do they plan to do it?
- Look for positive statements on both financial and nonfinancial matters.
- Ready the proxy statement for background information on top management.
- What you want is management that is motivated by a big ownership position in the company, not by big six-figure salaries.

Service

- Today's competitive world dictates that companies offer top-notch service.
- Repeat business because of excellent service is key.
- Call the company and put their service to the test. Ask questions and request information from investor relations.
- Try to get through to an executive of the company. Ask him the tough questions. How friendly and willing are they to give you answers?
- A company's customers and suppliers can inform you as to their quality of service. Perhaps you may even have been a customer of the company. If so, were you impressed?

Sponsorship

- Consider it a plus if a company has a small but growing number of followers, such as institutions and analysts.
- When regional or national brokerages start to follow a stock, it can shoot up in value. It is great to be invested ahead of them.
- Institutions generally stick to bigger stocks, unless they feel a small stock has unusual merit.
- Look for institutional ownership of perhaps 10% to 20% as a sign that they've started buying but have a long way to go.
- As time passes, increasing institutional interest can catapult your stock ever higher.
- Stock conferences and road shows can bring attention to a company. Watch for them in your area.
- A good public relations department can really help get the word out. Small companies need to market themselves with public relations, press releases, and articles in the press and in trade journals.

Sales/Revenues

- A good company should have products or services in great demand and they should show the characteristics that would lead you to believe this growth can be sustained, i.e., no fad products.

- Products or services should be in line with the macrotrends of the economy.
- Look for growth rates of 20% or above.
- If sales growth has accelerated recently, find out the reason. Has the company introduced a hot new product?
- Study quarterly and annual sales results. Check for seasonality. Find out why some quarters are better or worse than the normal progression. Give extra weight to annual figures.
- Break down sales (if possible) into different categories. Discover where sales are growing fastest. Perhaps a small part of a company's business is growing to where it may be its largest segment in a few years.
- Check international sales (if any); a global growth company is demonstrating an opportunistic view toward its future.
- With a service business, what's their approach to winning new customers? Discount? Merchandise? Home health care?
- Are a retailer's same store sales increasing? Are new stores being added at an impressive clip?
- What's the current level of market penetration?
- With product companies, what problems does the product solve? How does it make life easier or better?
- Is the product cheaper and/or better than a competitor's offerings?
- Look for products in a niche market. Is it a proprietary and valued product?
- What's the company doing to upgrade existing products and bring new products to market? What's the commitment to research and development?
- Trade journals can attest to or detract from the stature of a company's products? How does your prospect company's products rate?
- With a manufacturing company, are they operating at or near capacity? Will new and expensive plant and equipment need to be added anytime soon? If needed, are plans underway for the expansion of facilities?

Profit Margins

- Sales growth is not enough. Growing sales must be accompanied by stable or expanding profit margins.

- Expanding sales and margins together can fuel exceptional growth in a company's earnings.

- Profit margins can be useful in comparing the profitability of companies within the same industry.

- Net profit margins are most important—they measure a company's margins after taxes. After all, net income is what a business is left to work with after all expenses (including taxes).

- Look for positive trends. Even what appears to be a slight growth in margins can be very meaningful.

- Economies of scale and management efficiencies should help a good small growth company's margins to expand over the years.

- Remember that margins will eventually level off at some point in the future.

- Rapidly contracting margins can be disastrous to a stock's earnings.

- Why do stocks skyrocket? Sales growth + margin expansion + P/E expansion = a potentially huge gain in a stock's price.

Return on Equity

- Return on equity is a measure of the return management is able to earn on the money entrusted to it.

- Look for an attractive ROE of at least 15% to 20% in a small growth company.

- In some cases, ROE may run as high as 40% to 50% or more for a few years. Don't be too alarmed if it slows down somewhat from this lofty level.

- ROE is also a measure of how fast the company can grow annually without having to seek additional sources of capital.

- A high ROE causes a business's net worth to expand rapidly.

Dividends

- Small growth companies typically pay little or no dividends. Most, if not all, earnings are put back into the company to foster future growth.

- Earnings that go back to the company, in theory, allow your investment to compound tax-deferred.

- Even a small dividend may increase a stock's appeal, especially to some institutional investors. The declaration of a company's first dividend is a sign of maturity in a company.

- Expect small dividends to grow at a rapid rate. This growth may mirror the company's growth in earnings.

- Consider it a negative if a company fails to increase a small dividend— or worse yet, be very leery if the dividend has been cut or omitted.

- Over the long haul, a small but rapidly growing dividend could, based on your original investment, turn into a meaningful source of income.

QUESTIONS

1. Because there are thousands of small companies to choose from, a small growth stock investor should be: _____ .

2. XYZ Corporation has 4,500,000 shares outstanding. In the first quarter, XYZ had a net income of $360,000. During the second quarter, net income rose 12% and 2,000,000 additional shares were issued in a secondary offering of stock. What were XYZ's first and second quarter earnings per share (EPS)? By what percentage did they increase or decline in the second quarter?

3. Fast-growing international sales are a sign of an opportunistic management that is thinking global. Three years ago, ABC Corporation had total sales of $10.3 million; 14% came from international sales. At the end of the current year, ABC's sales had grown to $25.3 million, with international sales making up 28% of the total. By what percentage did each segment grow over the three years? Would you be very upset if management decided to issue more stock to fund overseas expansion?

4. A company is trading at 12 and has a net income of $1.4 million with revenues of $6.7 million. What is its net profit margin?

5. Service is critical for most small companies. What are some places you can check to see how they perform this critical function.

6. Each year a consistent small growth company reports above-average earnings gains of around 30-40%. Each year the P/E of the stock expands further and is now at 35 versus four years ago at 18. Why would the P/E now be so much higher?

7. You have discovered what looks like an interesting company but are concerned with the latest December quarter EPS, which at .17 is down substantially from the previous quarter. Should you drop this stock, or is there possibly a good reason for the decline?

Year	March	June	September	December	Annual
1	.12	.20	.22	.14	.68
2	.14	.25	.28	.15	.82
3	.17	.31	.40	.17	1.05

How much is EPS up in the June quarter (third year) versus the comparable quarter of a year ago?

8. What is Wall Street's number-one fundamental concern?

9. XYZ Corporation has recorded the following stream of sales and net income over the last five years. What can you conclude from this about the company's profitability and, thus, its attractiveness as an investment?

Year	1	2	3	4	5
Sales	4.2	5.5	7.0	9.0	12.0
Net Income	.6	.9	1.2	1.4	1.7

10. You are considering a small growth company for purchase and you find that it looks good from all angles, including EPS, which has progressed as follows over the last few years: .10, .15, .26, and .40. What are the percentage increases in the second, third, and fourth years? You are now a few weeks into the new year and the .40 earnings have just been announced. The stock is selling at 4 1/2. What is its P/E ratio? The P/E ratio for the S&P 500 is now at 18. The institutions own 4% of the stock. Why do you think the stock is selling at such a discount to the market?

11. A _____ product can help lock out the competition.

12. ABC Corporation is a small growth company that manufactures widgets. Its current plant is running at 35% of capacity. If unit sales are growing at an annual rate of 20%, how long will it take before the company will outgrow its current facility?

13. Name at least four of the things you would like to see mentioned in the CEO's letter in the annual report.

14. ABC Corporation has 8.4 million shares outstanding. Institutional investors now own 670,000 shares versus 310,000 six months ago. Should you be concerned about this activity? What is their current percentage of ownership? XYZ Corporation is another good growth company. It has 11.7 million shares outstanding, of which 4.7 million are owned by institutional investors. Based only on the information above, which stock looks like it has the most potential?

15. What are probably the two most important sources of sponsorship for a small growth company?

16. XYZ is a hot growth stock now selling at 18. XYZ has a 12 month's earnings of .75, resulting in a P/E of 24. Analysts expect XYZ's EPS to grow at 40% over the next two years. What is XYZ's P/E ratio at the current quote based on future earnings?

17. ABC Corporation sells high-tech products and spends 15% of sales on research and development versus the industry average of 10%. This rapidly growing young company has a 35% market share of a $120 million industry. The industry is expected to grow at an annual rate of 25% over the next three years. At that time, ABC expects to have 45% market share. How big will the industry be in three years, and what will XYZ's share be of total industry sales (in dollars)?

18. Should you be concerned if a company's sales growth rate slows from 100% to 50%?

19. ABC Corporation is benefiting from increased operating efficiencies. Five years ago revenues were $7.6 million and the company's net profit margin was 8.2%. Sales over the last five years have compounded at 24%. Meanwhile, the net profit margin has improved to 14.6%. Shares outstanding have grown from 1.1 million to 1.4 million. Meanwhile, the stock's P/E has expanded from 10 to 22. What was net income and EPS in the first and last years? What was the beginning

and ending price of ABC Corporation's stock? What percentage gain did it register over the last five years?

20. The founder and CEO of XYZ Corporation, which went public four years ago, now owns $6 million of company stock versus $3 million when the company went public. He recently sold shares valued at $400,000. The current market capitalization of XYZ is $25 million. The CEO has an annual salary of $220,000. Everything else considered, would you buy or not buy XYZ based on the information? Why or why not?

21. Sales at ABC Corporation were $2 million in 1985. Over the next five years they grew at the following annual rates (in order): 104%, 122%, 78%, 56%, and 47%. What were sales last year? How alarmed should you be because of the sharp drop in percentage growth over the last three years?

22. _____ is required if you want truly big winners.

23. XYZ Corporation has just reported earnings of .78. Earnings are projected to compound at 25%-30% over the next five years. If the low-end forecast is met, what would EPS be in five years? What would it be if XYZ grows at the more optimistic forecast of 30%? XYZ's stock is currently selling at 11. In five years, if ABC's earnings grow at 30% and the stock then commands a P/E of 16, what would the stock then be selling for? What percentage gain would the stock have made from the current price of 11?

24. You've just called ABC Corporation and asked to be put on their mailing list. Over the next 12 months, assuming ABC is interested in marketing its stock, what items would you expect to receive?

25. XYZ Corporation has 40 stores with average sales of $5,000,000 for the year just ended. They expect to open ten more stores this year. The new stores will average half of the income of the already existing stores. Same store sales are expected to rise 12% this year. What should XYZ Corporation's total sales be over the next 12 months?

26. If you purchased $15,000 worth of stock in a company that paid a dividend of $125 and the dividend grew at a 25% compounded rate over the next ten years, what would the dividend be, and what would it amount to as a percentage of the original investment?

27. A company wishes to grow at an annual rate of 25%. Based on these figures, is it earning the funds to grow on its own, or will it need to

obtain additional capital? Suppose it does need new capital. What would be two primary sources? (Use average stockholders' equity in your calculations.) Could this company afford to pay a dividend and grow at 25% without additional funding?

	December 31, 1989	December 31, 1990	December 31, 1991
Net Income (000)	1.5	2.0	2.7
Shareholders' Equity (000)	5.3	7.1	9.6
ROE	—	?	?

28. If a company has 6.8 million shares outstanding, a net income of $3.1 million and stockholders' equity of 22.4 million, what is its book value?

Chapter 4

HOW TO USE
FINANCIAL STATEMENTS

Small company growth stocks carry an extra degree of risk with them. For that reason, make sure that your purchase candidates are on sound financial footing before parting with your hard-earned dollars. If your potential "hot stock" has passed over all of the hurdles in Chapter 3, chances are you have a very profitable company with great prospects for growth. The next step is to check out a few facts and figures so that you can invest with complete confidence. Most of the numbers can be found in the company's annual and quarterly reports. For those who desire more facts, you can ask a company for their 10-K and 10-Q, which are filed with the SEC and contain more-detailed annual and quarterly information. This book will not make an accountant out of you, but at least you will be prepared so that your Hot Shot Industries will be able to weather a temporary slowdown in business and/or the economy.

BALANCE SHEET ITEMS

A dynamic young growth company is forever on the move, constantly changing on what seems like a daily basis. Despite this, there can be some value gained from stopping time for a moment and examining a company's financial records as of the date on the statements. When checking the statements, what you're looking for are trends, indicating if things are getting better or worse.

One of the most useful tools in assessing the financial wherewithal of a company is the balance sheet, listing assets, liabilities, and stockholders' equity. The most fundamental equation is: Assets – liabilities = stockholders' equity. Because a balance sheet must balance, the equation is restated as follows:

The Fundamental Equation

Assets	Liabilities
	Stockholders' Equity

Total Assets	=	Liabilities + Stockholders' Equity

In its most simplistic form, this is what a balance sheet looks like. In reality, this financial snapshot is broken down even further and usually

---

Figure 4-1
Breakdown of a Balance Sheet

ASSETS	LIABILITIES
Current Assets	*Current Liabilities*
• Cash	• Accounts Payable
• Cash Equivalents	• Short-Term Notes Payable
• Receivables	• Current Portion of Long-Term Debt
• Inventories	• Interest Payable
• Prepaid Expenses	• Taxes Payable
	Long-Term Liabilities
• Land	• Bonds Payable
• Plant and Equipment	• Mortgages
• Intangibles	• Notes Payable
• Goodwill	• Pension Liabilities
	• Tax Liabilities
	Stockholder's Equity
	• Capital Stock
	• Additional Paid-in Capital
	• Retained Earnings

---

includes the following items, and sometimes more, depending on the business in question (Figure 4-1).

Questions that can be answered from a balance sheet include how deeply the company is in debt and how easily it can meet its obligations. You will not only want to know the company's standing as of the date of the balance sheet but also how things stack up against previous quarters and years. What you should be looking for are positive trends, signs that the company's financial health is improving. As stated earlier, small companies rarely stay the same for very long, so unless things are improving they may be getting worse. It may also be useful to compare a company's financial condition to others within its industry. However, because many successful small companies operate within a niche, it is not always easy to find other businesses that are directly comparable.

Let's say you know that you're going to have to start preparing for your retirement, which is still 15 years away. At the same time, you need to feed, clothe, and house your family. You know what needs have to be addressed first. Similarly, a business is first and foremost concerned with meeting its short-term obligations, because if they cannot meet their near-term debts, there may not be a long term to worry about. A company's creditors will see to that.

CURRENT RATIO

You can determine a company's short-term financial strength (or weakness) by comparing its current assets to its current liabilities. Current assets include cash and those items that can be converted to cash within the short term, or one year. Current liabilities are simply those obligations which must be met within the next year. To arrive at a company's current ratio, which measures a company's short-term financial condition, you simply divide current assets by current liabilities.

$$\text{Current Ratio} = \frac{\text{Current Assets}}{\text{Current Liabilities}}$$

It has become accepted by financial analysts that, as a general rule, you want to see a company's current ratio at 2:1 or better to feel comfortable about its near-term financial condition. Again, owing to the volatility of small growth companies, you may wish to see your purchase candidates have a current ratio slightly in excess of this accepted standard. Table 4-1

Table 4-1

Current Ratio Calculation - XYZ Corporation

Year ended December 31,1991 (in thousands)

Current Assets:		Current Liabilities:	
Cash and Cash Equivalents	$1,273	Accounts Payable	$ 235
Accounts Receivable	$ 514	Short-Term Borrowings	$ 302
Inventories	$ 648	Current Portion Long/Term Debt	$ 175
Prepaid Expenses	$ 137	Income Taxes Payable	$ 423
Total Current Assets	$2,572	Total Current Liabilities	$1,135

is a sample of the current assets and liabilities portion of a balance sheet and the calculation of the current ratio:

XYZ Corporation's current ratio is listed below. XYZ Corporation appears to be in relatively good shape from a near-term perspective, as its current ratio of 2:3 is above the accepted minimum standard of 2:1. The company should, therefore, have no problem in meeting its short-term obligations.

$$\text{Current Ratio} = \frac{\text{Total Current Assets}}{\text{Total Current Liabilities}} = \frac{\$2,572}{\$1,135} = 2.3:1$$

QUICK RATIO

Some current assets won't be converted to cash for a while. Depending on credit terms, accounts receivable may not be collected for 30 to 60 days or longer. If times are tough, it is possible that some customers may not pay for quite a while if at all. Inventories are expected to be sold and turned into receivables, which are in turn converted into cash. As you can guess this may not happen overnight. Because of the potentially fickle nature of some current assets, many analysts also choose to calculate what is called a quick ratio, or acid test ratio. The quick ratio compares only a company's cash and cash equivalents to current liabilities.

$$\text{Quick Ratio} = \frac{\text{Cash + Cash Equivalents}}{\text{Current Liabilities}}$$

When using this test you will want to see a ratio of at least 1:1, indicating that cash and cash equivalents are equal to, if not greater than, current liabilities. The quick ratio allows for the fact that, in a worst case scenario, if accounts receivable are not collected and inventories will remain unsold, the company can still in the near term keep its head above water. In the previous example, the quick ratio would be as follows:

XYZ's Current Quick Ratio

$$\frac{\text{Cash and cash equivalents}}{\text{Total current liabilities}} \quad \frac{\$1,273}{\$1,135} = 1.1$$

XYZ Corporation has more than enough liquid funds on hand to meet its short-term obligations over their next 12 months, as evidenced by its quick ratio of 1:1.

INVENTORIES

A company with a current ratio of 2:1 should be considered in good financial condition, at least for the near term. However, does a 4:1 or 8:1 current ratio indicate that the company is exponentially that much stronger? Not necessarily. If you find a company's current ratio has been trending upward, it might be a sign that accounts receivable are growing. Perhaps customers are undergoing hard times and are slow in paying their bills.

Table 4-2
ABC Corporation's Inventory Buildup (in thousands)

	1991	1990	1989
Cash and Cash Equivalents	$4,125	$5,537	$4,879
Receivables	$2,040	$1,960	$1,642
Inventories	$5,553	$3,740	$2,965
Prepaid Expenses	$3,218	$2,857	$2,470
Total Current Assets	$14,936	$14,094	$11,956

An increase in the current ratio may also be a result of inventories piling up on the shelves as the product has lost its zip in the marketplace. It's okay if inventories increase in a growing business, but you don't want them to build up at a faster rate than the company's growth in sales.

Consider the case of ABC Corporation, which has been a fast-growing young company over the last few years (Table 4-2). Sales growth for 1990 and 1991 over the previous year was 28% and 18% respectively. Growth in inventories just about matched the growth in sales in 1990 as they were up 26%. However, 1991 was a different story. While sales were up 18%, inventories shot up 49%! Meanwhile, the company's cash position declined significantly. This huge buildup in inventories could very well mean that ABC Corporation's products are losing their appeal in the marketplace. To reduce inventory, ABC Corporation may have to reduce its prices, which will cut into its profit margins.

EXCESS CASH

A company doesn't need to have any pressing problems for its current ratio to be extra high. An above-average current ratio could also mean that some assets are going to waste. For example, suppose that a company's current assets and liabilities are as shown in Table 4-3.

The company's current ratio is 4.4:1, which provides more than adequate coverage for near-term obligations. In addition, its quick ratio is a rather hefty 2.4:1. Meanwhile, assume that the business's cash and cash equivalents are earning about 5% while the company's ROE is 25%. Obviously, a lot of cash is largely sitting idle on the balance sheet. A company in this position that is able to earn 25% on shareholders' equity should be looking for a more profitable way to invest these funds.

Table 4-3
Current Assets and Liabilities

Current Assets (000)		Current Liabilities (000)	
Cash	$ 5,448	Accounts Payable	$1,237
Cash Equivalents	$ 3,175	Short-Term Notes Payable	$2,416
Accounts Receivable	$ 3,366		
Inventory	$ 4,012		
	$16,001		$3,653

As you can see, there are no absolutes when using this or other financial measurements. They all must be viewed in context. And remember, what you are trying to monitor is the current trend: Is the company becoming financially stronger or weaker? Beyond all else, you want to make sure that your small company growth stocks can survive so that they can prosper.

ASSESSING THE LONG-TERM FINANCIAL CONDITION

A company's long-term financial condition can be determined by examining how it is capitalized. In other words, what is the relationship between stockholders' equity and long-term debt?   The more this relationship swings in favor of stockholders' equity, the more conservatively managed the company is and vice-versa. In the example below, stockholders' equity and the long-term debt of three different companies are presented.

	Company A	Company B	Company C
Long-Term Debt	0	$1,250,000	$2,500,000
Stockholders' Equity	$5,000,000	$3,750,000	$2,500,000
Debt to Equity	0%	33%	100%

Company A is extremely conservative, as they have no long-term debt whatsoever. Many times you'll find examples of superbly managed, highly profitable young growth companies that have no need to take on the added risk that comes with borrowing money. Perhaps the company has raised all the funds it needed to get rolling when it went public. Since going public, the success of the business has permitted it to be self-financing. It is possible that this young company may also have been successful in raising more capital via additional offerings of stock. Whatever the case may be, Company A provides you with a very favorable level of risk for a small growth company, assuming its short-term finances are in good shape. Companies like this are a prime candidate for taking on debt, should they need capital to meet short-term obligations or long-term plans for expansion. Eager lenders who are impressed with Company A's balance sheet would most likely be very willing to loan them money.

In the second example, Company B has taken on what most financial analysts would consider to be a prudent level of debt. Company B's debt to equity ratio is .33. The .33 ratio is considered (like a 2:1 current ratio) to be an acceptable level for most businesses. However, this is a rule of thumb only.

Some businesses that are very consistent in their performance can get away with more debt than a business that is highly unpredictable. Because of the higher degree of risk associated with small companies, you may wish to see an even lower ratio of debt to equity (such as .25), as this can provide you with an extra measure of safety.

Our final example, Company C, is probably in a very precarious position. In fact, the company's creditors have as big a claim to the assets of the business as do the stockholders, and they hold a preferred position regarding the company's assets. A company in this position may have tapped out its ability to borrow additional funds. Company C may be able to strengthen its balance sheet by offering more stock, or it possibly may be acquired by a stronger company that appreciates the inherent value or cash flow of the company. Regardless of the matter, if you come across a company as financially strapped as Company C, you will probably want to move on to the next one.

In addition to the total amount of long-term debt, you may also wish to take notice of how it is structured. This information is available in the footnotes of the balance sheet. The debt listing will give the interest rate and maturity date of all long-term (over one year) obligations. Provided the company's borrowing power is intact, it may be advantageous for some high-interest debt to come due within the next couple of years so that the company can possibly refinance the debt at lower interest rates and lower its interest costs. Debt that has been issued at favorable terms may have many years to go before the principal is due. The company should then benefit from this source of relatively cheap capital.

When comparing balance sheets going back a few years, if you find that the company is paring down its level of debt, consider that a plus. As long as the level of debt is within reason (debt to equity is .25 or better), you should then weigh the burden of the debt versus what the proceeds are providing for the shareholders. If the business is growing nicely, chances are that the interest cost, be it 8%, 10%, or 12%, is more than being paid for by the additional profits that the borrowed funds are enabling the company to generate. However, remember that leverage is a double-edged sword. Should a company's business slow appreciably, the debt burden could severely eat into corporate profits. Investors may want to be selling as this scenario evolves.

The discussion above has been of a general nature, highlighting some important items that should help to keep you from investing in a company that is stepping into financial hot water. There are certain other quality issues to be addressed concerning all balance sheet items, but that should be left up to analysts who devote the majority of their time to this task.

SUMMARY

- Small companies carry more risk, so you'll want to make sure your selections are on sound financial footing.
- Annual and quarterly reports and 10-K's and 10-Q's can give you the figures you need.
- The balance sheet can tell you the financial condition of the company.
- Look for positive financial trends in the companies you are considering for investment; when possible, compare them to other companies within the same industry.
- Calculate the current ratio to test the business's ability to meet its short-term obligations.
- The quick ratio compares a company's cash and cash equivalents to its current liabilities. It is the most stringent test of whether or not a company can meet its short-term obligations.
- A high current ratio can mean trouble, or it may indicate that some assets aren't being used productively.
- Inventories should not, in most cases, grow at a faster rate than sales.
- The relationship between stockholders' equity and long-term debt is an indication of conservative management or of a company with a risky financial structure.
- Many solid, fast-growing young companies do very well without any debt at all.
- Ideally, you should not invest in small growth companies with a debt to equity ratio above .25.
- A company's debt can be a plus or minus, depending on how it is structured. This information is in the footnotes to the balance sheet.

QUESTIONS

1. What would have to be the main characteristic of a business to justify a higher than average debt to equity ratio?

2. What is the basic balance sheet equation?

3. XYZ Corporation's inventories have trended up sharply in the last two quarters, quite a bit above the growth in sales. What would be an acceptable reason for this occurrence?

4. There are four companies within the same industry. Based on the information below, which company appears to be in the strongest long-term condition? Which is the weakest? Which company probably is the best overall from a combination of both the long-term and short-term perspectives?

Company	1	2	3	4	Industry Average
Current Ratio	2:1	3:1	1:5	5:0	2:9
Debt to Equity	.15	.45	.00	.33	.23

5. ABC Corporation is a fast-growing young manufacturing company. Sales in 1991 grew 25% versus those of 1990. The questions below are based on ABC Corporation's balance sheet (Figure 4-2).

- What are the current and quick ratios for each year?

- How would you rate the company's financial condition from a short-term perspective?

- How much were inventories up in 1991?

- How does this compare to the company's sales growth?

- What's the company's capital structure (debt to equity)?

- Is this a conservatively run company?

- Is ABC Corporation getting financially stronger or weaker, based on the information above?

- Based on the criteria presented in Chapter 3, would you be inclined to buy stock of ABC Corporation based on the information above?

Figure 4-2
ABC Corporation's Balance Sheet
Year End December 31, 1991 (in Thousands)

	1991	*1990*
Assets		
Current Assets:		
Cash	$ 4,175	$ 3,711
Cash Equivalents	$ 1,890	$ 1,653
Receivables	$ 4,064	$ 3,140
Inventories	$ 2,235	$ 1,788
Prepaid Expenses	$ 771	$ 599
Total Current Assets	$12,135	$10,891
Land	$ 3,750	$ 3,750
Plant and Equipment	$ 1,740	$ 1,835
Intangibles	$ 1,014	$ 963
Total Assets	$19,639	$17,439
Liabilities and Stockholders' Equity		
Current Liabilities:		
Accounts Payable	$ 1,712	$ 1,461
Short-Term Notes Payable	$ 2,123	$ 2,125
Current Portion of Long-Term Debt	$ 676	$ 1,088
Total Current Liabilities	$ 4,511	$ 4,674
Long-Term Liabilities:		
Bond Payable	$ 1,156	$ 1,832
Mortgages	$ 954	$ 976
Stockholders' Equity	$13,018	$ 9,957
Total Liabilities and Stockholders' Equity	$19,639	$17,439

Chapter 5

MARKET AND STOCK TIMING

The graveyards of Wall Street are filled with those who thought they possessed the fastest gun in town, those market practitioners who believed they were next to infallible, who thought they could call each twist and turn in the market with unerring accuracy. Sometimes a guru will get hot and stay hot for years on end, only to undo much of the good with an erroneous call that keeps followers out of stocks during a bull market or in stocks during a bear market.

Of course, it is fun to try to play guru, to forecast market turns, to predict the future and see if you can be right. And if you are right, if you could consistently be right, you could make a fortune. The trouble is, no one can call the turns with any great degree of accuracy forever. Interestingly enough, however, a new sage will come along with a bold and well-publicized prediction and hit it right on the nose. This will create a following for this guru for years to come, long after he's probably issued a costly forecast or two along the way.

For the sake of argument, let's say you do choose to use a timer to help you enter and exit the market. How are you going to know when to ditch him when he finally cools off, as they all do? Do you know what problem this approach creates for you? Now you have to time the market timers. Now the success of your investments will rest on moving from timer to timer as the years go by, which should prove, at best, to be equally as difficult as the job you've paid them for doing in the first place.

Also keep in mind, as shown later in the chapter, that if your success depends on being in or out of the market at the right time, chances are you may succumb to those natural human tendencies—greed and fear. You'll sell your stocks at the bottom out of fear of even greater losses, as pundits convince you that the next Great Depression is around the corner. And of course, when gloom and doom reign supreme, you will fail to muster up the appropriate courage necessary to buy stocks at huge discounts. At the other extreme, when the economy is sailing along and stocks are reaching new highs, greed will keep you in stocks that have become severely over-valued. You'll also be tempted to buy on the slightest rumor of a stock's surefire potential.

Hopefully, at this point you have come to realize that market timing is a tough way to go, and your own human tendencies to be in or out of stocks could prove to be your undoing. Don't get depressed. There's plenty of evidence to support the thesis that you don't have to worry about the market's ups and downs to make money in stocks. Let's go over a few points one by one.

First of all, the economy spends over three times as long in an expan-sion mode as it does in recession. Typically, the good growth years more than compensate for the down years, so over the long haul our economy has a definite upward bias. Not coincidentally, corporate earning over time shows the same tendencies for growth as does the economy. And because higher corporate profits mean higher stock prices, it follows that stocks over the long haul have the same upward bias as does the econ-omy. (Please refer back to Chapter 1 for the market's average annual gains.) In short, the house odds are in your favor just as they are for the owners of casinos in Las Vegas. In the long run, betting on the health of the American economy has proved to be a wise wager. The doubting Thomases who stick to cash will, over time, be left behind as they always have been.

Although market timing is discussed in this chapter, this book is about stock selection, not market timing. Not surprisingly, unless you're the manager of an index fund, you invest your money in stocks, not the mar-ket. You would do well to remember the old bromide that it is a market of stocks, not a stock market. In a good year some stocks will clobber the market averages, some will post modest gains, and some will even decline in value. Turning this upside down, not all stocks will go down in an off year. Although the good stocks may be held back by a weak overall mar-ket, the ability of the strongest of the strong to continue their upward

move even in a bad year is evidenced by the stocks in the software industry. You may gain even greater comfort from the "buy good stocks and
hold them for years" approach because it is endorsed by some of the
country's foremost and most successful investors.

The legendary John Templeton heads up a group of mutual funds that
bear his name. The long-running flagship Templeton Growth Fund has
compounded investors' money at better than a 15% annual rate for over
30 years. During this time Templeton, perhaps with tongue in cheek, has
stated that he is still searching for a forecaster who, over a long period of
time, has been right over two-thirds of the time. To date he says he hasn't
found one! Looking ahead, Templeton takes a broad brush approach and
sees a glorious age ahead, especially now that capitalism is sweeping the
globe and the cold war is history.

The 1980s were, on balance, a great decade for stock investors. No fund
manager did more to enhance his shareholders' net worth than Peter
Lynch, who ran the Magellan Fund for Fidelity. This fund compounded
throughout the 1980s at an annual rate in excess of 28%. What was Mr.
Lynch's secret? Stick to picking stocks and forget about the market. His
fund was nearly 100% invested in stocks for the entire decade. In his best-
selling book, *One Up on Wall Street*, Mr. Lynch candidly admitted that if it
was up to market timing to make any money in the market, he wouldn't
have made any.

Our third proponent of the buy good companies approach is the re-
nowned Warren Buffet of Berkshire Hathaway out of Omaha, Nebraska.
Mr. Buffet has become one of the richest men in America, and along the
way has made a ton of money for those who invested with him in Berkshire Hathaway (NYSE). Mr. Buffet's approach has nothing to do with
timing the market or the economy. Rather he picks companies with great
businesses and superior management and normally sticks with them for
many years.

As you move through the 1990s, the philosophies of the men mentioned
above should stand you in good stead. In fact, it is quite possible that the
1990s will prove to be one of the especially great decades for the buy and
hold investor.

Interest rates and inflation made a secular peak in the early 1980s and
have been trending downward ever since. In early 1992, interest rates
reached their lowest levels in 28 years. Students of previous market history will remember that stocks as a whole have done very well under
these conditions. All during the 1950s and up until the mid-1960s, low
inflation and low interest rates were major factors in one of the great
sustained growth periods for stocks and the economy in this country's

history. If these current megatrends hold true, stock investors could be in for another era of exceptional returns. But as stated, the emphasis in this book is on stock selection. Therefore, regardless of what happens in the economy, in the years ahead good stocks should continue to earn handsome returns for the patient investor.

As investors, it is one thing to have the beautiful and theoretical beliefs of the buy and hold investor behind you. But in the real world of investing there are going to be times when it is tough to pull the trigger, when you will shy away from investing no matter how much you like any particular company. More often than not this fear of stocks, this tendency to procrastinate on a buy decision, will happen at precisely the time when you should be putting any excess cash you have to work in stocks.

In the years ahead the market will fluctuate, as will the economy. They are closely linked together over the long run. In the short run, stocks will usually lead the economy into and out of periodic recessions. When stocks do decline, be on the lookout for some especially attractive bargains. This chapter will help you to recognize some of the signs that stocks have gotten particularly cheap. Again, market timing should not be your modus operandi. But from time to time the market does provide some great buying opportunities. It will only enhance your returns if you can learn to take advantage of opportunities and keep your cool when others are panicking.

It's quite possible that when the market looks bleak you will have money coming to you from the sale of real estate, or a bonus from work that is ready to be put to work. The pages ahead will teach you how to put these funds to work at the times of greatest potential profitability. Economic recessions are a fact of life. Over the last 35 years, the economy has suffered through seven slowdowns, or about one every five years. These contractions in business activity are never pleasant. Businesses go under, people lose their jobs, and a feeling of pessimism sweeps across the nation. Recessions more than likely will continue to occur every so often. History shows us that no trend, no matter how powerful, will periodically experience a move counter to its prevailing direction. And so it goes with the U.S. economy. Since 1960, the U.S. economy, in constant dollars (noninflated), has increased more than 900% to over $5 trillion by the end of the 1980s. However, this fantastic record of growth has not been accomplished without some pain along the way.

When recessions grab hold, they have a tendency to affect all of us. And yet times of crisis also create opportunities. So when a recession appears, realize that it will bring some longer-term good for the economy. The system is being cleansed of its excesses from the previous expansionary cycle. As investors, recognize that downturns in the economy have presented some of the greatest bargains in common stocks.

GROSS DOMESTIC PRODUCT

When you add up all of the pluses and minuses of economic activity, the sum total has historically been represented by the percentage change in Gross National Product, GNP. From 1992 on, the government has chosen to use Gross Domestic Product as the new standard of economic activity. For the purposes of this discussion, GNP will be used. Just remember that the change has been made. This oftentimes controversial barometer of the country's output is, in the final analysis, still considered as the bellwether of economic activity. When GNP is on the rise, the economy as a whole is expanding. Over the last 35 years (1957-1991), the score of quarterly results reads as follows: 110 expanding, 27 contracting, 3 unchanged. In other words, 79% of the time the economy has been in a growth mode. Recessions are normally a succession of negative quarters, with a positive quarter sometimes interspersed along the way. Table 5-1 is a table of prior recessions which will give you an idea of what the GNP numbers looked liked during some previous slowdowns.

Figures on the GNP are released about a month following the end of each quarter. A few weeks later this announcement is followed up with a revised number. Your local paper's business section will feature GNP when it is released. *Barron's Financial Weekly* and other business publications also print the quarterly results. After several years of expansion, if you read that GNP has turned negative, it is a warning that a great stock

---

Table 5-1
GNP During Recessions

Quarter	1969–1970		1973–1974–1975		1980	1981–1982		1990–1991	
1st	—	-2.4%	—	-2.2% -7.6%	+4.1%	—	-5.9%	—	-2.8%
2nd	—	-0.3%	—	+1.1% —	-9.1%	—	+1.2%	—	-0.5%
3rd	—	+5.0%	—	-5.1% —	+0.3%	+1.8%	-3.2%	+1.4%	—
4th	-1.6%	-3.6%	+3.6%	-3.5% —	—	-5.5%	+0.6%	-1.6%	—
Total Quarters	5		6		3	6		4	

Note: Underlined number is the quarter that the stock market bottomed.

buying opportunity should arrive soon. In the table above, please note the quarter that stocks bottomed during each of these recessions. In every case, it was several months or longer before the economy turned up again.

BEAR MARKETS DEFINED

Stocks have proven time and again to be a great lead indicator for the economy. They go down prior to a recession and advance before a new expansion has begun. During bull markets, the popular averages such as the Dow Industrials will periodically suffer through a correction in the range of 10% to 15%. When the Dow's decline exceeds 20%, it is typically a sign that the economy is headed for, or already in, a recession.

During the last seven bear markets, including two that were not accompanied by a recession (and calling a bear market a 20% decline in the Dow from its previous peak), the Dow Industrials have declined an average of 30.6%. So when the economy has gone sour and the Dow is off over 20%, you are now getting close to the bear market's lows. You then need to get ready to do what will prove to be the hardest thing for most people at that time: Buy more stocks and increase your commitment to the market. Again do not use market timing as your method of making money in stocks. Buy when stocks are cheap and you have idle funds that need to be put to work. By averaging your way into stocks you'll make sure not to buy all your stocks at the top when the economy is humming and it is the easiest thing to do.

You might even want to consider the following as a rule of thumb: When the Dow declines 20% or more, consider that as a buy signal. You won't catch the bottom (who does anyway?), but at least on a historical basis you'll be pretty close. And if you have done your homework well, the growth stocks you buy should shoot up ahead of the averages when the market turns for the better.

Figure 5-1 briefly mentions the seven bear markets that have occurred since the mid-1960s. In the past, bear markets have lasted for nearly a year or longer. Interestingly enough, however, the last two bear markets were over with in less than three months. As a matter of fact, some will argue that the crash of 1987 and the decline of 1990 weren't really bear markets at all. At this point it becomes a matter of your definition of a bear market. Let's stick for now with the description of Dow declines over 20%. What you are looking for are great times to add to your holdings. Those who bought during or anytime soon after the crash have been amply rewarded for their bravery. Investors who followed the 20% rule for buying stocks

---

Figure 5-1
Bear Markets 1966-1991

Dow Decline	Years	Comments
–25.1%	1966	A pause in the long-term mega-growth trend from post–World War II to late 1960.
–35.8%	1969–1970	The end of the growth stock era—higher interest rates and inflation rates start to accelerate.
–45.1%	1973–1974	The grandfather of all bear markets since the Great Depression—higher interest rates and inflation; the buying opportunity of a lifetime.
–26.9%	1977–1978	Blue chips decline, but growth stocks do well.
–24.1%	1981–1982	Super-high unemployment, long, deep recession as record high interest rates are used to combat double-digit inflation.
–36.1%	1987	The great Crash of 1987—a bear market or super bull market correction of temporarily overvalued stocks.
–21.2%	1990	Relatively mild, short bear market belies severity of first economic contraction following the longest post–World War II expansion.

---

in 1990 would have purchased stocks within 1.2% of the Dow's eventual closing low.

CHARTS OF BEAR MARKET BOTTOMS

At important market lows, the Dow will look like it has just tumbled over Niagara Falls. Investors will give in to scare stories on the economy and bail out at any price. Buyers will be in short supply. There will seemingly be nothing left to prop up stock prices as the market continues straight downhill. Miraculously enough, however, is that the market does end what is known as the capitulation stage. Enough is enough. Despite the gloom and doom prevalent everywhere, stocks begin to head higher again. The bottom has come and gone. And like the Wall Street adage says, "No one rings a bell at the bottom." Very few buy stocks there either. But if he buys anywhere near the lows, the long-term investor can certainly enhance his returns. It might be of interest to look at some snapshots of bear market bottoms. When you see something similar again (as most assuredly you will), you'll know what a bottom looks like. From the charts you can see that most of these bear markets ended with a waterfall-like decline that sent the Dow plunging to new depths.

The culmination of the 1969-1970 bear market was a classic plunge straight downhill (Figure 5-2). If one were to look at the chart it would be hard to imagine that stocks bottomed out where indicated, but they did. Certainly it is hard to guess the exact low, but if the Dow is down over 20% and you see a pattern like this, there's a good chance that the market is near a low point.

The end of the super bear market of 1973-1974 featured a similar water-fall type of decline. The low shown here is when many of the popular averages hit bottom. The Dow made a slightly lower low a couple of months later. Anyone who bought stocks anywhere close to these severely depressed levels got stocks at the lowest point in the last 30 years.

The next bear market was primarily a blue chip affair. While the Dow bottomed out twice at approximately the same level in 1978 and 1980, the majority of other indicators performed much better, as they moved to new highs (Figure 5-3). Both of these bottoms were the result of steady, persistent declines in the Dow Industrials.

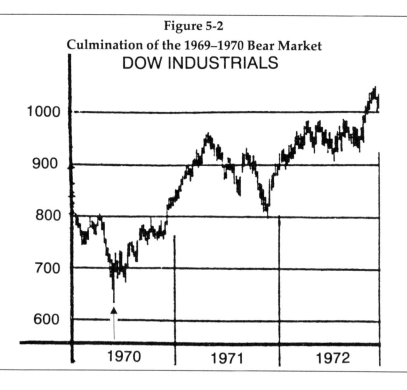

Figure 5-2
Culmination of the 1969–1970 Bear Market
DOW INDUSTRIALS

As the bull market ended in 1987, one of the sharpest, most devastating bear markets was to begin—the decline that set the stage for the crash of 1987. Indeed, the other declines pale in comparison to this bear market smash that took the Dow down 36% on a closing basis from its peak less than two months earlier (Figure 5-4). By now, even casual students of market history know that this financial panic set up a great buying opportunity for those with the courage to go against the tide and step to the plate.

After eight straight years of expansion, the economy finally took a breather in 1990. This coincided with a relatively short and mild bear

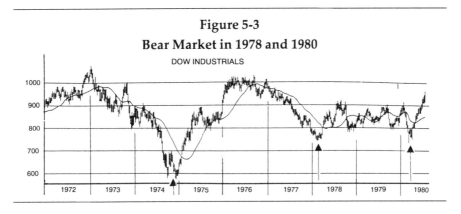

Figure 5-3
Bear Market in 1978 and 1980

Figure 5-4
The Crash of 1987—Dow Industrials

Source: Reprinted with permission from Bloomberg Financial Services.

Figure 5-5
1990 Bear Market—Dow Industrials

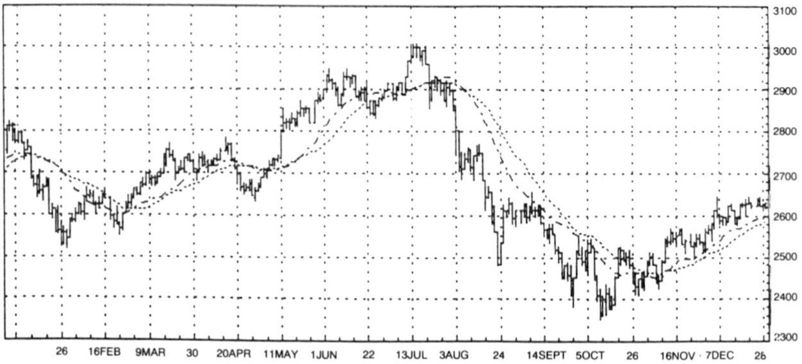

Source: Reprinted with permission from Bloomberg Financial Services.

---

market. In fact, the Dow's decline from peak to trough lasted a little less than three months (Figure 5-5). This mini-bear market was much harder on small growth stocks. In fact, the NASDAQ Composite fared far worse, having topped out in October 1989. However, the decline in the OTC market did set up one of the best buying opportunities in this sector in a long while. Once the 1990 bear market took hold, the averages entered into a textbook waterfall decline until the Dow hit bottom after losing about 21%.

39-WEEK MOVING AVERAGES

In addition to watching a chart of the Dow, there is another useful technique for helping to identify when the market may be near its lows. Many leading chart services will print what is called a moving average along with the Dow Industrials. A moving average is computed by adding up a preset number of closing prices and then dividing this total by the number of days or weeks chosen. One of the most commonly used moving averages for analyzing long-term trends is a 39-week moving average.

Each week you add in the new closing price and drop the one from 39 weeks ago. Unless you want the precise figure, you can approximate where the Dow's M.A. is at on one of the chart services or in *Investors Business Daily*. When stocks are trending lower, the market averages for the most part will remain below their moving average.

Table 5-2

Bear Markets and Moving Averages

Date of the Bottom	Dow	Percent Below 39-Week Moving Average
October 7, 1966	744.32	–17.0
March 26, 1970	631.16	–19.9
December 6, 1974	577.60	–23.5
February 28, 1978	742.12	–11.9
April 21, 1980	759.13	–10.0
August 12, 1982	776.92	–7.3
October 19, 1987	1738.74	–27.3
October 11, 1990	2365.10	–12.8

Should the Dow, for example, fall significantly beneath its moving average, it could be signaling that the decline has been overdone, and that a bottom could be near.

Table 5-2 lists eight bear market lows (counting the 1978-1980 as two separate bottoms). In every case but one, the Dow fell at least 10% below its 39-week moving average. When a sell-off reaches this kind of extreme, the market could be fast approaching a bottom. True, the market will probably head lower still, but the worst of the bear market should be behind you.

STOCK MARKET CYCLES

There are a number of advisors who base their market calls on cycles that have repeated themselves over and over again. For your purposes, the cycles that have relevance are the ones that can help you identify multi-year market lows. Stocks have shown a propensity to bottom out somewhere in the fourth year from the previous low.

Table 5-3 lists the timespan between the low points of all bear markets dating back to 1962. While reading cycles has a mystical quality to it, it is rather amazing to see how these cycles have worked out. Because nothing stays the same, there is the possibility that today's new economy may alter these cycles somewhat. For example, the lengthy expansion following the recession of 1981-1982 led to a five-year and two-month time span between important market lows. Perhaps the most valuable lesson to be

---

Table 5-3

Time Between Bear Market Lows

Low Point	Years-Months from Previous Low
1966	3 years - 7 months
1970	3 years - 8 months
1974	4 years - 6 months
1978	3 years - 3 months
1982	4 years - 5 months
1987	5 years - 2 months
1990	3 years - 0 months

---

learned here is that once you've seen a low point, the odds favor that you'll have to wait awhile before stocks get pummeled again.

INVESTOR'S INTELLIGENCE INDEX

One thing you can count on at market lows is that bears will be out of hibernation. Like clockwork, bearish sentiment runs to extremes when the averages are scraping bottom. Human nature being what it is, the fear of losing money replaces the hope that profits can still be earned in stocks.

Market gurus have cooked up a whole host of indicators to measure when bearish sentiment is running at an extremely high level. Without bogging you down with market indicators, one of the oldest and most reliable tests of investors' sentiment is presented here.

Each week, *Investors Intelligence* (located in New Rochelle, New York), runs a tab on the prevailing opinion of over 140 investment advisors, called the Investor Intelligence Index. Sentiment is divided into three categories: bulls, bears, and those looking for a correction in prices (i.e., neither bullish nor bearish). As you might expect, at important turning points the index is used as an indicator of contrary opinion. So when the advisors are heavily bearish, that's the time to buy (and vice versa). Why would these pros who write advisory letters be so bearish at market lows? There are a couple of reasons that may account for this. For one, many are trend followers. Until an important change in direction has been registered, they will continue to go with the flow. Secondly, even they can fall prey to the same emotions that plague the average investor.

By examining the indicators reading at or near previous bear market lows, you can arrive at what level of bearishness there needs to be to garner a buy signal. Like any indicator of this kind, you will come up with certain readings for buys that have worked in the past. You should understand that close is often good enough. These arbitrary levels of bearish sentiment may or may not necessarily occur at the next important low. This is often the case with indicators that have worked so well in the past. Nevertheless, the Investor Intelligence Index, (I.I. Index) has an excellent track record dating back to the early 1960s. An analysis of how it has performed previously is presented, as well as tips on how you can use it to help identify important market lows.

When about 60% of all advisors are bearish, that's the kind of reading that says the market is near a bottom. The end of the bear market of 1966 was signaled perfectly as the Investor Intelligence Index hit 61.0% the week of the low. The next 60%+ reading came within a couple of weeks of the bottom—a bull market correction that had lopped over 12% off of the Dow. The indicator gave its only truly false signal during mid-1969 with three readings of 60% that came about ten months prior to the bear market bottom in May 1970. At the 1970 lows, the I.I. Index hit a peak of 59.3% just five weeks after the bottom.

The end of the devastating bear market of 1973-1974 was first signaled three months prior to when most market indicators bottomed out. The extremes of bearish sentiment were registered with a reading of 69.6% just ten weeks prior to the bottom for the majority market averages.

Five weeks before the lows of 1978, the I.I. Index reached 60%+ and stayed there for eight straight weeks, forecasting very accurately the ensuing market rally. The market bottom of April 1980 was signaled six months early with a reading of 61.6%. However, the Dow at that time was within about 6% of its bear market lows. When the market hit bottom, the index checked in at 52.7%.

The bear market that accompanied the painful recession of 1981-1982 came to an end in August 1982. At that time, the I.I. Index was at 53.9%. Five months prior to the market bottom, the I.I. Index peaked at 60.9%. At that time, the Dow was within about 4% of its eventual lows.

Interestingly enough, the I.I. Index failed to signal the lows following the horrendous crash of 1987. However, the index did remain above 37.5% from October 30, 1987, to February 10, 1989, the longest period of sustained bearishness in the history of the indicator. This certainly gave a clue that stocks were undervalued at that time.

The bear market of 1990 was too short and shallow to develop the kind of bearishness seen at other important lows. Despite this, the I.I. Index did reach a peak of 56.5% within a month of the bottom. As stated earlier, indicators are not perfect. The I.I. Index must be considered part of your overall analysis of the market. In sum, when the bearish component of the I.I. Index starts trending higher while the markets are heading down, be on the lookout. Should the Dow's decline reach 20% and the I.I. Index register a bearish reading of around 60%, a bear market bottom may be close at hand.

INVESTOR SENTIMENT

Investor sentiment can also be measured by the opinions of your friends and business associates, as well as your own feelings about the market. These gut reactions as to what's going on in the economy and the market can provide you with valuable input on just where you stand during a bear market. As shown, the market bottoms out well ahead of the economy. This has been proven time and again, yet so many have failed to learn that lesson. Instead, most equate the market with what is going on in the economy. Of course, the result is that these investors (or would-be investors) never take advantage of the bargains that the market periodically presents them. Instead, they continue to worry about the economy while stocks start soaring as a new bull market is born.

To find out if stocks are nearing bargain basement levels, ask yourself how you feel about stocks. Are you making plans to commit money to stocks, or are you shying away from them for fear that things may get worse? If you discover you are fearful about investing, step back and reconsider your thinking. Oftentimes it can be profitable to go contrary to your own negative beliefs when things look bleak. So learn to play the devil's advocate with your own thoughts. Try to recall what you were thinking in a similar circumstance. Did you fail to buy out of fear in the past? Have you let the doomsayers keep you from stocks at the time of greatest opportunity? Then try your hardest not to let this happen to you again.

Once you have completed your own evaluation, you are ready to move on and sample the opinions of your friends and business associates. This opinion gathering can now be a much more useful exercise. You will be armed with the belief that a true buying opportunity may be at hand. With this new perspective, you can listen with great interest as those you know tell of the horror of investing in stocks. But rather than agreeing with them and deciding to avoid stocks altogether, you will be gathering useful information that may in fact help you to buy stocks near their lows.

You should then take your own opinion poll. Find out what your friends and business associates are doing now with their money. If they are scurrying into T-Bills and CD's while cursing stocks and swearing off the market forever, it is time to double check the indicators discussed previously for signs of an important turning point in stocks.

SOURCES OF INFORMATION

The basis of our opinion and beliefs can largely be influenced or determined by our sources of information, by what we choose to read, or what programs we decide to watch. Like the opinions that we gather from our friends, these sources of information, if believed, can lead you to cash out of stocks when you should be doing precisely the opposite. It is not necessarily the fault of the media that they are typically very negative of stock market bottoms. Their job is to report the news, not to forecast the market.

However, the media will often unwittingly provide you with an extremely negative viewpoint on investing just when stocks are ready to turn for the better. Some of the samples of the types of headlines you'll see at market lows are listed below. Judge for yourself. Would you buy stocks based on these headlines? If not, you are probably like most investors who let the media influence them. Now that you have seen how this can work against your own financial self-interest, vow not to have your opinion shaped by the media again. Rather, consider their headlines and tales of gloom and doom as signs that opportunity may indeed once again be knocking.

Headlines You Can Expect to See at Bear Market Bottoms

- Stock buyers in short supply.
- Recession looks more like a depression.
- Dow slumps to three-year low.
- Analysts advocate defensive moves.
- Dazed investors put money in T-Bills.
- Bear market slump continues, economy worsens.
- Auto sales off sharply.
- Housing starts lowest in fifteen years.
- Stocks plunge as investors panic.
- Investors bail out amid mounting losses.

I had the privilege of working with Don Summerell, whose career in the brokerage industry dated from the Great Depression until a couple of weeks before he died in December 1990. Obviously, this man had been through it all. When stocks were getting pummeled in the fall of 1990 and the news couldn't have been worse, I asked him what he thought of the market. He turned and looked me in the eye and said, "All you need now is money and guts."

We can all learn the lessons of time from this man. So the next time you are ready to panic and sell all of your stocks, stop, and consider buying more instead.

INTEREST RATES AND OTHER ECONOMIC DATA

As a group economists do a fairly good job of following and predicting business conditions. Individually, however, they are prone to making errant forecasts, just like the stock market gurus. The most troublesome of their predictions are those that call for the next Great Depression or something similar. These are the types of forecasts that can keep you on the sidelines during a bull market. But as stated, most economists do a credible job. The trouble is, many investors equate movements in stocks to those of the economy. In the long run this is true. However, if you're looking to prosper by buying stocks during periodic bear markets, you can all but forget the economists. The economy lags behind the stock market. So just when economists are super bearish, stocks should be at or close to their lows.

While you shouldn't rely on economists to help you time the market, nevertheless there is some economic data that may prove useful to you. At all times various investments are in competition for investors' dollars. Because so many investors have an inherent fear and distrust of stocks, trillions of dollars are parked in short-term cash instruments (for example CDs, T-Bills, or money markets). In addition, the bond market attracts huge amounts of investors' capital.

When interest rates are relatively high, investors tend to go for the sure thing provided by interest-bearing instruments. High rates prove to be stiff competition for stocks. Interest rates are periodically increased to fight off inflation and cool off an overheated economy. Just the opposite takes place when the economy is in recession. In an effort to get the economy going again, the Federal Reserve Board will begin to drop the discount rate. By making money cheaper, businesses are encouraged to borrow once again. As interest rates decline, stocks become more attractive, relatively speaking. At some point in time interest rates become so low, and stocks appear so undervalued, that a crossover takes place. Stocks begin to rally and a new bull market is underway. You should learn to view interest rate movements as a lead indicator for the market. When the economy is weak and stocks are in retreat, look for declines in several key interest rates. They can give you some useful clues as to a coming market bottom.

The aforementioned discount rate probably gets the most attention because it is a reflection of a conscious decision by the Fed to either ease or tighten credit. In contrast, other interest rates are determined by market forces. The prime rate nearly always follows the discount rate in lockstep. This is the interest rate that banks charge their most creditworthy customers, including the blue chip, AAA-rated companies in the Fortune 500.

The banks' profits are tied into the spread between what they pay for money (the discount rate) and what they charge (the prime rate). Both the discount rate and the prime rate tend to stay in well-defined trends, which helps their forecasting ability. When either or both, as a rule of thumb, are cut two successive times, that is a good indication that money is going to be easier to come by for quite a while. These strongly trended indicators are quite different from the daily and weekly fluctuations seen in the bond market and with short-term cash instruments. Investors who choose to follow these other rates may fall victim to a number of false and misleading signals.

The figures on unemployment are a reliable indicator as to whether or not the economy is in recession. Unlike some indicators, the unemployment rate stays in a fairly well-established trend during a downturn. So if the market has been heading south for a while and unemployment has been steadily rising, you have a strong indication of a recession and a bear market. You also have another confirmation that an important stock market low point could be in the making.

Other economic data which you may want to keep tabs on are auto sales and housing starts. These are both classic cyclical industries. When they start to decline in a meaningful way, it is another sign that the economy is in the midst of a slowdown. *Barron's Financial Weekly* presents an excellent recap of these and other economic data of interest each week in its comprehensive statistical section.

Hopefully, this discussion on coping with and profiting from market declines will achieve a twofold objective: (1) To keep you from selling out when stocks are getting near an important low, and (2) To give you confidence to add to your positions when stocks in general are trading at bargain basement prices. This book is about stock selection first and foremost. However, your results can be augmented by buying stocks at all times and not just when the market has been going up for a while and therefore buying stocks seems like the easiest thing to do.

SIGNS THAT THE MARKET HAS TURNED UP

Once an important low has been reached (as demonstrated by the indicators discussed above), the market should be on sound footing and ready for another multi-year bullish trend. You should receive several signs that the market is back on its way up again. Things to look for in the approximate order they would occur include:

- Investment advisors start to turn bullish again.
- Volume swells dramatically on a number of very positive trading sessions.
- Advancing stocks greatly outnumber decliners.
- The Dow and other key indicators move above their long-term moving averages.
- Interest rates continue to drift downward—the Fed doesn't want to abort a recovery attempt.
- GNP turns positive.
- Unemployment starts to decline.
- Many on the sidelines now feel it is safe to buy stocks again.

USING STOCK CHARTS TO HELP TIME YOUR PURCHASES

One of the most frustrating things you can do as an investor is buy a fundamentally sound stock, only to watch it tumble several points shortly after you've purchased it. Possibly you bought the stock when its chart pattern resembled a flagpole—straight up. Assuming the stock is a winner in the long run, admittedly it will recoup these losses and then some. However, if you are able to fine-tune your buying, you have an opportunity to improve on the results of your portfolio. The rest of this chapter reviews some common chart patterns. These should assist you in your assessment of when it is time to buy shares in a fundamentally attractive business.

Before you start, remember that charts should be looked at as a tool or as a part of your overall analysis. Also keep in mind that charts are not infallible. Certain patterns do repeat themselves over time, but however repetitious they may seem, there most certainly will always be exceptions to the rule. No, reading charts is not like reading tea leaves or palms as some would suggest. They can and often will serve as a useful aid in helping you to make a better purchase. In addition to helping you buy smarter, a stock's chart pattern may alert you to the possibility that something that has gone wrong at the company. If the pattern has turned decidedly negative, perhaps you should recheck the fundamentals to make sure there isn't something you overlooked. A stock that appears cheap and buyable may have its worst days ahead of it.

In a perfect world, a stock's price would go up in tandem with the value of the company. With good solid growth companies, the worth of the company would be steadily rising. In the real world, a company's stock will fluctuate between extremes of over- and undervaluation.

For example, look what happens in Figure 5-6 if you buy at Point A and the stock retreats from there. If the company is fundamentally strong, the stock will eventually recover and exceed your purchase price. However, notice how much better off you would be by buying at Point B when the stock becomes undervalued. You won't necessarily want to always wait to buy shares with a truly strong stock. After all, the strong have a way of getting stronger. But do keep in mind that buying opportunities will present themselves in the stocks of the companies you favor.

Figures 5-7 to 5-16 show some common patterns that appear regularly. Small growth stocks will often trade in a fairly wide range as they build a base while waiting to be discovered. Figure 5-7 shows you what this pattern might look like. The advantage to buying here is that you can purchase stock at your leisure, taking advantage of periodic dips to add to your position. You won't feel the anxiety of chasing a stock that is running up in value. The disadvantage to buying during base building is that it may take some time for the stock to become noticed. Meanwhile, your funds could possibly be working better for you elsewhere. However, patience does pay off and if your stock has merit, it could very well be worth the wait.

If you want more immediate gratification, you may wish to wait for a stock to break out of a base formation. Figure 5-8 shows a stock exceeding several previous peaks where it had topped out before. This breakout may be triggered by a positive news announcement concerning record earn-

Figure 5-6
Progression of a Growth Stock
Perfect World Versus Actual Stock Performance

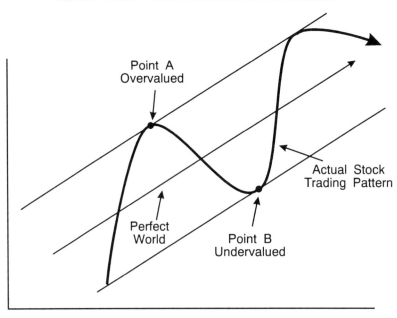

Figure 5-7
Basebuilding

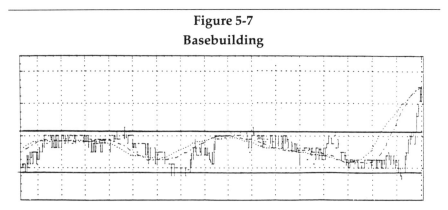

Source: Bloomberg Financial Services.

Figure 5-8
Breaking Out of a Base Formation

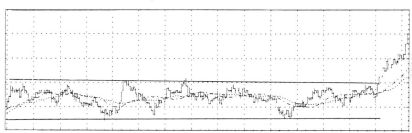

Source: Bloomberg Financial Services.

ings or an exciting new product. The breakout should be accompanied by a substantial increase in volume. This surge in trading might come from institutions that have just begun to take notice of your stellar selection.

Growth stocks that are on the move may enter into a prolonged pattern of rising prices. Some are what you could call steady risers (Figure 5-9). These stocks will enter in a well-defined uptrend as they head steadily higher. This kind of progression offers you little chance to buy on a meaningful correction as long as this pattern holds. Sometimes you may want to jump aboard after a stock has risen steadily from $10 to $20, for example, because it may continue rallying straight to $40.

Should the steady riser break its uptrend, you may be given a chance to jump on board at reasonably lower levels (Figure 5-10). This break in price may take the appearance of a free fall. While the stock is dropping, do the

Figure 5-9
Steady Riser

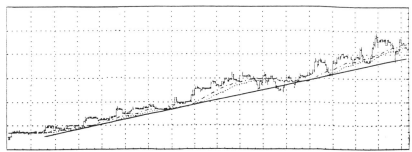

Source: Bloomberg Financial Services.

Figure 5-10
Breakdown of a Steady Riser

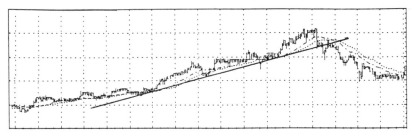

Source: Bloomberg Financial Services.

following: Recheck the fundamentals to make sure the company is still a solid choice. Then wait for the stock to bottom out and start to take a turn for the better. If the fundamentals check out and the stock is on its way up again, it is time to buy.

Some growth stocks will form what is called an uptrend channel. The channel is formed by connecting successive peaks and low points together as shown in Figure 5-11. Uptrend channels have a much wider percentage variation than stocks that demonstrate characteristics of a steady riser. You might want to take a pilot position if the stock breaks out above the upper limits of the channel, or at the lower limits of the channel.

Often a super strong stock will proceed in a configuration that resembles going up a flight of stairs (Figure 5-12). The stock will run for a while, then consolidate in a sideways trading range for a short while before

Figure 5-11
Uptrend Channel

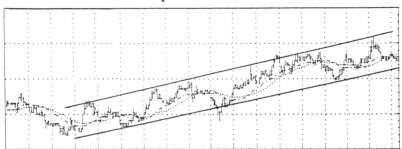

Source: Bloomberg Financial Services.

Figure 5-12
Stair Step

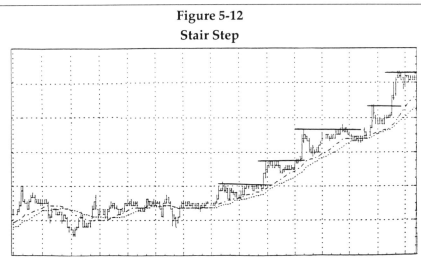

Source: Bloomberg Financial Services.

shooting up again. Sometimes the consolidation pattern will have a slight downward bias to it. In either case, you are given little chance to buy at a price much lower than the current quote. With a stock like this, if you feel it is not too overpriced, fundamentally speaking, you should consider buying at any time. You might also want to buy when the stock starts to run again following a brief consolidation.

Sometimes a top young growth stock will suffer through what seems to be a rather sizeable decline, dropping perhaps 30%-40% from its recent peak. Reasons for this include: the overall market is weak; the stock got too far ahead of itself; or perhaps the company is experiencing an off quarter or two. When this happens, the stock may suffer through a sharp decline and then enter into a period of base building. You can follow the rules discussed earlier for dealing with a stock in a base formation. You can buy during the base building (Figure 5-13), or wait for the stock to break out of the base and begin a new advance. If you buy during the base building period, watch out to make sure that the stock doesn't break below the lower limits of the trading range. If it does, recheck the fundamentals. It is possible that the stock will have to be sold quickly, should your fundamental analysis be in error.

The next two patterns could be caused for the same reasons that applied in the previous example. Following a sharp decline, the stock in Figure 5-14 has formed a double bottom. This is an especially positive

Figure 5-13
Consolidation Base

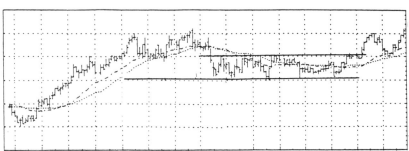

Source: Bloomberg Financial Services.

reversal pattern. You can buy shortly after the stock has started up from the second bottom (A). However, for extra assurance that the stock has indeed hit its lows, you may consider waiting until it breaks above its prior rally high (B). A similar formation is presented in Figure 5-15. The difference here is that the stock's second bottom is higher than the first. Again, you can consider buying at point A or B.

Another bullish pattern to be on the lookout for is a stock in an extended period of high level consolidation such as seen in Figure 5-16. Following a sizeable advance, this stock is trending in a sideways pattern in the shape of a wedge. The highs are about the same, but each new low keeps getting higher. With this pattern you can buy after the stock has

Figure 5-14
Double Bottom

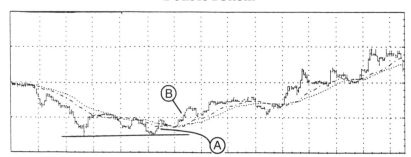

Source: Bloomberg Financial Services.

Figure 5-15
Double Bottom—Higher Second Low

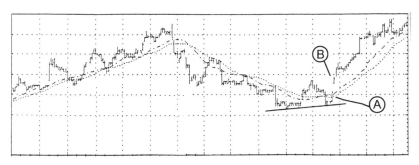

Source: Bloomberg Financial Services.

been in the wedge for a while, as this pattern shows a strong likelihood that it will be resolved to the upside. For extra safety, you can wait for the upside breakout to take place. Of course, this extra measure of safety may cost you a couple of points.

Figure 5-16
High Level Consolidation

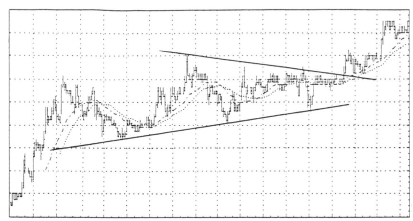

Source: Bloomberg Financial Services.

The chart patterns presented may prove useful in helping you to buy your growth stocks at more advantageous prices. In addition, you will come across others that may be helpful, as this listing is by no means comprehensive. But do keep in mind that fundamental analysis always takes precedence in the long run. A fundamentally strong stock will do just fine in the long run (several years), even if you time your purchase poorly. On the other hand, a stock that looks ripe for the picking according to the charts won't succeed for long if it is fundamentally weak.

SUMMARY

- Calling market turns consistently is tough to do; one big mistake can be very costly.

- Using a market timer, the question becomes: How do you time the timers?

- You don't have to time the market to make money in stocks. In the long run, the stock market and the economy historically have an upward bias.

- Remember the old bromide: It is a market of stocks more than it is a stock market.

- Good stocks can go up in a bad year and vice versa.

- Some of the country's most successful investors endorse the buy and hold approach.

- Learn to overcome your fears and buy stocks near market lows.

- Don't engage in panic selling when things look bleak.

- Economic recessions are a fact of life. Accept them and learn to invest profitably when they occur.

- GNP is the final score on the condition of the economy; it totals up all of the pluses and minuses.

- The stock market has proven to be a great lead indicator for the economy.

- Declines in the Dow Industrials in excess of 20% from a prior peak are a sign the economy is headed for, or already in a recession.

- Have the courage to put idle funds into stocks when the market is down and the economy is in the tank.

- All bear markets (defined as a decline in the Dow of at least 20%) are different in their length and the magnitude of the decline.
- The crash of 1987 was a great buying opportunity for those with courage and a long-term perspective.
- Thirty-nine-week moving averages can help you identify when the market has sold off to an extreme.
- Market bottoms have tended to occur about every four years.
- Sentiment indicators (such as the Investors Intelligence Index) can help you to identify when negative psychology has reached an extreme.
- When stocks are heading down, check your own feelings about the market, then survey friends and business associates. If gloom and doom prevail, you're probably getting a good contrary buy signal.
- Beware of the influence your sources of information have on you—try to emphasize sources that will help you develop confidence in the long-term prosperity of American business.
- Learn to identify the type of scary headlines you will find at important market lows.
- The economy lags the stock market, therefore, you shouldn't necessarily use economic forecasts to predict the market.
- Declining interest rates have historically been a good lead indicator for a turnaround in the market. Cuts in the prime rate and discount rate have been among the most reliable signs of a coming market low.
- Learn to recognize the signs that the market has made a long-term turn for the better.
- Frustration can build when you buy a fundamentally sound stock and then watch it tumble; charts can help you avoid this.
- Charts should be viewed as a tool; they can help, but they are by no means infallible.
- Certain chart patterns tend to repeat themselves.
- Charts may alert you that something may be fundamentally wrong with a stock.
- In a perfect world, stocks would go up in tandem with the value of the company. In the real world, they fluctuate between extremes of over- and undervaluation.

- Familiarize yourself with the chart patterns that commonly repeat themselves.

- Keep in mind that a stock's fundamentals take precedence in the long run.

QUESTIONS

1. Seven months ago the Dow Industrials were at 3122. They have just hit a new yearly low of 2404. How far is the average down from its peak? What should you, as a long-term investor, be doing now? Buying? Selling? Given this decline, what most likely is the condition of the economy?

2. What's one of the biggest problems with exclusively using the services of a market timer?

3. Bear markets are defined by a decline in the Dow Industrials of at least _____%.

4. Declining interest rates are often a sign of the Fed's desire to stimulate the economy. What are two rates to watch closely? What do they need to do to give a positive signal?

5. At nearly all bear market lows, the Dow will fall at least _____% below its _____ average.

6. The market appears to have reached and passed a bear market low. Explain what you should expect to see from the following:
   - Investment advisors
   - The Dow Industrials and other key market indicators
   - Interest rates
   - GNP

7. The percentage of bearish investment advisors (according to *Investors Intelligence*) has reached a new high of 58.2% as the Dow has declined from 2834 to 2125. The Fed has just cut the discount rate for the third straight time. Should you wait for a 60% reading (which usually signals a bottom) before buying more stock?

8. We're all influenced by our sources of information. What are yours? Have they helped you to make money in stocks in the past?

9. Which usually comes first—a decline in the stock market or a slow-down in the economy? An economic recovery or a new bull market?

10. You've just read the following headline in the business section of your local paper, "Dow dives 57 points to new low as fears of a weakening economy mount." What should you do?

11. The crash of 1987 was a traumatic event for many. For experienced investors it proved to be a ___/___/___.

12. How should you view the use of charts?

13. Stocks will normally fluctuate between the extremes of ____ and _____.

14. If you like the fundamentals of a company, but its stock breaks below an important support zone or trendline, what should you do?

Chapter 6

SOURCES OF INFORMATION

Short-term traders require very little information before making a buy/sell decision. Give them a chart and/or a hot news story they can play for a few days and they're off and running. Once they have captured a 10%-20% profit they have most likely gone off to the next hot ticket. These investors are at one end of the information spectrum. In sharp contrast are those investors who wish to make gains of possibly several hundred percentage points over a period of years. Unless you're extremely lucky and by chance come across a big winner, you will need to do your homework to find multiple gainers. In addition to first helping you identify a potentially rewarding stock, doing your due diligence will give you the confidence to hold on to a winning stock. If you luck into a stock that doubles, odds are you'll feel fortunate to have made that kind of gain. What happens next is that, not knowing why the stock has gone up, you'll probably take a nice profit and move on to something else. This will short-circuit your ability to have that truly big winner that can do wonders for your retirement fund.

Information, wherever it's gathered from, leads to the forming of opinions. By now you know that the philosophy of this book is tied to the long-term bullish outlook for America's economy, as well as the potential for growth stocks in the years ahead. So before going on to some positive sources of information, a warning needs to be issued so that the whole investment process will not be derailed. Negative stories grab the headlines. No one can argue much with that. After a while, it's easy to believe that a lot of bad thing are going on. This in turn leads to the decision to procrastinate, to put off investing until things get better. The problem with this is that, in our incredibly complex economy, good and bad things are happening constantly. When you add it all up, stocks have done very well in the long run. So don't rely too much on what you read or hear if it keeps you from investing in stocks. Learn to take a positive outlook instead and begin your search for the next winners on Wall Street.

There's certainly no doubt that this is the information age. Furthermore, the quantity and ease of access to this information only seems to grow daily. One of the skills you'll need as an investor is a nose for what information is of value and what is not. You will need to ferret out superfluous data while at the same time learn to cherish good solid, reliable information that can help you find winning stocks.

This chapter covers some sources of information that are readily available and that can help you make some wise investments. Some of the sources to examine include a company's literature, meeting a company firsthand, brokerage reports, investment services, magazines, business papers and periodicals, newsletters, and chart services. Taking the long-term fundamental approach, the areas that you'll want to examine from these sources (in descending order of importance), include the following: (1) the company, (2) the industry, (3) the market, and (4) the economy. In the long run, a super stock will outperform the market by a wide margin. Because this is true and because timing the market consistently is tough to do, stock selection should rank first in priority.

Growth industries spawn winning stocks, so quite naturally it's possible to do well by buying a hot stock in a hot industry. However, even in the best performing industries, some stocks will lag behind. In addition, as an industry grows, competition can begin to eat into the profits of even an industry's leading stocks. Do pay attention to the industry your stocks are in. This will also help you to properly diversify your portfolio. But make the proper analysis of the company your greatest concern.

Chapter 5, on timing, covered some ways to improve your results by recognizing the great buying opportunities that come along every few years. If you have any cash sitting on the sidelines or funds coming due that are earmarked for stocks, these low points in the market can serve you well. Some services are covered in this chapter that can give you a perspective on the market's current trend. Knowing what the economy is doing can also help you to put idle funds to work with confidence. When the economy is at its worst, most stocks are at or near their lowest prices. This chapter shows where to look to get the economic data you'll need. When you do decide to buy or sell a stock, a chart of its recent price and volume trends can help you pinpoint times to make your entry or exit. Some of the top chart services will be listed later in this chapter. The following sections discuss some other sources you'll want to know about and how to use them.

COMPANY LITERATURE

When you feel you've come across an idea that's worth investigating, you'll want to review the company's literature. It can and should be the foundation for your decision-making process. The most commonly read document is the company's annual report. Go right to the CEO's letter to shareholders. What does he have to say about past performance? Are there any negatives? Because management is usually quite optimistic, you should put anything that appears to be a negative under a microscope. Possibly, there's a good explanation for why a company lost money in the second and third quarters. On the other hand, if something has gone wrong, it could be the beginning of the end. So don't treat negatives lightly.

The CEO's message should contain positive and believable comments on why the company has been successful, why it will continue to be so, and how the company is going to grow. Remember, for the most part you are looking to invest in solid growth companies with a prior record of success and ones that give every indication that this growth will continue. You should not be looking for growth from beaten down turn arounds, unless an extremely strong case can be made that they will be entering into a new dynamic growth phase.

You should consider a company's annual report from a marketing perspective. Small growth companies need good press; they need potential new investors to become impressed with them so that they will invest in a somewhat unknown quantity. Smart growth company management knows this and pulls out the stops to make sure they present a good image. That's not to say they will prosper on image alone. They still have to do the job and tend to business. Nevertheless, good marketing helps to bring in new investors. Ask yourself, does the quality of the report impress you? Is it easy to read and understand? How about the graphics? Does it exude a tasteful degree of salesmanship? Or is it as exciting as vanilla ice cream? If the company's annual report is a dud, consider the source—management. If you are impressed with the annual report, chances are other investors are too. Consider this another plus for your prospect company.

By all means do proceed beyond the flowery statements to the cold hard facts in the back of the report. (Some pertinent figures may also be displayed in the front and throughout the report. If you've got it, flaunt it!) The calculation of some key ratios has been covered in Chapter 4 and some important fundamental data was presented in Chapter 3 to help you. The information you need for this type of analysis will be provided for the last several years. Basically, are the numbers good and getting better? Are the financial trends positive?

If the numbers aren't good, and they may not be in all cases, seek out a reasonable explanation. It's probably okay if sales grew only 30% last year versus 33% the year before. However, if they were up only 10%, that's enough to make you wonder. Annual reports have a positive bias. Make sure you recognize this and learn to look at them with a discriminating (not jaded) eye.

A company with a lot of good things going on that's marketing its stock properly will let the investing public know about them by issuing press releases. These are just one of the many ways that a company communicates with current and prospective investors between annual reports. Ask for copies of the last few months' press releases when you call for the annual report. Are there any new product announcements or have any service contracts been awarded recently? Did they just report record earnings? If you are strongly considering a company as an investment, you should request to be put on their mailing list for press releases and quarterly earnings reports. A quarterly earnings report is kind of a mini-annual report. It usually has a few comments from a corporate officer as well as the most recent three months' financial data. Like the annual report, you will want to see positive trends and comparisons.

Some of the best public relations that a company can get comes from trade publications and other third parties that give glowing testimonials as to the company's product or service. These will often be included in the package the company sends you.

If other independent, unbiased, and reliable sources are enthusiastic about what a company's doing, you can add another big check to the plus column. Should you be getting a ton of literature while on a company's mailing list, and you've dropped it from consideration as an investment, do yourself and them a favor and ask to be deleted from the list.

MEETING COMPANIES FIRSTHAND

In addition to the literature discussed above, many public relations-minded companies will employ means of direct communication with investors to promote their stock. Growing in popularity are a number of growth stock conferences held throughout the country. These conferences typically last two to three days and provide a forum for 20 or more companies to tell their story. The conferences also give you an opportunity to ask questions and meet executives personally. Companies that attend these conferences often pick up meaningful sponsorship from investors, including some institutional investors. Chapter 3 explained what the big boys can do to a stock when they climb on board.

Companies that seek to be in the spotlight alone will often take to the road and go from city to city doing what have come to be known as "dog and pony shows." In essence, these presentations allow these resourceful companies to tell their story in great detail (often accompanied by colorful slides and videos). Find out if the stock you are looking at is going to have one near you at some time in the near future. The meeting should answer a lot of the questions you may have on the company.

Each year all publicly traded companies are required to hold a meeting for stockholders. If you live nearby and own the stock, you should try to attend it. Should you still be evaluating the company, call them to see if you can attend the meeting. Indicate that you are considering making a substantial investment. They just might let you attend. Don't think of this as deceitful. After all, if you're taking this business of investing seriously, any amount you are able to invest is substantial to you. Stockholders' meetings have come to be known as a means for shareholders and professional hecklers to grill and embarrass management, if at all possible. If the meeting you attend has little or no shareholder dissent, chances are management is doing a pretty good job.

Some, but not all companies provide tours of their facilities. Do take advantage of these tours and go visit the company if it's reasonable to do so. How they greet you at the door, the condition of the facilities, and the looks on the workers' faces will tell you a lot about their operation. While you're there, try to gain at least a brief audience with one of the top executives. Visiting a company can help give you that warm fuzzy feeling and the confidence to make a serious commitment to a potentially rewarding stock.

BROKERAGE RESEARCH REPORTS

A company is almost always optimistic about its future. Reports issued by brokerages at the local, regional, and national level can often be a very rewarding source of information on small growth companies. Brokerage analysts tend to be more realistic in their appraisal, but they also tend to be, as a group, optimistic about the stocks they follow. For example, local brokerages may have a great number of stocks to choose from, simply because small stocks greatly outnumber the big blue chips. The research they conduct is geared toward providing their brokers with stocks they can recommend for purchase to their clients. Buy recommendations are looked on more favorably and inspire far less controversy than do reports urging customers to sell stocks short (a technique used to profit from a decline in a stock). In addition, a company may eventually turn around and be a potential buy some day. However, they may not be too coopera-tive with a firm that wrote a negative report on them in the past.

   For the most part, local brokerages will just ignore a stock rather that put a sell out on it. As you move up to the regional level and especially at the national level, the big firms may not be offered as much of the luxury of picking and choosing which stocks to cover. Yes, they can follow some smaller companies. But as a practical matter, their research is geared to providing advice to large institutional investors.

   Larger brokerages also must provide research to a network of possibly 5,000-10,000 brokers or more nationwide. The institutions, as well as the retail clients of these brokers as a whole, own massive positions in IBM, GM, and American Telephone, to name a few. Their clients want an opin-ion on these stocks at all times. So to some extent, the larger brokerages are forced to follow the biggest stocks. It is also not cost effective for them to follow very many small growth companies. Figure 6-1, a cycle of a stock's growth, is another way to visualize the type of stocks brokerages of different sizes follow. Please recognize that this is an approximation and that coverage does overlap to some degree.

Local brokerage. Most emphasize stages 1, 2, and 3. They are usually first or second to get the story. Although there is a higher risk in some selec-tions, there is also a higher reward to get in on ground-floor opportuni-ties.

Regional brokerage. Brokerages at the regional level emphasize stages 3 and 4, some in stage 2. They pick up on small but emerging winners after local brokerages do but before the nationals. They generally need to see

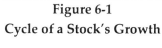

Figure 6-1
Cycle of a Stock's Growth

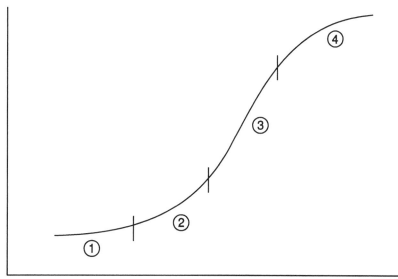

① Undiscovered

② Early Growth Phase

③ Established Growth

④ Mature Company

some size in a stock and a record of success before recommending it to institutional and retail clientele.

National brokerage. Almost all of their recommendations will come from stocks in stages 3 and 4 where the stock is now fairly large and well established. To the credit of these firms and their clients' desire for small growth stocks, their coverage seems to be expanding to stage 2 stocks in some cases.

To get an idea of what type of stocks a brokerage covers, give them a call and ask them to send you a summary report of their recommended list. These lists are often broken down into different categories (income stocks, blue chips, aggressive growth, etc.) so make sure you get a summary for all groups that they follow. The summary on small growth stocks (if they follow them) will give you an idea if this particular firm has research that could be of value to you.

If you do plan to seek research directly from a firm and invest in their recommendations, in all fairness to them and yourself you should buy the stocks they research from them. When their opinion changes on a stock, you'll be one of the first to know. Remember, though, that the purpose of this book is to help you make informed decisions. To that extent, broker- age reports should be looked at as a tool in your decision-making process, just as the company literature is.

You can use the yellow pages to find listings of the brokerages that serve your local area. Unless you live far from a major metropolitan area, you'll no doubt recognize the names of some of the national brokerages. You may also see some names that you are not so familiar with. These may very well be a local or regional brokerage that can help you get reports on some exciting young growth opportunities. To carry this proce- dure a step further, assume you live in Florida but are interested in high- tech stocks located in the Silicon Valley. You could go to your library and look in the yellow pages for brokerages in the Bay area. After a couple of calls you would come to learn that Hambrecht and Quist, located in San Francisco, are specialists in this area. By taking this tactic you can learn about companies in areas of the country other than your own backyard. Again, this will be necessary if you live in an area that's not heavily populated with publicly traded companies. As a word of caution when calling around to different brokerages, avoid getting involved in penny stocks. If you get research from a firm and their reports all recommend stocks under $1 or $2, it is caveat emptor.

There are several things to look for once you have a broker's report in your hands. For starters, to what are they recommending that you do with the stock—buy, hold, or sell? Obviously, what you want to see is a buy recommendation. If it is qualified in some way, such as a long-term buy, or accumulate, it doesn't carry with it the same sense of urgency in the analyst's opinion as an outright buy. Sell recommendations are so uncom- mon that you can almost look at a hold, but not in all cases, as if it's a sell. If the analyst who has spent a great deal of time researching this stock doesn't recommend buying at current levels, you probably shouldn't ei- ther.

Should the stock rate a buy, next read the summary and opinion of the company. This will tell you in a nutshell why you should buy the stock. Does the analyst's reasoning make sense to you? Is the company a growth company or not? Because you are looking for above-average earnings growth, you will want to take notice of the company's EPS over the last few years. Does the analyst expect earnings to continue to grow impressively over the next couple of years? What are his estimates? Does his forecast tend to be conservative or overly optimistic? Listed below are a number of other questions you will want to have answered in the report.

- What is the company doing that is working?
- Where is the additional growth going to come from?
- Any new products coming on stream?
- Does the company possess leading-edge technology?
- Are new markets being approached and will existing ones be more fully exploited?
- Are profit margins expanding?
- How is the competition doing? Is the stock over- or underpriced in comparison to its leading competitors?
- Do the risks seem minimal and manageable?
- Is the company on financially sound footing?
- Is the company's background covered?
- Are there any recurring sources of revenue?

These are some of the questions you'll want answers to. You should also see if the report covers the many tests of an ideal growth stock covered in Chapters 3 and 4. Don't forget that analysts are human and do make mistakes. The ultimate responsibility for making good buy-and-sell decisions is up to you.

INVESTMENT SERVICES

There are a couple of services available by subscription that offer excellent presentations of fundamental data on growth stocks. The most comprehensive in terms of the number of stocks covered is offered by Standard and Poor's Corporation. Separate coverage is available for stocks on the NYSE, AMEX, and Over-the-Counter market. Over 4,000 stocks are covered in the three editions, including over 2,000 OTC issues. Information is updated four to five times annually. An example of a two-sided report is given in Figure 6-2. Fundamental data covers nine to ten years. You can

Figure 6-2
Standard and Poor's Stock Report

Adobe Systems 3017T

NASDAQ Symbol ADBE   (Incl. in Nat'l Market; marginable) Options on Pacific (Jan-Apr-Jul-Oct)

Price	Range	P–E Ratio	Dividend	Yield	S&P Ranking	Beta
Oct. 3'91	1991					
52³⁄₄	63–26³⁄₄	24	0.32	0.6%	NR	NA

Summary
The systems and application software designed and marketed by this company are used to print integrated text and graphics for high-quality electronic printing and publishing. Adobe derives almost two-thirds of its revenues from the licensing of its PostScript interpreter. Earnings growth continued into fiscal 1991, despite difficult conditions in the industry.

Business Summary

Adobe Systems Incorporated designs, develops and markets systems and application software used to print and display text and graphics for high-quality electronic printing and publishing and for general computer use.

The company's principal product, the PostScript interpreter, executes page descriptions generated from application programs that support the PostScript language to produce documents containing multiple typefaces and graphics, including charts, diagrams, drawings and photographic images. Because the PostScript page description language is device-independent, application programs that have been written to support the PostScript language can be used interchangeably with any raster output device that contains a PostScript interpreter.

The PostScript interpreter is typically implemented on a dedicated processor (controller) that has direct control over a printer. Adobe licenses the PostScript interpreter and associated controller designs to computer, printer, typesetter and film recorder manufacturers for incorporation into their products. As of January 31, 1991, Adobe had contracts with 38 OEM customers. Royalties derived from the licensing of the PostScript interpreter amounted to 62% of revenues in fiscal 1990. Apple Computer was the largest OEM customer, accounting for about 23% of revenues.

The Display PostScript system is a high-performance interactive version of PostScript software technology for use on workstation displays. This software is an extension of the PostScript language that incorporates a PostScript interpreter with other system software.

Approximately 340 software companies have introduced or announced the development of application programs that support the PostScript interpreter. More than 4,000 application programs currently support the PostScript interpreter.

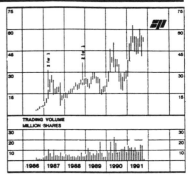

In addition to the PostScript interpreter, Adobe's products include application software packages and downloadable typeface software programs that are licensed through retail distribution channels and directly to end-users. Revenue from product sales amounted to 33% of the total in fiscal 1990.

Important Developments

Oct. '91— Adobe announced that it will begin selling a computer chip that greatly speeds up the process of printing text and displaying text on personal-computer screens. The new chip marks the company's first major move into the vending of hardware.

Aug. '91— The company acquired a digital video-editing software product known as ReelTime from SuperMac Technology. The companies will work together on development of software designed for use with Apple Computer's Macintosh personal computers.

Next earnings report expected in early January.

Per Share Data ($)

Yr. End Nov. 30	1990	1989	¹1988	1987	1986	1985
Tangible Bk. Val.	³5.14	2.93	2.14	1.15	0.68	d0.06
Cash Flow	2.05	1.72	1.08	0.48	0.22	0.05
Earnings	1.83	1.55	0.98	0.43	0.19	0.03
Dividends	0.23	0.19	0.08	Nil	Nil	Nil
Payout Ratio	13%	11%	8%	Nil	Nil	Nil
Prices²—High	50³⁄₄	30	25¹⁄₂	28	7	NA
Low	17	14	11³⁄₄	6³⁄₈	2⁷⁄₈	NA
P/E Ratio—	28–9	19–9	26–12	66–15	37–15	NA

Data as orig. reptd. Adj. for stk. divs. of 100% Nov. 1988, 100% Mar. 1987, 100% Jun. 1986. 1. Refl. merger or acq. 2. Cal. yr. 3. Incl. intangibles. NA-Not Available. d-Deficit.

Standard OTC Stock Reports   October 11, 1991   Standard & Poor's Corp.
Vol. 57/No. 117/Sec. 2.   Copyright © 1991 Standard & Poor's Corp. All Rights Reserved   25 Broadway, NY, NY 10004

Figure 6-2 (continued)

3017T   **Adobe Systems Incorporated**

Income Data (Million $)

Year Ended Nov. 30	Revs.	Oper. Inc.	% Oper. Inc. of Revs.	Cap. Exp.	Depr.	Int. Exp.	Net Bef. Taxes	Eff. Tax Rate	Net Inc.	% Net Inc. of Revs.	Cash Flow
1990	169	67.0	39.7	7.40	4.86	NA	66.3	39.6%	40.1	23.7	44.9
1989	121	55.3	45.6	5.20	3.73	NA	54.9	38.6%	33.7	27.8	37.4
'1988	83	36.2	43.4	4.95	2.09	NA	35.8	41.0%	21.1	25.3	23.2
1987	39	17.2	43.7	3.03	1.05	Nil	16.9	46.8%	9.0	22.8	10.0
1986	16	7.4	46.1	1.23	0.54	Nil	7.2	50.3%	3.6	22.3	4.1
1985	5	1.0	21.2	0.51	0.34	Nil	0.8	40.8%	0.5	10.8	0.8

Balance Sheet Data (Million $)

Nov. 30	Cash	Assets	Curr. Liab	Ratio	Total Assets	% Ret. on Assets	Long Term Debt	Common Equity	Total Cap.	% LT Debt of Cap.	% Ret. on Equity
1990	69.7	109	37.0	2.9	146	32.9	0.25	108	109	0.2	47.4
1989	49.7	77	34.1	2.3	94	42.7	0.50	59	60	0.8	66.2
1988	35.2	52	19.0	2.7	65	42.9	0.86	44	46	1.9	61.9
1987	17.4	25	7.9	3.2	32	34.3	Nil	24	24	Nil	48.2
1986	12.9	17	5.1	3.2	20	18.2	Nil	14	15	Nil	57.0
1985	2.8	4	1.1	3.8	6	NA	Nil	NM	5	Nil	NA

Data as orig. reptd.   1. Refl. merger or acq.   NA–Not Available.   d–Deficit.   NM–Not Meaningful.

Net Sales (Million $)

13 Weeks:	1991	1990	1989	1988
Feb.	52.6	37.2	25.5	14.2
May	57.1	35.3	28.1	18.8
Aug.	57.2	42.8	30.0	25.2
Nov.		53.4	37.7	25.3
	168.7	121.4	83.5

Revenues for the 39 weeks ended August 30, 1991, advanced 45%, year to year, reflecting continued strong demand for PostScript software and an increase in application product revenues. Operating costs rose at a more rapid pace, due in part to continued investment in new technology, and the gain in pretax income was limited to 35%. After taxes at 38.7%, against 39.8%, net income was up 37%, to $38,464,000 ($1.68 a share), from $28,029,000 ($1.28).

Common Share Earnings ($)

13 Weeks:	1991	1990	1989	1988
Feb.	0.55	0.48	0.32	0.17
May	0.58	0.36	0.35	0.21
Aug.	0.55	0.45	0.41	0.29
Nov.		0.55	0.48	0.31
	1.83	1.55	0.98

Dividend Data

A "poison pill" shareholder rights plan was adopted in July 1990.

Amt of Divd. $	Date Decl.	Ex-divd. Date	Stock of Record	Payment Date
0.06	Dec. 20	Jan. 9	Jan. 15	Jan. 29'91
0.08	Mar. 18	Mar. 22	Mar. 29	Apr. 12'91
0.08	Jun. 20	Jun. 26	Jul. 2	Jul. 16'91
0.08	Sep. 18	Sep. 25	Oct. 1	Oct. 15'91

Finances

In August 1991, Adobe announced plans to work with Apple Computer to implement a cooperative font strategy. Late in 1989, Apple and Microsoft Corp. had agreed to produce a set of products to compete with Adobe's offerings. However, no competing products were produced and Microsoft subsequently disbanded its printer business unit.

In March 1991, the company introduced a new generation of software technology that it said will significantly improve electronically printed characters. HBO, a major cable channel, plans to use the new software for both printing and on-the-air video.

In May 1991, Adobe and Lotus Development reached an agreement whereby Lotus would use Adobe's typeface software in all Lotus software. In March 1991, Hewlett-Packard Co. agreed to bundle Adobe's software with its new computer printer.

In March 1991, the company and Electronics for Imaging Inc. agreed to settle their patent dispute. Adobe would receive a nonexclusive license to a color-imaging technology for which EFI had been the exclusive licensee, while EFI would become a PostScript licensee. Adobe also made an investment of an undisclosed amount in EFI.

Capitalization

Long Term Debt: $174,000 (5/91) of lease obligs.

Common Stock: 21,645,898 shs. (no par).
Institutions hold about 85%.
Shareholders: About 1,155 of record (1/91).

Office— 1585 Charleston Rd., Mountain View, CA 94039-7900. Tel—(415) 961-4400. Chrmn & CEO—J. E. Warnock. Pres & COO—C. M. Geschke. VP-Fin, CFO, Treas & Investor Contact—M. Bruce Nakao. Secy—Colleen M. Pouliot. Dirs—D. C. Evans, C. M. Geschke, W. R. Hambrecht, L. W. Krause, R. Sedgewick, J. E. Warnock. Transfer Agent & Registrar—Manufacturers Hanover Trust Co., San Francisco. Incorporated in California in 1983. Empl—508.

Information has been obtained from sources believed to be reliable, but its accuracy and completeness are not guaranteed.   Sylvia B. Privel

Reprinted by permission of Standard & Poor's Corp.

tell at a glance how the company stacks up financially. A chart covering the last six to seven years' price behavior will alert you as to whether or not this company has been successful. (Please refer to Chapter 5 on timing your purchases.) Recent important developments are summarized as is the company's basic business. You will also find out how much stock the institutions and insiders currently own. Should you wish to contact the company for further information, the report makes it easy to do by providing its address and telephone number.

Value Line is another fine source of information on growth stocks. However, their coverage is limited to about 1,700 stocks, including all of the important big capitalization issues. A growth stock has to have something special going for it to be included in the Value Line's coverage, at least initially. So those stocks that have made it into Value Line's realm should welcome this increase in status and they may deserve your attention. Figure 6-3, a sample Value Line report, will give you an idea of the depth of their coverage.

Basic fundamental data going back as far as 16 years will allow you to easily determine how well the company meets your criteria. Value Line does analysis on all of their stocks and assigns each stock a letter rating for financial strength. A written summary discusses recent developments at the company and offers the analyst's opinion (name at the bottom) on the investment merits of the company. Logarithmic charts present over ten years of the stock's price history. Like the S&P reports, you are given the company's phone number and address should you wish to get more information.

MAGAZINES

The search for winning growth stock ideas can also be aided by a number of publications that periodically publish lists of top performing companies. These lists are typically compiled by applying some specific criteria to the stocks being screened. Usually a company's financial performance over the last few years is evaluated, on a preset formula based on crunching the relevant numbers. This approach will certainly identify an above-average number of stocks in the fast track that could turn out to be big winners for several years to come. However, because these lists are merely a screening device, you should not purchase stocks solely on the basis of their numerical standing or even on the basis that they are included on the list. Instead, what you are looking for are some ideas that you can research

Figure 6-3
Sample Value Line Report

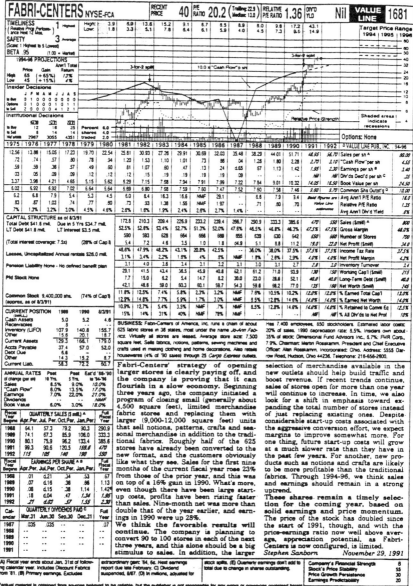

Source: Reprinted by permission of Value Line Investment Survey.

further. If they meet the standards outlined in this book, you may then have found yourself another hot stock for your portfolio.

When perusing a list, keep in mind that it was prepared solely on the basis of past performance, and that the information may be a little bit dated. Things can happen quickly with small growth stocks. Some that appear on the compilation may already be heading in the wrong direction by the time you get your hands on it. If you keep this in mind, it may help save you some time when you begin your investigation of some individual issues. So don't be surprised if you have to drop a stock from consideration that you gleaned from one of these magazines two days previously. They're not all going to be winners just because they are in the top 100 or 200.

Each fall, *Forbes* magazine publishes its list of the top 200 best small companies. The statistical breakdown covers about a dozen critical numbers regarding the financial strength and performance of each company. Also of interest is the table listing pertinent facts on each company's CEO. To start your screening process, you will want to compare the CEO's annual salary to the market value of the shares he owns of company stock. Remember, as an indication of a motivated management, what you want to see here is a modest salary compared to the value of his shares. Stocks on the *Forbes* list are compared to their standing the previous year. Not surprisingly, there's a lot of change going on in the oftentimes volatile world of small stocks. In 1991, only 88 of 200 stocks were repeaters from 1990's findings. Repeaters that have moved up smartly on the list may warrant further scrutiny. You may also want to pay special attention to newcomers that rate highly. For example, Cambex, a computer equipment and software manufacturer, debuted at number one. Cambex stock shot up 290% in value in 1991.

Another interesting presentation of growth stock candidates appears each May in *BusinessWeek*. A good number of the stocks on their list of 100 best small companies are in the earlier, more volatile stages of growth than those *Forbes* ranks. Evidence of this is provided by the fact that only one-third of the companies on the list for 1990 made the grade again in 1991. Five companies did manage to outgrow the list $150 million sales limit. Therefore, as with the *Forbes* list, you will need to use due diligence after picking stocks from those screened by *BusinessWeek* for their top 100. You will find some stocks that make both magazines' lists. For example, *BusinessWeek* ranked Cambex number 10 in 1991.

Although *Forbes* and *BusinessWeek* are perhaps the most prominent of the growth stock rankings, you will want to scout for other publications on both the local and national level that provide a similar service. *Califor-*

nia Business publishes a list each year of what it feels are the best 100 small companies within the state. *Barron's Financial Weekly* will periodically run a computer screen to see which growth stocks are most undervalued.

Fortune magazine has a section each issue called "Portfolio Talk," which features a successful money manager. Every so often the interview will be with a growth stock manager who discusses his top picks and why he thinks they will do well. The interview also explains his philosophy of investing. This will alert you as to whether or not he practices the long-term fundamental approach advocated in this book. Although *Fortune* is geared to America's largest companies, it will occasionally do features that highlight additional promising growth stocks. You can also gain confidence from the magazine's positive comments about the current condition of business in America. *Fortune* doesn't necessarily skirt the negatives as they exist, but they do a better than average job of letting you know the good things going on in the world. *Fortune* will also provide you with comments on various industries of interest as well as reviews and forecasts on the economy.

BusinessWeek has commentary on virtually everything going on in the world of business. Regular features cover politics, industry analysis, legal issues, personal business, and much more. At the front of the magazine they have an easy to read, concise, presentation of economic information that can keep you abreast of current business conditions. The magazine regularly contains special features and excellent charts on the major trends that can affect your investments. *BusinessWeek* annually publishes a comprehensive review of mutual funds.

Those who like hard-hitting, pull-no-punches commentary on individual companies and the world of business will really appreciate *Forbes* magazine. Right or wrong, the magazine definitely takes a stand. If you find a story in *Forbes* that is less than flattering about an investment you are in or thinking about for investment, consider yourself forewarned. They have a good nose for eyeballing the lesser lights (i.e., incompetents and crooks) of the business scene. If you want someone to play the devil's advocate for you, consult *Forbes*. The magazine gives you excellent industry reviews. Although *Forbes'* emphasis is on big cap stocks, it also gives good coverage to small growth stocks of above-average promise. Mutual fund investors will gain value from *Forbes'* annual fund rankings. They evaluate each fund's performance in both up and down markets. The best funds tend to resist market declines while outperforming the averages during bull markets.

Money magazine is an excellent resource for the average investor who seeks advice on financial planning. The magazine offers useful suggestions on things like saving for your children's college education, how to reduce your taxes, and how to make the most out of your retirement account. *Money* is a mainstream publication that is usually on top of the major trends in finance. Mutual funds are emphasized both in articles and in the ads that appear in the magazine. Fund recommendations are issued in virtually all categories, including small company growth funds. *Money*'s annual fund rankings appear each year in the February issue. Their table contains much of the data this book recommends you use to select the best small company mutual funds.

Kiplinger's Personal Finance magazine ranks right up alongside *Money* in providing the individual investor with the "how-to" of managing their personal affairs. *Kiplinger's* gives regular coverage to such areas as taxes, real estate, insurance costs, and more. The magazine periodically provides small growth stock ideas from investment professionals that may be worth looking into further. Again, like *Money* magazine, *Kiplinger's* gives ample coverage of mutual funds in all categories. Those of you who wish to participate in small companies via a mutual fund will find *Kiplinger's* mutual fund ranking in the September issue to be of value.

Serious investors wishing to keep tabs on the latest trends in corporate America will appreciate *Financial World*. The magazine profiles mostly large companies but does feature small companies occasionally. *Financial World* conducts a number of interesting surveys, including awards to the top CEO and to the company that issues the best annual report. The magazine issues forecasts and provides interesting commentary by respected analysts. Each August, *Financial World* publishes a list of the 500 fastest growing companies in America, based on a five-year rate of earnings growth. Although not restricted to small growth companies, you may still be able to identify some candidates for further review from the listing. Every three months, *Financial World* publishes a list of mutual funds which feature the fund's current asset size and three-year performance ranking.

BUSINESS PAPERS AND PERIODICALS

The Wall Street Journal is undoubtedly the best known daily paper that is devoted primarily to finance. *The Wall Street Journal* provides a wide variety of coverage on topics such as politics, business news, opinions, legal matters, and personal finance. Special features inform readers of the latest trends developing in the financial markets, including topics such as small growth stocks, mutual funds, interest rates, portfolio management, and big cap stocks. The earnings digest presents the latest reports on individual companies' profits or losses. Charts going back a year and a half give you, at a glance, the recent trends in stocks, bonds, interest rates, and the U.S. dollar. Charts on Dow Jones market indicators and volume show the last six months' daily trading activity. *The Wall Street Journal* gives you a very comprehensive set of stock tables.

Investors Business Daily, published by William O'Neil, is gaining in popularity among stock market participants. The paper gives you a concise presentation of the latest breaking stories in the world of business and includes comments on various investments, the economy, and the opinions of a wide variety of leaders in business. Daily price activity is given in a series of excellent stock and mutual funds tables. A series of charts on NYSE, AMEX, and NASDAQ stocks in the news give you snapshots of the hottest stocks in each market. Corporate earnings are reported daily. Charts going back nine months give you daily changes in several leading market indicators, including the Dow and S&P 500. The last six months' percentage changes are listed from top to bottom for 200 industries. This will inform you as to which sectors of the economy are doing best and those which you may wish to avoid. In the back of each issue, the paper devotes extensive coverage to a stock and industry that it feels warrants your attention.

For the serious investor, *Barron's Financial Weekly* is a must. *Barron's* statistical section is in a class by itself. Approximately 85 pages are devoted to data on stocks, bonds, interest rates, market indicators, the economy, and much more. Since this book's approach is geared to the long term, in most cases you can get by with weekly data. Barron's weekly stock listings provide the most information on stocks on the major exchanges. Charts on the indicators cover four months of daily price movement. Barron's regularly publishes feature articles on the opinions of leading financial pros covering a variety of topics, including occasional talks with top small growth stock advocates. These may give you some ideas worth looking into. Newly issued research reports are summarized each issue and may provide more stock ideas for you to consider further. Barron's gives extensive coverage to mutual funds including their very detailed quarterly fund reviews.

The usefulness of your local daily newspaper as a reference source varies greatly from paper to paper. Indeed, not all business sections are created equal, so for the most part you should look at your local daily as a complement to your other sources. Because the philosophy of this book is investing in stocks you can get to know well, it follows that many of the stocks that you will invest in may be close to home. As a result, your local paper will provide you with detailed coverage on these stocks that you might not find elsewhere. Therefore, you'll want to make a practice of at least scanning through the business section daily so you won't miss any important developments in local stocks that you own. The quality of the stock tables and market barometers will again vary. You may, however, find the prices of small local stocks that may not be readily available elsewhere.

Another useful source of news on local stocks is business journals that give very specific coverage to nearby communities. These journals will often provide insights and information on hometown companies that you won't find elsewhere. They are not available in all areas, but if there is one where you live, you will probably want to subscribe to it.

NEWSLETTERS

There are literally hundreds of newsletters available on every topic of finance imaginable. The quality of these advisory services varies greatly, so if you choose to use newsletters as a source of information, proceed with caution. Fundamental stock recommendations should be backed up by some solid evidence that the letter writer has done his homework. Look at his report as you would that of a brokerage analyst. If the letter looks more like a tout sheet for the racetrack, you will have to conduct a more detailed analysis on your own of any ideas that appear to be of interest.

The cost of newsletters varies. Some can run into hundreds of dollars per year. An inexpensive way to sample several at a time is through a company called Select Information Exchange. For about $12 you can receive trial subscriptions or samples of 20 newsletters. Letters with a history of success will more than likely be able to show you a good track record as part of their effort to convert you into a long-term subscriber. There are some good newsletters, but be careful which guru you hook up with should you use this approach. (Select Information Exchange, 244 West 54th St., New York, New York 10019, (212) 247-7132)

FRIENDS, BUSINESS ASSOCIATES, ETC.

In your search for winning growth stocks you should always be open to potentially rewarding new ideas. These ideas can often come when you least expect it. An associate informed me that he was putting in the air conditioning on AST's new manufacturing facility. He reasoned correctly that AST's business must be expanding. AST wound up the top stock (among those that began the year over $5) in the United States in 1990 with a gain of 259%. By now you probably get the point. Your sources of information should include not only the services mentioned previously but also the people you come in contact with on a daily basis. Friends, spouses, co-workers, business associates, in short, anyone could be the originator of a worthwhile idea.

At this point you should recognize the distinction between these sources and taking stock tips. You've probably heard of someone who has done well on a stock tip. What you might not know is all of the times they've been burned by these suggestions. Perhaps you've lost money on some sure-fire stock that you bought only on a rumor. In sharp contrast, look at the potential sources mentioned in this book as the starting point for your investigation. If a friend likes the service he got at an auto supply store, it's possibly worth checking further. The idea is the starting point. It may lead you to a big winner. Just make sure that you follow through with the tests covered in earlier chapters. Should the idea pan out, fine. If not, move on to the next one.

CHART SERVICES

Chapter 5 discussed how charts can help you time your purchases. In Chapter 7 you will be given some ideas of how you can use charts to help you sell. Listed below are some of the best chart services for the small growth stock investor. Most of them offer relatively low-cost trial subscriptions that will allow you to gauge the usefulness of the service.

Daily Graphs. Charts cover 1,600 NYSE issues (700 go back 1 year), 400 AMEX issues (200 go back 1 year), and 560 OTC leaders. Charts cover daily price action and use an arithmetic scale. Each chart presents a wealth of fundamental and technical data, including earnings going back several years as well as analysts' estimates for the next couple of years.

Long-Term Values (Published by William O'Neil and Company). Approximately 4,000 stocks are presented on semi-logarithmic charts going back 15 years. These charts give monthly high-low and close on 1,600 OTC issues and 2,400 listed stocks (NYSE and AMEX). Charts are arranged by industry group. Each stock is covered, on a rotating basis, every six weeks.

Securities Research Corporation, Security Charts. Each month, 1,100 listed stocks and 1,000 OTC issues are presented in separate chart books. Charts give weekly price action going back over one and a half years and use semi-logarithmic graph paper. Earnings are plotted along with the price of the stock.

Securities Research Corporation, Cycli-Graphs. Published quarterly, these charts cover 1,000 OTC issues and over 1,100 listed stocks. Semi-logarithmic charts cover 12 years of monthly price activity and also include each stock's earnings history.

R.W. Mansfield. Charts cover all NYSE and all Amex issues in two separate editions; 4,200 OTC stocks are presented in three separate editions. OTC issues are divided according to their size. Mansfield charts come out weekly and cover two and a half years of weekly price activity. The charts also present recent earnings history and other useful fundamental data.

Standard & Poor's Chart Guide. Over 4,400 charts appear in each monthly edition covering stocks from the NYSE, AMEX, and OTC. Charts contain a one year history of each stock's weekly high-low-close.

REFERENCE SOURCES

The names and addresses of the sources discussed in this chapter are listed below. Phone numbers and addresses are subject to change, so be sure to call the 800 operator if you find one of these lines is no longer in operation.

Magazines, Periodicals and Investment Services

Standard & Poor's
Attention: Customer Service
25 Broadway, 17th Floor
New York, NY 10004

Phone: 1-800-853-1640
Phone: 1-212-208-8768

Fortune Magazine
P.O. Box 60001
Tampa, FL 33660-0001
Phone: 1-800-628-8993

Value Line Investment Survey
711 Third Avenue
New York, NY 10017

Phone: 1-800-833-0046

Forbes, Inc.
P.O. Box 10048
Des Moines, IA 50309

Phone: 1-800-888-9896

Business Week
P.O. Box 421
Highstown, NJ 08520

Phone: 1-800-635-1200

Money Magazine
P.O. Box 61790
Tampa, FL 33661-1790

Phone: 1-800-633-9970

Financial World
Attention: Circulation Dept.
1328 Broadway, Floor 3
New York, NY 10001

Phone: 1-800-666-6639

Barron's Financial Weekly
200 Burnett Road
Chicopee, MA 01021

Phone: 1-800-328-6800

Wall Street Journal
200 Burnett Road
Chicopee, MA 01021

Phone: 1-800-628-9320

Investor's Business Daily
P.O. Box 25970
Los Angeles, CA 90025

Phone: 1-800-831-2525

Kiplinger's Personal Finance
 Magazine
Editor's Park, MD 20782-9964

Phone: 1-800-544-0155

Chart Services

Daily Graphs and Long-Term Values
Daily Graphs
P.O. Box 24933
Los Angeles, CA 90024-0933

Phone: 1-310-820-2583

Securities Research Company
Babson United Building
101 Prescott Street
Wellesley Hills, MA 02181-3319

Phone: 1-617-235-0900

R.W. Mansfield
2973 Kennedy Blvd.
Jersey City, NJ 07306

Phone: 1-800-223-3530

Standard & Poor's/Trendline Chart Guide
P.O. Box 992
New York, NY 10275-0417

Phone: 1-212-208-8768

SUMMARY

- Doing your homework gives you the confidence to hold on to a winner for big gains.
- Don't be influenced by negatives in the media if they keep you from investing; instead, emphasize positive sources of information.
- Learn to distinguish what information is of value and what is not.
- First and foremost, emphasize information on companies.
- Get the company's literature and study it carefully. It should be the foundation of your decision-making process.
- Pay particular attention to any negatives in the annual report.
- Company literature should be a marketing tool.
- Get on the mailing list of companies you are interested in.
- Check out trade journals and other third-party endorsements for a company's products or services.
- Stock conferences and road shows can inform you of promising stocks; they also allow you to rub shoulders with the key executives.

- A stockholders' meeting gives you the chance to ask questions and hear the company's story firsthand.
- Call company headquarters and ask questions, and if possible visit the company.
- Call for brokerage reports on the stocks you're interested in and obtain a summary of their small stock recommendations.
- Small and regional brokerages tend to be your best source of information on small growth stocks.
- Watch out when a "buy" recommendation turns into a hold.
- Use out-of-town yellow pages to locate brokerages out of your immediate area.
- Make sure to stay clear of the penny stock brokers.
- Learn to read brokerage reports including the analyst's future predictions.
- Standard and Poor's Corporation offers extensive and detailed coverage of small growth stocks.
- Value Line Investment Survey gives coverage to some of the most promising small growth stocks.
- Promising young companies are in the small stock lists published by magazines such as *BusinessWeek* and *Forbes*.
- Interesting growth stock candidates often appear in magazine articles, but be sure to do your homework.
- *The Wall Street Journal* is the best known daily business newspaper.
- *Investors Business Daily* is a concise presentation of business news and information that is geared to stock market participants.
- Each week *Barron's Financial Weekly* provides the serious investor with a wealth of statistical data as well as commentary from a broad cross section of investment professionals.
- Your local newspaper can be a useful source of information on local companies of interest.
- Business journals also give excellent coverage on local stocks.
- Newsletters may prove to be a useful source of new stock ideas. Be sure to check out each idea thoroughly.

- Avoid investing based solely on stock tips from friends and business associates; do your own homework.
- *Money* magazine provides tips on financial planning and gives extensive coverage on mutual funds.
- *Kiplinger's Personal Finance* magazine gives you good ideas for managing your personal affairs and gives extensive coverage to mutual funds.
- Each year, *Financial World* presents its list of the 500 fastest growing companies in America. The magazine emphasizes corporate developments.
- There are a number of excellent chart services. You may want to test them with trial subscriptions to see which one is right for you.

Chapter 7

WHEN TO SELL

Purchasing a stock for long-term profits should not be a decision that is easily arrived at. As shown, there are a number of key fundamentals that need to be checked out before you can feel confident that you're looking at a potential big winner. You need to know enough about your stocks so that you'll feel confident enough to ride them to big profits. Once your homework is done and you've bought a stock, you've now taken on the responsibility for your new investment. After all, your dollars are now at risk.

If things work out as planned, your stock will have a long and profitable journey. However, the best laid plans of even the finest stock investors often go astray. Therefore, from the outset, you must plan to monitor every stock you buy from purchase until it is sold (hopefully many years later at a substantial gain). Monitoring a stock does not mean calling your broker three times a day for quotes, nor should you be concerned with each day's closing price. What monitoring your stocks means is to keep on top of the key fundamental developments which could, should they turn for the worse, change the status of your holding from a buy to a sell.

Most small growth stocks will eventually lose their steam and need to be sold. For the truly successful companies, this may take years. Those that grow to the status of the Fortune 500 are the real exceptions to the rule. However, your growth stocks don't need to reach that level to make you a lot of money. If they do, so much the better.

When you purchase small company growth stocks, you may find your-self susceptible to the emotions of fear and greed. To counteract these often times ruinous emotions, you will need to develop a rational approach to selling your stocks. Fundamental analysis will be the most important factor in deciding when to sell a stock. Technical analysis should be used to augment the fundamental decision-making process. Of course, it would be great if all your stocks turned out to be winners. Unfortunately, however, it is also important to know how to handle a losing position.

WHAT TO DO AFTER YOU BUY

Once you buy a stock, hopefully the next trade will be an up-tick and your new position will never again trade lower than where you bought it. This rarely happens. In the short run, the ebb and flow of a stock's price will quite possibly carry it lower than where you bought it. Providing this movement is not pronounced, you should not be overly concerned. Growth stocks, particularly if they are low priced (perhaps under $10-$15) can show a high degree of volatility. So you must learn to live with these short-term fluctuations. You don't, however, want to get locked into holding a loser. Some investors will marry a stock and find all kinds of reasons for holding on to a loser that should be sold. It's true that you want to have a certain feeling for the stocks you buy. But don't forget that there will be a time to sell.

In the worst case scenario, you may be faced with a sell decision within possibly days or weeks after investing. Nobody's crystal ball is 100% accurate when it comes to forecasting conditions in the business world. Some unforeseen disaster may strike your company. Maybe the CEO, who has been vital to the company's success, will have a heart attack, or possibly a competitor will suddenly announce a product that's far superior and cheaper. All of these developments and more could turn the fundamental outlook of your company upside-down overnight. In addition, there's a chance that you may have overlooked a key point in your analysis, and it may be the one negative that's going to undermine the stock.

So right from the start, be sure to follow any important developments in your new stock. If all goes well, the marketplace will soon recognize the value of your stock and it will begin to trend higher. Should the stock show any appreciable weakness after you have invested, you may want to double check the fundamentals in the absence of any new developments. Also check out the chart patterns discussed in Chapter 5 on market timing. If you bought the stock in what appears to be a low-risk zone, and then it breaks an important trendline or violates a proven level of support (see examples below), the market might be telling you something by the price action of the stock that you may not have noticed in your original appraisal.

If you found that you've made a mistake, don't hesitate to cut your losses and run. Don't let your ego or belief that the stock will get better stand in your way; sell and be done with it. And after you've taken a loss, try to learn something from it. We all make mistakes, so just try not to repeat them.

Many investors like to use mechanical means to limit their loss in a new stock. For example, some will decide to sell if a stock declines 10% or 20%. This kind of disciplined approach will keep your losses in check. The big weakness of this approach is that you may sell out just at the time when you should, if anything, be adding to your position. When you factor in the bid/ask spread and the volatile nature of small growth stocks, you will understand the need to give them more leeway.

For example, suppose you just bought a growth stock for $10 and a blue chip for $50. You might want to consider selling the blue chip if it dropped 10% to $45, using a discipline of limiting your losses. The same approach with your $10 stock would have you selling out at $9, or 10% below your purchase price. Lower-priced stocks tend to have wider percentage fluctuations. Therefore, you should allow lower priced stocks to decline further on a percentage basis than you would blue chip issues.

Because OTC stocks are more thinly traded, you may wish to consider using a "mental stop" to protect you from large losses. Should the $10 stock decline to $8 1/2, or 15% below your purchase price, that should alert you to strongly consider selling the stock. With a mental stop, you will need to follow the stock's price to make sure that it gets off to a good start. If the stock hits your mental stop, you will need to call and place your sell order. If and when your stock does hit a mental stop, that doesn't mean you should automatically sell your shares. It does mean, however, that you should undertake a serious reappraisal of the company. Should it pass your inspection, continue to hold on to it. Keep in mind that the best insurance you can have against a big decline in a stock is to invest in fundamentally solid stocks in the first place.

DEALING WITH A WINNER

The second scenario is a much cheerier one. The stock you've chosen has begun to advance in price, and you now have a winner on your hands. For some investors, dealing with a winning selection can be as hard if not harder than taking care of a loser. One big mistake is to sell too soon. By doing so you will short-circuit your chance of having that truly big hit that can do wonders for your portfolio. Winners take time to register several-fold gains, so you must learn to develop the confidence and patience in your better stock selections so that you can ride them to big profits.

The year 1991 was one of the best years in history for small growth stocks. The number-one stock in the Over-the-Counter market (among those that started the year at $5 or above) was Synergen Pharmaceuticals. Over the course of the year, Synergen skyrocketed 496%. It would be interesting to know how many investors had the patience to stick with Synergen for the full year. To carry this a step further, how many investors will hold on to their shares for another one, two, or five years in search of 20- or 30-fold gains? The pressure to sell a big winner is enormous.

Eventually, however, you will come to a point where you will need to consider selling your superstar growth stock. Either the company will peter out, or it will grow in size to where it's no longer a small company growth stock. Perhaps your growth stock will evolve into a sure and steady performer and become a consistent, if no longer spectacular, performer as it was in the early years. You may even want to continue holding on to it if it becomes another Bristol-Myers or Coca Cola. But remember these extra large and successful companies are the exception, rather than the rule.

FUNDAMENTAL SELLING

The fundamental condition of your stock will be the single most important ingredient for its success in the long run. Chapters 3 and 4 covered a number of positives to look for in a promising young company. When it comes time to consider selling your winning stocks, you will need to basically reverse the questions that led to your original decision to buy.

The selection process taken in this book started with a conceptual approach to evaluating a company's business. Periodically, you will want to review the basic questions: Why was the business successful at the start? Are they still on the same pathway? Has the business taken on an added dimension that's a plus? Has the business begun to flatten out, or worse yet, lose touch with today's realities? The computer industry is full of examples of promising young growth companies in the early 1980s that were involved in mainframes and failed to adapt to the new trend towards personal computers fast enough. And, as might be expected, many of these promising young hopefuls have seen their stocks plummet in value.

The sixth sense you've developed about sizing up a business will not only help in buying good stocks but will also prove to be of value in assisting you to make a wise sell decision. When you've given a stock the once-over to find out if it still feels right to you, it's time to move on to more objective criteria.

MANAGEMENT

In the beginning, you want management to be motivated by a large ownership position in the company, especially in view of large salaries. The top executives' success at making the company grow could well affect their plans for retirement, or some other such financial goal. As the years pass and the company's stock progresses higher, you should not be surprised to see these insiders periodically sell off sizeable blocks of stock. As long as such selling stays within reason, it should not be viewed as a negative. After all, it's only prudent for a chief executive officer and/or founder of a growth company to diversify his assets and to, at least partially, cash in on his efforts. For example, assume a CEO owned 20% of his company's stock that had a market value of $4 million. Over a few years' time, the stock went from $10 to $50 per share. During this period he sold half of his shares. Based on the higher stock price, the CEO, despite his selling, would still own $10 million worth of his company's stock!

Even though insiders do sell shares occasionally, don't let that lead you to believe the stock is ready for a fall. The alarm bells should go off, however, if an executive's ownership position has dwindled from 20% to 2% while his salary has gone from $200,000 to $1,000,000 annually. At some point, when the fire has gone out, a management that's no longer highly motivated could prove to be the undoing of your favorite stock. Don't forget that money is not the only motivator. Some executives may still get a kick out of running a business successfully, even if their financial stake in it has shrunk dramatically. There are a number of places you can check to keep tabs on the ownership position of the key executives in your stock. The company's annual proxy statement will list the insiders' ownership position as well as their current salaries, including bonuses.

Interestingly enough, sometimes you will find that management has succumbed to a weak economy and/or falling stock price and sold a big block of stock right near an important low. Because they may be so wrapped up in running a business, they may fail to remember that their company's stock price may bear little resemblance when it is down to what the company is really worth.

In their efforts to help a business grow, management will seek to acquire other business. When 1+1=3, that's great! That's called synergy, and it's achieved when management buys other businesses that can serve to complement their efforts. Perhaps the company they're acquiring has a complementary product line or some existing and valuable channels of distribution. In contrast, a red flag should go up if management acquires a totally unrelated business. That can result in 1+1=1 or worse. When management begins to stray from their basic business, disaster could be around the corner.

EARNINGS PER SHARE

Wall Street literally falls in love with stocks whose EPS is trending seemingly ever higher. A stock that posts consistently higher earnings year after year is rewarded with an expansion of its P/E multiple. As you might suspect, this process is a two-way street. Should earnings growth start to slow appreciably, the market may then assign the stock a correspondingly lower multiple. And if earnings actually fail to meet previous quarters, and there's no good explanation that would suggest this decline is only temporary, look out below.

Unpredictable or erratic earnings have a way of casting a pall over a stock. Even when business is good and earnings are soaring ahead, most investors will still look at the company with suspicion. That's why some very fine companies whose businesses are cyclical in nature fail to achieve the P/E of small growth companies that show consistent growth. If your stock starts to show cyclical (not seasonal) tendencies—beware! Your stock has been transformed from a growth stock to a cyclical stock.

In the early years, growth stocks can record some rather astounding percentage gains in EPS. You should not be too alarmed if a stock with a 100% growth rate slows to 50%. Chances are the market won't be either. However, as the company matures and EPS growth slows, you should keep in mind the prevailing trend. This will vary, of course, from stock to stock. With the stock mentioned above, if the growth in EPS were to fall below perhaps 30%, the stock may lose a lot of its former luster (i.e., some investors might start selling out).

Growth stocks that have exhibited a degree of consistency over the years are to be coveted. If you've found a solid grower that keeps tacking on 25%-30% EPS gains each year, then you just might have a stock you can hold for several years. However, when this growth starts to slow (possibly to 15%) because all of their markets are saturated, you should begin to consider selling your shares.

No one quarter should make or break any good long-term business. Nevertheless, you will want to keep tabs on the quarterly data. Should an off quarter pop up, it's time to recheck the company's fundamentals. Good solid growth companies entering or in their prime will almost never post negative annual comparisons. So if it looks like a whole year is going to be flat or down, you can no longer consider that as an ideal growth stock. Disappointing earnings may go hand-in-hand with a sell-off. In that case you are now looking at a turnaround and not a growth stock.

SALES GROWTH

Growth companies are, by definition, those whose demand for their product or service increases rapidly over the years. From a small base, sales can grow at rates of 50% more. But as with earnings, the rate of increase will normally slow to a more realistic rate within a few years. You can't expect 75% annual growth in sales forever, but when the inevitable leveling off takes place, sales should still be growing at perhaps 20%-30% a year. This is just a rule of thumb. What you're looking for are signs that the company's products or services are losing their grip or ability to grow in the marketplace.

A service company may have saturated its market and failed to develop new ones, or possibly they may have lost a couple of large customers and were unable to replace them. How are same store sales growing, if at all? Are new outlets or franchises being opened regularly? In a product-oriented company, research and development may have failed to come up with any hot new ideas lately. Has the company's leading product lost its pizzazz? Has it fallen in stature in trade journals when compared to other companies with a similar product? You might also want to know if the company plans an expensive new facility if the present plant is already running at or near full capacity. This kind of expenditure may not pay for itself for a while, especially if sales are slowing down.

Take some time to review the company's sales strategy. What are their plans for expansion? Does their marketing plan have any new twists to it that could reignite sales? When all is said and done, if the demand for a company's product or service is on the wane, or if its rate of growth has slowed to unacceptably low levels, it could very well be time to sell your shares and move on.

PROFIT MARGINS

While a growth company needs to show rapidly growing sales, that is not enough. To fuel a commensurate rise in earnings, the profitability of those sales must stay stable, or better yet increase. The benefit of rising sales and increasing profit margins was covered in Chapter 3. A company's profit margin can rise for many years before eventually leveling off. Hopefully, when margins do slow their ascent it is at a high and sustainable level. What you don't want is a serious and prolonged decline in profit margins. If that were to occur, the volume of sales would have to shoot ahead to keep earnings from stagnating.

Declining margins can be attributed to increased competition which may in turn lead to price wars. In addition, a company may start to sell a large volume of products that may have less profit than other product lines. Whatever the reason, a sustained fall-off of margins and the subsequent impact on earnings is generally viewed as a serious negative by Wall Street. To give you an idea of what falling margins can do to a company's earnings, consider the following example. In each year, sales grew 20%.

Year	1	2	3	4
Sales (000)	$10,000	$12,000	$14,400	$17,280
Net Profit Margin	15%	15%	14%	13%
Net Income (000)	$1,500	$1,800	$2,016	$2,246
% Growth-Net Income	—	20%	12.0%	11.4%

In the second year, margins remained flat, while sales and earnings both grew by 20%. Unfortunately, in both the third and fourth years, margins started to slip. As you can see, this led to a big drop in earnings growth, even though sales kept increasing at a 20% annual rate. Keep in mind that the trend is always your friend, as long as it is upward, but when a company's profit margin starts to slip, unless sales are now sky-rocketing ahead, it just may be time to unload your shares

RETURN ON EQUITY

The ability of a business to remain self-financing depends largely on its return on equity (ROE). If the business wishes to expand at 30% per year, and its ROE is at that level or beyond, then the company may not need to burden itself with debt or dilute itself with additional offerings of equity. As with several other tests, a company's ROE could be unusually high in the early going. When it does settle down, it should still be running at 15%-30% or more, depending on the business.

SPONSORSHIP

The big institutions represent one of the biggest sources of demand for a stock when it is in its dynamic growth phase. Conversely, they also represent a large potential source of supply when a growth stock reaches maturity. Heavy institutional ownership is a healthy sign of acceptance, but it can also be a large negative should the banks, mutual funds, and pension plans turn sour on a stock and start dumping shares. The example below is a rough guide as to how the ownership of a company can change as it moves up the ladder of success.

Percentage of Ownership

	Start of Growth Phase	At Maturity
Insiders	30%	10%
Individuals	60%	30%
Institutions	10%	60%

When your growth stock reaches about 60% institutional ownership, it means that these investors have largely gained control of the stock. Insiders are usually restricted as to how much stock they can sell at any given time. And the individual investor, perhaps because of higher commissions and tax consequences, tends to hold stocks longer than the institutions. So with the big boys buying and selling your former growth stock like crazy, they can represent a powder keg ready to go off.

Sometimes you will discover that a stock that is heavily owned by the institutions keeps advancing in price anyway. The reason for this is that even bigger institutions, with their liquidity requirements, will be attracted to a solid growth company. Your former small growth stock may now have become a respected member of the institutional community. When this happens, recognize that you now own a medium to large capitalization stock. If you're still investing for above average growth that small companies can offer you, then it's time to move on. On the other hand, you might just find yourself owning an industry leader such as Wal-Mart, that seems to keep steadily growing despite its size and institutional dominance.

As your growth stock grows in size and reputation, you may want to keep a watch on the current opinion of brokerage analysts toward the company. Their reports may serve as a useful means for keeping you abreast of important developments. Their earnings forecasts, although always subject to error, can give you a consensus view of the future earnings potential of a stock. Earnings forecasts are also available on Daily Graphs Charts and Value Line reports, among others. Also be on the lookout in case an influential brokerage or two changes their rating to a hold. This could precipitate an abundance of sell orders by both their retail and institutional clients.

DIVIDENDS

Small growth companies will almost never pay a dividend, especially in their early years. All available earnings are being plowed back into the company to foster future growth, as it should be. There are, however, some investors (including a number of institutions) that won't invest unless a company pays some sort of dividend, no matter how small. So if your company starts to pay a dividend, you might want to recheck the story again. It's possible that the stock has now reached a level of maturity that no longer qualifies it as a small growth stock.

If your stock pays a small dividend, it should be rising annually at a rapid rate, or else it will forever represent a token payment. If a company that pays a small dividend (usually 1% or less of the current stock price) fails to increase the payout one year, or worse yet reduces or eliminates the dividend, that's a sign that management has lost confidence in the company's earnings capability. It could be time to unload your shares.

FINANCIAL CONDITION

Chapter 4 discussed the importance of examining a company's financial condition from both the short-term and long-run perspectives prior to purchasing shares. Ideally, the financial strength of the stocks you buy will only get better as they reach a size where they gain added stability and profitability as well. Unfortunately, however, circumstances will change and the finances of some of your selections may ultimately take a turn for the worse. The bad news is that, by the time the balance sheet has taken a serious turn for the worse, the stock in question may already be down sharply from its peak price. The good news is that by spotting a deteriorating balance sheet you may be able to sell (if you haven't done so already) before a bad situation gets worse. If you are really lucky, and/or skillful at detecting the first signs of a weakening financial structure, you may be able to sell before the crowd has run for the exits.

Make sure to periodically check the company's current ratio. Is it still running at better than 2:1 in favor of current assets over current liabilities? What's the trend like over the last several quarters? If the company also has long-term debt, its creditors may call in their loans if the current ratio dips below an agreed-upon level. Be sure to check out the company's inventories to make sure that they aren't growing any faster than sales. With the aid of computers and new techniques of manufacturing, there is no reason why inventories should reach unacceptable levels, unless, of course, trouble is brewing.

Another consideration includes finding out about the current status of the accounts receivable. Have they been trending sharply higher? Has the company been accepting poor credit risks in a effort to bolster sagging sales? You will also want to figure the company's quick ratio to determine if cash or cash equivalents are equal to or greater than the short-term liabilities. Remember, if a company's finances are starting to weaken in the near term, it's possibly a sign that the long-term financial prospects are also turning down.

Successful growth companies are often able to expand without taking on the burden of debt. Indeed, their success often allows them, when needed, to raise capital via the issuance of additional shares of stock. So if your company has recently taken on some long-term debt, find out exactly what it's being used for. If it's for something such as the financing of an acquisition of an unrelated business, chances are you should consider selling your stock. Again, check the structure of the debt. Are there any large amounts of debt coming due in perhaps 12-24 months? And don't forget to calculate the relationship between stockholders' equity and long-term debt. Has equity fallen below 75% of a combination of stockholders' equity and long-term debt? If so, this may be a red flag concerning the long-term financial condition of the company. Should any of the negative financial criteria be met, and your other fundamental evaluation is also less than thrilling, it's time to take your profits and move on to something else.

TECHNICAL SELLING

Charts, as shown in Chapter 5, can help you time your purchases. Similarly, charts can assist you in your selling if your fundamental evaluation tells you the stock may have seen better days. Some common chart patterns are presented that are useful in identifying stocks that have reached their peak and are ready to enter into a prolonged downtrend. This presentation is by no means complete, but it should give you a feel for some of the topping formations that you'll run across.

An uptrend line is formed by connecting a series of low points on the chart of a stock that has been steadily rising in price. Each periodic decline in the stock will have had, for quite some time, the tendency to brake itself on the uptrend line. Following an extended rise in price, once a stock breaks a trendline there is a distinct possibility that the stock has reached an important long-term top (Figure 7-1). When one of your long-term holdings breaks a significant trendline, don't hesitate to check the fundamentals of the stock. If they are a bit shaky also, the market is telling you that it's time to sell. On the other hand, if the fundamentals are still in good shape, a trendline break could only mean that the stock is going to

Figure 7-1
Breaking an Uptrend

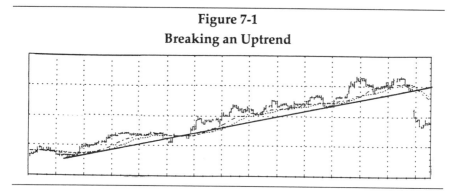

Figure 7-2
Distributional Top

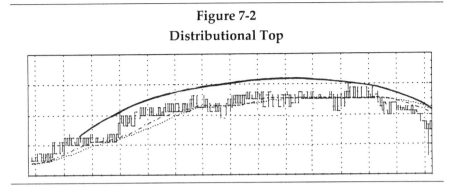

suffer through a mild and normal correction before resuming its march to an even higher high.

Often a stock that is running out of gas will form a distributional (or rounding) top (Figure 7-2). After a prolonged advance, a stock will start to move only slightly higher, reach a peak, and begin to very gradually head lower. All the while, smart money is supposedly distributing stock to unwary latecomers to the stock. If you find yourself in a stock that's gradually turning for the worse, prepare to place your sell order. Once the sellers gain the upper hand, the stock will be ready to head sharply lower.

A technical formation that can signal the end of a stock advance with a fairly good degree of regularity is called a double top reversal. As the name implies, this chart pattern consists of a stock reaching a peak, declining for a while, rallying once again, only to reverse itself in the vicinity of the previous high. You should give added weight to those double top patterns that have a reasonably long period of time between peaks, such as a couple of months or longer. Double tops with only a few weeks between them may produce an inordinate amount of false sell signals. Figure 7-3 demonstrates what a double top looks like.

A head and shoulders formation is an offbeat name for another reliable indicator that can help you sell a stock somewhat near its peak (Figure 7-4). You will note that with this pattern, as well as the ones just covered, you will never sell at the exact top. Rather, what you are trying to accomplish is that the sale of your stock is close enough to its peak while assuring that you retain the majority of what will hopefully be a substantial profit. With the head and shoulders pattern, when a stock reaches a peak, it will enter into a short-term decline. This forms the left shoulder. This decline is then followed by a rally to a new high slightly above the previous peak. This rally will also fail, and the stock will decline back to about the level of the previous low, which creates the head. One final rally

Figure 7-3
Double Top

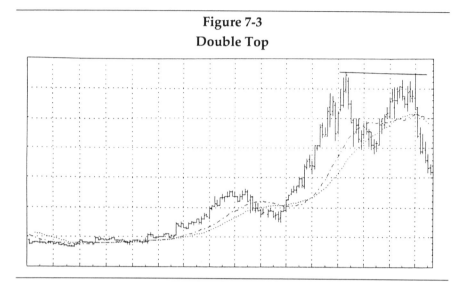

attempt will also be aborted. The next decline will take the stock below the previous two bottoms. This action will complete the right shoulder and the topping action. The stock is now poised for a prolonged slump.

The patterns presented are some of the most common technical signs that a stock is ready to enter into a downtrend. When your favorite growth stock assumes the characteristics shown above, and this is combined with a deterioration in the company's fundamental outlook, you know what to do next: sell. Remember, learning to sell wisely is perhaps more difficult but easily as important as picking winning stocks in the first place.

Figure 7-4
Head and Shoulders Top

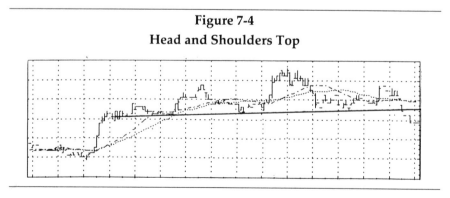

CASE STUDY - L.A. GEAR

L.A. Gear designs, develops, and markets fashionable, high quality athletic and leisure footwear and apparel. The company was highly successful in the late 1980s in riding the crest of the trend toward athletic clothing. Sales reached a peak in fiscal 1990 of $902 million, up from $10.7 million just five years earlier. Meanwhile, earnings jumped from $.02 per share in 1985 to $3.01 per share in 1989. As you might expect, L.A. Gear was a hit on Wall Street. From a low of $2 in 1986, L.A. Gear shares skyrocketed to a high of 51 3/4 in May 1990.

The chart pattern of L.A. Gear's stock gave some early indication of coming fundamental weakness in the company. After reaching the first significant peak in September 1989, at nearly $50, L.A. Gear's shares slumped to under $24 (Figure 7-5). This decline was accompanied by a slippage in L.A. Gear's net profit margins, which dropped from 9.8% in 1988 to 8.9% in 1989. Nevertheless, EPS was still up sharply in 1989 as it came in at $3.01 versus $1.29 in 1988.

L.A. Gear's shareholders were given another chance to sell slightly above the previous peak as the stock rallied to a new high of 51 3/4 in May 1990. As the stock turned down from this new high, the technical pattern of the stock chart suggested the possibility that L.A. Gear had formed a long-term double top. With a gap of eight months between the two peaks, the double top took on added validity. The proverbial shoe finally dropped on June 1, 1990, when the company announced that sec-

Figure 7-5
Price Chart for L.A. Gear

Source: Bloomberg Financial Services.

ond quarter 1990 earnings would be off sharply. Management's explanation for the drop in earnings was that the company's sales gains had been largely attributed to sales of low priced, low margin sneakers. L.A. Gear's stock sold off sharply the day of the announcement, and wound up closing at 30 3/4, off 8 1/2 points for the day.

Obviously, L.A. Gear violated Wall Street's number-one fundamental for a high flying growth stock: consistent gains in earnings per share. As the stock slumped, management expressed the belief that margins would be on the rise again thanks to its coming line of high-priced footwear endorsed by Michael Jackson. This strategy, based on the faddish impulses of consumers, failed to work out. Over the next two quarters, the earnings comparisons were as follows:

	Third Quarter	*Fourth Quarter*
1989	1.21	.58
1990	.71	(.36)

The technical pattern first turned for the worse, followed by the substantial drop in earnings. Was it then too late to sell L.A. Gear, after the negative earnings surprise? Not really, for L.A. Gear's troubles grew and the stock continued to drift lower. By January 1991, the stock reached a low of $9. Since its stock peaked, L.A. Gear's troubles continued to mount. For fiscal 1991, the company lost $3.49 per share as the company underwent an expensive reorganization and consolidation of its operations. In addition, new management has taken over the company. Will L.A. Gear regain its former luster? Who knows for sure?

SUMMARY

- When you buy, you've taken responsibility for your new investment. You need to then be prepared to sell whenever appropriate, whether it is one week or ten years later.

- Keep tabs on the stock's fundamentals first and foremost, but follow the price as an indicator of its continuing fundamental condition.

- Learn to deal with fear and greed.

- Don't let a stock's normal short-term fluctuations throw you.

- After buying, watch the chart to make sure your stock gets off to a good start.
- If you make a mistake, cut your losses — sell.
- Learn from your mistakes.
- Don't sell your winners too soon; let your profits run and develop the patience and confidence to stay with a winner.
- In the long run, fundamentals are key. To arrive at a sell decision, reverse the questions that led to your initial purchase.
- Has the basic concept of the business changed? Have they stopped following the success formula of the past?
- Are management's salaries way up while their ownership position has dwindled substantially?
- Have acquisitions been synergistic, or are they in unrelated businesses that aren't working out?
- Has earnings growth slowed appreciably, and have they been erratic?
- What's the sales trend for a company's products or services? Have they lost their grip on the marketplace? No new products? Are they losing customers (service company)?
- Have profit margins peaked, remained stable, or have they started to decline? Can sales increases make up for a slippage in margins? Has competition created price wars?
- What's the trend in return on equity? Is it still running at a high level? Will the business be able to largely finance itself versus adding shares or taking on debt?
- Has institutional ownership risen to 50%-60%?
- Have a number of regional or national brokerages picked up the stock? Have any of them downgraded the stock from buy to hold (or even sell)?
- Has the company started to pay a dividend? Have they failed to increase it in the last twelve months? Worse yet, has it been cut or omitted?
- Keep a close watch on the financial condition of your stocks.
- If a company's current ratio dips below 2:1, that's a sign that its short-term finances are getting weak; a quick ratio below 1:1 is another red flag.

- Successful small growth companies often can grow without taking on long-term debt. If they do take on long-term debt, make sure that equity remains above 75% of a combination of stockholders' equity and long-term debt.

- Charts can alert you in advance to a deterioration in a company's fundamentals. If you find one of your stocks has formed one of the topping patterns discussed in the text, double check the fundamentals. If they have also gotten weaker, sell!

QUESTIONS

1. A product company has been spending between 15% and 17% of sales annually on research and development to keep its products up-to-date, and to bring new ones out to market. Over the last 12 months, sales were up 12% versus an average gain of 25% over the last five years. Research and development spending represented 14% of sales. What can you conclude from this? Based on this information alone, would you sell this stock if you currently owned it?

2. You bought a stock two weeks ago at $9 and it has since dropped below its support zone on the chart to $7 1/4. There has been no news to account for this decline. As a long-term investor, what should you do now?

3. You've owned an outstanding small growth stock that manufactures medical devices for several years now and have a substantial profit. The outlook for the company still looks good. In an effort to accelerate growth, the company has announced plans to acquire a company that provides maintenance services to hotels and motels. What do you think of this move? Should you hold or sell your stock?

4. You've just gotten the latest balance sheet from one of your current holdings. Current assets and liabilities are as follows:

Current Assets	1991	1990	Current Liabilities	1991	1990
Cash	$435	$1,275	Notes Payable	$575	$465
Receivables	$1,365	$1,265	Accounts Payable	$625	$620
Inventory	$785	$565			
Total	$2,585	$3,105		$1,200	$1,085

Sales grew 18% in 1991. What do you like about this? What concerns do you have about this balance sheet when compared to last year's. Should you consider selling based on this?

5. ABC Corporation has been a successful small growth company for several years now. They have just finished another fiscal year and have released their latest financial results. Below is a summary of some key figures going back several years. Which do you consider as positive and which as negative? Would you continue to hold or sell based on this information?

	1987	1988	1989	1990
Sales (000)	$10,475	$16,236	$22,893	$31,363
Net Profit Margin	12.5	13.1	12.9	14.1
EPS	.11	.18	.25	.37
P/E Ratio	14	22	21	26
% Institutional Ownership	18%	36%	44%	62%
Dividend	.10	.13	.16	.22

6. You've just sold a stock at a loss of 20%. What's a wise thing you can do now?

7. Once you've bought a stock, what two emotions do you need to learn to deal with?

8. CEO and founder of ABC Corporation, Bill Jones, has managed a highly successful small growth company. Listed below are his salary and holdings of company stock, both when the business went public eight years ago and today. The company's stock has risen from $5 on the IPO to the current price of $22. Based on this information, would you want to continue to hold this stock?

	1983	1991
Salary	$75,000	$675,000
Shares Owned	2,000,000	100,000

9. Charts can help you determine when to sell a stock. However, the most weight when making a sell decision should be given to a company's _____ .

Chapter 8

MANAGING YOUR SMALL GROWTH STOCK PORTFOLIO

The quality of management is one of the key variables when considering the purchase of stock. Similarly, you should look at the management of your stock portfolio with the same businesslike attitude that top corporate management uses in obtaining superior results. This chapter explores some strategies that should help you to get the most out of your portfolio while at the same time staying in control of risk.

ASSET ALLOCATION

The first decision you must make is to figure out what your level of commitment is to growth stocks. How much can you invest? How much should you invest? How much will you invest? The answers to these seemingly simple questions will go a long way toward determining your success as an investor. In terms of percentages, it is possible to feel that you are doing quite well in stocks. When you compare your results to a benchmark like the S&P 500, you may in fact be performing very well. However, if you invested $10,000 and it grew to $15,000 (or 50%) while the

S&P 500 was up only 15%, the $5,000 gain wouldn't have much impact on your financial well-being if your net worth is $1.5 million. Unless you view investing as nothing more than a game, you should plan to make your efforts pay off for you in meeting your financial objectives.

To arrive at where you want to go financially, you will need to properly allocate your assets. Your tolerance for risk will probably be the single most important factor in determining your success as a growth stock investor. If you can become comfortable with the idea of taking well-calculated risks, you will increase your potential to make money in stocks. On the other hand, if you meekly place just a minute portion of your assets in stocks, as described above, don't expect any significant change in your lifestyle or net worth.

The 1990s have the potential to be an outstanding decade for the growth stock investor. To take advantage of this, you will need to commit the appropriate amount of assets to growth stocks. Learn to believe in America's long-term growth potential and ignore the constant barrage of scare headlines in the media. Your results will be enhanced tremendously if you prudently calculate what you should have in growth stocks, and then follow through with a commitment to invest the amount you've chosen.

As a rule of thumb, the younger you are, the more you should commit to growth. How young you are as an investor is purely an individual matter. You can't simply lump investors into age brackets and call them young or old. One man of 35 who has been extremely successful in his business, has a stock portfolio of $2 million, and plans to retire in five years, may be considered old as an investor, at least in terms of the risks he can or should take. In contrast, another investor is 40 years old, in good health, and expects to work another 20 years. Furthermore, his stock portfolio amounts to only $30,000. This gentleman would be considered a relatively young investor. He has plenty of time for his investments to grow prior to retirement, and with his relatively small portfolio, he will need to take some risk in search of the long-term rewards offered by growth stocks.

You will need to carefully consider what your long-term goals are and then devise a strategy to meet them. If you are an older investor who has met or is close to his objectives, obviously you won't want to go overboard and put 100% of your money in small growth stocks. At the other extreme, a young investor should not shy away from risk and undercommit to growth stocks.

As the years go by you will want to periodically assess your allocation to the various categories of investments. The older you get, and the more successful you've been, the more conservative you'll want to be with your money. Although this is prudent, make sure you don't become overly cautious in your later years, as is the natural tendency. Even the most well-to-do investor probably should have some growth investments. After all, if you switch to fixed-income investments only, inflation will eventually reduce your dollars in real terms.

BUILDING YOUR PORTFOLIO

Now that you've decided on what you can, should, and will commit to stocks, it is time to start building your portfolio. It is not necessary that you invest all your money at once into stocks. But understand that if you take too long (for the sake of argument let's say six months) you will start to lose out on the compounding effect of time on top quality growth stocks. Start doing your homework, and when you find stocks that you really like and they're priced right, make a positive decision and invest.

There are no hard and fast rules on how many stocks you should own. However, one of the reasons for taking a portfolio approach versus putting all of your eggs into one or two baskets is to manage risk. Nobody is infallible when it comes to selecting stocks. Even the best investors will have their clunkers. To win in the long run, you want a good batting average. If you do fall prey to the temptation of overinvesting in one stock and it works out great, consider yourself very lucky. Even the top pros don't ever know for sure which stock is going to go up 500% or 1000%.

The danger in the nondiversified approach is that you'll get blown out of the water right at the start. Most likely, due to the substantial financial wound you've suffered, you'll join those who have sworn off stocks for good. You may come to regard the market as a crapshoot. Then you'll miss out on the opportunity afforded by America's top long-term investment. Don't let this happen to you!

To adequately control risk and properly diversify your holdings, you will want to own at least 10-12 stocks. A study on portfolio diversification has shown that owning more than 12 stocks does very little to incrementally reduce your risk. However, this study does demonstrate that every stock you add from one to ten produces a measurable decline in portfolio risk.

If you are just starting out, or do not have the time to research and select ten or more stocks, you should at least begin with five or six. This will smooth out your returns considerably versus the one, two, or three stocks only approach. However, plan to eventually get up to ten or more.

With the long-term fundamental approach advocated in this book, you should not be overburdened by tracking ten or more stocks. After all, they really don't need to be followed with the scrutiny of a commodities trader in pork bellies. If you've done your homework well, hopefully you can sit back and enjoy the ride.

Once you have built your initial portfolio, you will want to keep on looking for new ideas. In the stock market nothing (or almost nothing) is forever and you will eventually sell the majority of stocks at some point. Some will be held for years, while others will bomb out (remember, nobody's perfect) and you may have to dump them six months or even three weeks out of the gate.

Let's suppose you own 12 stocks and the average hold period is two years. That means that on average you will sell and buy six stocks per year. The turnover ratio is calculated by dividing 6 by 12 to get .50. This would be, compared to the average investor, a relatively low rate. However, do not forget that you are investing for big long-term gains. You can also calculate a turnover rate that measures the dollar volume of stocks bought and sold annually as compared to the total value of your portfolio. If either of these ratios gets too high, your stock-selecting skills need honing; your stocks are not of the buy and hold vintage that you'd like them to be. Over the years, you will begin to see some trends develop that will reveal your success or failure at picking stocks that can be held for long periods of time.

In addition to the number of stocks you decide to own, you'll also need to figure the dollar amount that should go into each one. Here you can take a couple of different approaches. Let's say you have $100,000 and you are going to invest equally in ten stocks. That would work out to $10,000 each. In reality, it wouldn't be quite that precise. It is advisable, but not mandatory, to stick to investing in round lots of 100 shares. These round lots tend to be more marketable than, say, odd lots of 22 or 57 shares. Therefore, when taking the equal weighing approach, you may wind up with $9,200 in one stock and $10,600 in another. Don't let this overly concern you, because investing isn't exactly a precise science.

Do you recall that stock that you wanted to put all of your money into? If this temptation still exists, you will want to adopt our second approach, and that is to overweight certain stocks. In the real world of professional money management, this is the common approach. But don't go hog wild into one stock just because you feel very strongly about it. In our $100,000 portfolio of ten stocks, this can't-miss stock should still be held to perhaps no more than 15%-20% of the total. Once you start playing favorites and overweight a stock too heavily, it can be an open invitation to disaster.

Remember, if you do invest that $20,000 into one stock and it goes down 50% to $10,000 before you decide to sell out, its replacement will have to go up 100% (from $10,000 to $20,000) just to get you back to even. Big losses in a position you've overweighed can be hard to come back from. They could set your portfolio back a couple of years.

INDUSTRY DIVERSIFICATION

Proper diversification is achieved by investing in a number of different and unrelated industries. It is not accomplished by investing in six biotech stocks and four pharmaceuticals. Industry diversification is additional portfolio protection. When one industry is hot, another may be sitting still. Just like the economy, different industries have their ebb and flow. If all of your stocks are in closely related industries, your portfolio will have a volatility that may prove to be unsettling. Besides, in this highly diverse economy, there are a number of different industries that offer excellent growth potential. Why short-change yourself by concentrating on just a few? When you see that an industry is emerging into a dynamite growth phase, why limit your stocks to medical service and software only?

On top of missing out on the potential gain, you'll probably kick yourself for not participating in an area of growth with such obvious potential. As this is being written, biotech stocks have been particularly hot. Wouldn't it have been nice to own industry leader Amgen, which has sales and profits (as opposed to just dreams) and which gained 265% in 1991 alone? If you really do like one industry in particular you may want to buy more than one stock in it. For our $100,000 portfolio, you might put $10,000 in each of two stocks from the chosen industry. This approach can be called double-diversification. It is achieved by investing in a number of industries and different stocks within these industries. If your portfolio grows to 15-20 stocks or more, you'll surely want to employ this tactic. In Chapter 3, there is a listing of a number of industries that you'll want to consider when building your portfolio.

BUYING STOCKS

When you find a company that you really like but aren't sure if it is fairly priced, check out the chart patterns described in Chapter 5. It is possible the stock may be overextended in the short run and due for a pullback. Market timing and charts are not infallible, but a chart can tell, at a glance, if a stock has run straight uphill from five to ten in two weeks' time. If you feel the stock has the momentum and fundamental justification to keep going and you can't resist buying, strongly consider taking a pilot position. There's no law that says you have to buy your entire position at once. Buy half now, then see what happens next. Should the stock continue higher, at least you are partially in it, which is better than nothing. If it goes down you can employ a tactic called dollar cost averaging. After all, if the fundamentals are still rock solid and you liked the stock at $10, you should love it at $8. However, remember not to abandon your discipline that calls for carefully rechecking the fundamentals on a stock that may have reached your mental stop, which in this case may be at $8 or $8 1/2 per share.

If things have changed for the worse, then by all means sell. Providing the story is still good, you may wish to add to your pilot position. For example, let's assume you bought 500 shares at $10. By adding 500 more at $8 (following the price correction) you would now own 1,000 shares at an average cost of $9 per share. You should learn to keep a stock's decline in perspective. The decline could well be just a short-term jiggle on the long-term chart. Don't forget, the nature of a company's business will often determine the size of the jiggle. A seasonal or cyclical business will have bigger fluctuations than a company whose products enjoy a steady demand. Make sure that you don't let normal short-term fluctuations scare you into selling out of a solid long-term holding.

HOW TO HANDLE BIG WINNERS

There's an old saying on Wall Street that you should cut your losses and let your profits run. All too often, however, the novice investor is tempted to immediately grab every 30%-40% profit that comes along. Meanwhile, this same investor will sit for years with a losing stock in the hopes that it will finally get its act together. Don't let this happen to you. When you have a good stock, give it time to develop into a truly big winner. A big winner can overcome several small losers and maybe even a big loser or two. However, small profits will seldom make up for the bummers in your portfolio. It takes patience to ride a stock to a five- to tenfold gain, but it's a must for truly superior results. Let's look at the following two mini-portfolios to demonstrate this point.

Portfolio A		*Portfolio B*	
Stock A—Up 200%	$30	Stock A—Up 30%	$13
Stock B—Down 80%	$2	Stock B—Down 30%	$7
Total Value	$32	Total Value	$20

Both portfolios started with two stocks at $10 per share each. Portfolio A gained 60%, or $12, while Portfolio B broke even. The first portfolio had a big winner, which more than overcame a substantial loser (which, hopefully, you would have sold long before it got this bad). Portfolio B's small loser canceled out the equally small winning stock. Although taking big losses is not recommended, you will be better off by taking the patient approach of Investor A, who is willing to hold on to stocks that in his judgment are fundamentally sound.

Chapter 7 discussed fundamental and technical guidelines for selling stocks. From a portfolio management viewpoint, this chapter gives some additional guidelines on selling a big winner. One strategy to help you cope with a successful stock is to sell part of it after it has reached an initial target price. Because you are investing in potentially explosive growth stocks for the long term, your first sell point from a portfolio management standpoint should be substantially above the purchase price, for example, after a rise in price of perhaps 100%-200%. The sell part/keep part strategy accomplishes a number of objectives. It enables you to lock in a handsome profit, which will protect you and make you feel better should the stock begin to decline. Furthermore, you won't feel left out if the stock continues to march higher. Reducing a large holding also lowers your risk in your portfolio and frees up funds for other promising stocks. Table 8-1 demonstrates how selling part of a big winner can help you re-establish prudent portfolio diversification.

At the start, let's assume you had a $100,000 portfolio invested in ten stocks with some modest over- and underweightings. You began with $12,000 in Stock A. One year later, Stock A had tripled in value while the other nine stocks were up 20% on average. As you can see, the one big winner lifted the overall portfolio to a gain of 41.6%. This shows clearly why you want to let your profits run. We can also see that Stock A has now become over 25% of the total portfolio. At this point, it would be wise to adopt the keep part/sell part strategy. After selling half of the position and reinvesting the proceeds in two additional stocks, you once again have an ideally diversified portfolio.

Table 8-1
Keep Part/Sell Part Strategy

	At the Start			*1 Year Later*	
Stock A	$12,000	12%	Stock A	$36,000	25.4%
Other Nine Stocks	$88,000	88%	Other Nine Stocks	$105,600	74.6%
Total	$100,000	100%	Total	$144,600	100%

After Selling and Reinvesting

Stock A	$18,000	12.7%
Other 11 Stocks	$123,600	87.3%
	$141,600	100%

TAKING LOSSES

From a portfolio management perspective you'll also want to periodically make that tough decision to sell a stock that isn't working out. If the fundamentals have turned against you and the stock is technically weak, get out. Look at your portfolio the way a gardener looks at a yard he's working on. Just as he prunes the trees and weeds the yard to give it a better appearance, you should do the same thing with your stocks. You will rid yourself of a cancerous stock, and you will also gain a psychological boost from not having the constant reminder of that losing stock on your monthly brokerage statement. When you do sell, try to learn from the experience. Perhaps you will gain some new insights that will keep you from making the same mistake twice.

ASSESSING YOUR RESULTS

The reason for reading this book is to help you make money in growth stocks and be a winner in the market. Stock investments are also a viable means of helping you meet your goals. Therefore, you need to have some criteria for evaluating your results. Investing is a serious business where you need to know how you're doing. But life should be fun, so you can also look at investing as a game that you are trying to win. When your hard work pays off and you find a big gainer or two, you will no doubt experience a thrill as exciting as hitting a home run.

As in any game, you need to have a means of keeping score, a sensible way of determining just how well you are doing. If your stocks are climbing out of sight, congratulations are in order. On the other hand, if your results are less than what they should be, perhaps you need to work on your stock-picking skills. Perhaps you're not managing your portfolio properly. In any case, it will help you greatly if you know how well you are doing. Are you on track, or even ahead of schedule, in the pursuit of your objectives? Or are you starting to fall behind the pace?

All professional money managers' performances are tracked against certain market indicators, as well as each other. You should also try to attain the status of a professional, at least in terms of the management of your assets. To compare your results with this elite bunch you will need to learn how to assess your results properly. The Dow Jones Industrial average is the most widely watched market indicator. Because of its psychological significance to the vast majority of stock market investors, it is the indicator used to identify market bottoms in Chapter 5. As a benchmark for the investor in growth stocks, however, it leaves much to be desired.

Companies in the Dow are huge blue chips that have been household words for generations. Because of their sheer size, they no longer can grow at an accelerated pace. After all, when your sales are $69 billion, as IBM's were in 1990, it is all but impossible for that total to grow by more than a few percentage points at best each year. In contrast, it is not impossible for the growth companies you are looking at to have sales of $20 million grow 25% or 50% in a year to $25 or $30 million. Therefore, it makes no sense to compare your growth stock results to the performance of the behemoths in the Dow.

One step removed from the Dow is the Standard and Poor's 500. This index is the standard of performance for the majority of money managers that invest in large capitalization issues. Often the results of the managers of small growth stock portfolios are also compared to the S&P 500. However, this index is also inappropriate for the investor in small company growth stocks. As the name implies, the S&P 500 is a measure of the performance of 500 stocks. If the index was equally weighted among all stocks, it might have some validity as a benchmark for the growth stocks in your portfolio. This is not the case. The S&P 500 is weighted by market capitalization. Each stock's value to the index is computed by multiplying its current price times the total shares outstanding. Because of this, the index is dominated by large capitalization stocks. This includes almost all of the stocks that are in the Dow. As a measure of performance of your growth stocks, both the S&P and the Dow are out.

Growing in popularity as a measure of small growth stock activity is the NASDAQ Composite. This index contains all of the stocks trading in the national market system of over-the-counter stocks. Investors seem to like indexes with larger values. As this is being written the NASDAQ has climbed above 600 for the first time in history. Providing growth stocks do well in the 1990s, this index may one day cross 1,000. With the growing importance of growth stocks in general, perhaps reaching this level will give the NASDAQ a stature close to the Dow. The senior average spent from 1965 to 1982 bumping up against the 1,000 barrier before breaking through in a big way. For now, the NASDAQ Composite is the most well-known and widely used benchmark for growth stock performance. However, it does have its flaws. Like the S&P 500, the NASDAQ Composite is a capitalization-weighted index. Obviously, the big NASDAQ stocks carry the most weight. As of September 1991, the top five stocks in the index represented over 10% of the total value.

These stocks include Apple Computer, Microsoft, Intel, MCI, and Amgen, all of which are becoming big household names, much like the Dow 30. During 1991, the NASDAQ Composite shot up a blistering 56.8%, riding on the coattails of these five stocks. As a group, they were up 130% on average in 1991. This performance tended to distort the index and make it higher than it normally would have been. As a result, very few growth stock managers were able to match the NASDAQ that year. Despite its shortcomings, the NASDAQ will most likely continue in the years ahead to be the standard-bearer for growth stock performance.

A lesser-known index, but one gaining in acceptance is the Russell 2000. This index measures the value of the country's 1001-3000 largest stocks. Each June, stocks that have fallen out of this range are dropped from the index. Their place is taken by those that now fall within these parameters. Like the NASDAQ Composite and the S&P 500, the Russell 2000 is a capitalization-weighted index. It is not, however, dominated by a few large stocks. As of the middle of 1991, the market capitalization of the stocks in the index ranged from $23 million to $300 million. Meanwhile, as of December 31, 1991, Microsoft, a component of the NASDAQ Composite, had a market value of nearly $20 billion.

The stocks in the Russell 2000 are not penny stocks nor are they the monsters of the Dow. Rather, the index contains a great number of the type of growth stocks that you will want to be investing in. We would suggest that you familiarize yourself with this index and consider using it as a benchmark for the performance of your portfolio. If you're not totally comfortable with this index, perhaps you will want to use both the Russell 2000 and the NASDAQ Composite as reference points. In 1991, the Russell

2000 gained 43.7%, which probably was a more representative measure of the performance of small growth stocks.

There are some interesting and important differences between the relative performance of an index as compared to that of your portfolio. Indexes don't pay taxes, nor are they charged commissions for buying and selling stock. An index does contain all stocks within its realm. In other words, an index is a measure of performance of the average stock of its component issues.

When you buy and sell stocks, you incur transactions costs. In addition, you must pay taxes on your winners (unless it is a tax-deferred account). However, you can use losses to save on taxes. The most significant difference between an index and your portfolio is that you get to pick and choose the stocks you think will do best. An index has all the winners but is also stuck with the losers. With the cost items mentioned above, it would appear to be difficult to beat the market averages. However, your ability to select stocks should enable you to overcome these costs and, with skill and patience, allow you to beat the averages in the long run.

Should you own various categories of stocks, you will want to segregate them into appropriate groups, then compare them to an index that represents them best. In other words, if you own blue chips and small growth stocks, don't lump them all together and compare them to the Dow Industrials. Instead, put them into two different groups. Measure your blue chips' performance by comparing them to the Dow or S&P 500. Check the performance of your growth stocks with the NASDAQ and/or Russell 2000.

As stated earlier, over time you will want to beat the appropriate index. By doing so, you will feel you are winning the game. You will be making significant progress towards meeting your financial objectives. At this point you may be wondering just how much you should beat the NASDAQ by to be considered a successful investor. The answer is probably by a lot less than you think. This is where reasonable expectations come into play. Don't invest in stocks thinking you'll double your money every year and run circles around the market indicators we've just talked about. Forget it. It is not going to happen, at least not unless you've taken some extraordinary risk or overconcentrated in one or two stocks and gotten lucky.

Using the portfolio approach, your goal should be, over the years, to steadily compound your money. To be considered a successful investor, your money will need to grow only a few percentage points beyond a market index. Why, you may ask, should you set your sights so low? You're not really doing so, as you'll see shortly. However, the experience of some of the market's most talented investors has taught us that even the best investors do only modestly better than the market on an annual basis. Consider the following example, which admittedly is a crude approximation of the skill level demonstrated by various groups of investors over a long period of time (five to ten years plus).

Beat an Index Annually by . . .	*Status as an Investor*
10+%	Superstar - Hall of Fame Material
5-10%	Excellent - You Are a Top Pro
2-5%	Feel Proud - You Are Better Than Average
0-2%	Barely Worth the Effort
Below 0%	Buy a Mutual Fund or Improve Your Skills

As you can see, you don't need to triple your money in six months to join the ranks of the nation's most successful investors. Rather, you can do very well for yourself by staying a few percentage points ahead of the game. Earlier in the book the historical record was given for small growth stocks dating back to 1926. On average this group has gained about 12.1% annually. Of course, this record includes periods when growth stocks flourished, as well as times when they lagged behind the blue chips and other investments.

In Chapter One, there is an example of the possible returns you can earn in small stocks over the long term. As can be seen, the power of compounding over a long period of time combined with above average stock selections can produce some wondrous results. Using the historical average, $10,000 grows to $98,200 in 20 years. Although that is respectable, observe what happens to that original $10,000 if you are able to beat this bogie by 3%, 5%, or 10% annually. Our mythical superstar investor would have turned $10,000 into over $1/2 million! This should sufficiently motivate you to perfect your stock picking skills. You should also take comfort in the fact that you don't have to do the impossible—just buy stocks that are better than average and over the long run you should do quite well for yourself.

The benefit of beating the indexes in the long run has been shown. Along the way to achieving this, you'll want to check your results to see how your portfolio stacks up against the norm. With the aid of a computer you could check your progress daily. This may be fun to do, especially if your biggest position reports record earnings and shoots up from $12 to $15 in one day. Because the approach taken in this book is to make money in the long haul, such daily scrutiny of your stocks is really unnecessary. Unless you just plain enjoy watching your stocks like you do the standing of your favorite ball team, you can easily get by with checking your results every three months or so.

Rather than concentrating on how much money you've made or lost each day, it is far more important to be kept apprised of any development that could affect the status of one of your holdings. Even using three-month time intervals to check your results versus the index can prove to be misleading. One or two of your stocks may be in a lull for one reason or another. Maybe they will play catch-up in the next quarter and put you back on track to beating the NASDAQ for the year. Don't be very concerned with short-term results; however, be extremely cognizant of how you are doing on an annual basis.

One of the mysteries of investing is that the typical investor has no idea of how he is doing. If you asked him by how much his portfolio lagged the NASDAQ Composite or beat the Russell 2000, he wouldn't have a clue. Yet, this same investor will shop every savings and loan in town to get 1/4% more interest on a six-month CD. It hardly makes sense, does it? Since your financial future is tied into how your investments turn out, you need to know how things stand. Don't take the monitoring of your results lightly. At the other extreme, don't lose sleep at night worrying about every little jiggle in your portfolio's value.

Due to the vagaries of the overall market, there will be periods when you will actually witness your portfolio go down in value. These periods may last several months—even a year or longer. If the overall market is weak enough, it can drag down even the strongest of stocks. Since market timing is not advocated here, don't let these declines rattle you. The pure fact of the matter is that all of the major stock market averages were at new all-time highs in early 1992. It shouldn't surprise you that quality stocks also will reach new highs following a down market.

After assessing your results and finding that your stocks are down 8% over the last year, you may still in fact be doing better than average. Suppose the Russell 2000 has declined 20% in the same time frame. Your portfolio has actually shown superior relative performance to the market as a whole. In addition, when the market rebounds, your stocks may be some of the stellar performers in the next big market rally. The following year the Russell 2000 might rally 30% while your stocks gain 42%. If you consistently beat the averages in good markets and bad, year after year, you should do just fine in the long run. And remember, the long term is what is most important and profitable.

TAX DEFERRAL

One major benefit of taking the long-term fundamental approach is that you may wind up holding winning stocks for years, which shields you from current taxation. Almost all small company growth stocks pay little or no dividend, as earnings are plowed back into the company to finance future growth. In essence, this is similar to reinvesting interest that would normally be taxed, without current taxes being deducted. Compounding your money via a winning long-term growth stock is what you should be trying to accomplish.

In addition to taxes, inflation is also one of the enemies to beat in order to achieve a satisfactory real rate of return. Consider the following example:

Interest-Bearing Investments			*Small Growth Stocks*	
6%	Interest		12.1%	Historical Growth Rate
–3%	Inflation		–3%	Inflation
–2.1%	Taxes (assumes 35%)		–4.2%	Taxes (assumes 35%)
.9%	Real Rate of Return		4.9%	Real Rate of Return

In this example, 6% interest is assumed in a very conservative taxable investment. After taxes and inflation of 3%, your net return is .9%. Twenty years later, your original dollar at this rate of growth would be worth only $1.22! Obviously, this isn't much of a way to improve your lifestyle or prepare for retirement. The investor who earned the historical rate of small growth stocks dating back to 1926 would now have $2.60 versus his original dollar. Your minimum goal should be to beat inflation and taxes by a meaningful amount over the long haul. Although it is not possible for us to control the rate of inflation, hopefully it will remain low, as it has for the majority of the time since the inflationary spiral was broken in the early 1980s.

However, you can minimize the impact that taxes have on your investments. Let's take a look at what tax deferral can do for you in the long run. Investor A invests $10,000 and sells each year after a gain of 20% (we'll leave commissions out for now). He then pays 35% of the gain in taxes. Investor B also makes 20% annually on his investments; however, he avoids paying taxes until he sells out his position several years later. If Investor B sells after five years and pays his taxes, he would have 6.8% more money than Investor A. The advantage grows steadily as the years go by. If Investor B sells after ten years, he now has nearly 29% more money than Investor A, who paid as he went. You might also notice that holding stock a long time steadily increases your compound rate of return after taxes. In Table 8-2, the pay as you go investor made 13%. Clearly, deferring taxes allows more of your money to work for you for a longer period of time. Yes, there is a time when even winners must be sold. However, if you invest in stocks you can hold for a while, it can reduce your taxes and improve your bottom line. The buy and hold investor's ten-year compound rate was 15.9% versus 13% for the investor who paid taxes annually.

To further the cause of reducing taxes, you will want to take advantage of any accounts that offer tax deferral. Included in these would be IRAs 401(k)s, and SEP IRAs. Ideally, you will want to have a flexible plan that you can maintain complete control over, so you can employ the strategies for stock selection in this book. If that is not possible, carefully review the options available. These typically include various funds within a family of mutual funds. If you have several years to go before retirement, you will want to be more aggressive. The closer you get to retirement age the more you'll lean toward conservative choices. But always try to keep some growth in your tax-sheltered retirement account to help combat inflation.

Perhaps you will wind up maxing out on your tax-deferred accounts (assuming you don't use annuities). You might then wind up with both taxable and nontaxable investment accounts. At this point you should consider your strategy regarding which type of investments to put in each type of account. In the first scenario, let's assume that you have five to ten years or more until retirement. You own both growth stocks and bonds and utility stocks, which pay attractive dividends. You may wish to place your bonds and utility stocks in the nontaxable account, where their interest and dividends can compound tax-deferred. Meanwhile, your growth stocks are in a taxable account; if you lose money on a stock, you can sell it and deduct the loss. On the other hand, you may wind up holding your

Table 8-2
The Benefits of Tax Deferral

Time	Pay Taxes Annually Compound	Annual Compound Return	Buy and Hold	Annual Compound Return
Five Years	$18,424	13%	$19,674	14.5%
Ten Years	$33,945	13%	$43,742	15.9%

winners for years, thus avoiding current taxation (as we explained previously).

A second scenario finds you in retirement. You are now spending dividend and interest income. Since this income is taxable anyway, you might as well have these investments in a taxable account. Because you'll still need some growth, you may wish to put these investments in a taxable account. Your buy and hold strategy now might not be for as long as previously when your main objective was for growth. Therefore, you can benefit from selling and buying more often without paying current taxes.

These strategies depend on a number of variables, such as your total assets, risk tolerance, and whether you are retired and spending income or not. Your tax advisor should be able to help you here.

TAX LOSS SELLING

Naturally, you are not in this business to lose money, nevertheless, it happens to even the best investors. Fortunately, Uncle Sam will help soften the blow when you do take a loss. This is only fair since he shares in your profits. Let's say you bought a stock at $20 and it is now trading for $10. You've given up on it fundamentally and feel that it will go still lower. Take the loss now and write it off. If you are in the 35% tax bracket, the tax benefit would be $3.50 per share. You can compute the tax saving by multiplying the loss times your tax bracket ($10 x 35% =$3.50). Current tax law limits the amount of losses you can deduct in any year over and above those that you match off against gains. Again, because tax laws are always subject to change, consult your tax advisor on how to best handle the tax aspects of losses.

In the previous example, you sold a stock you didn't like anymore. Now assume that you still like a stock that has fallen from 20 to 10, but you don't think it's going to head north again in the immediate future. You can sell the stock and take the loss for taxes, then reestablish your position after 30 days. Be sure not to buy it before then or you will violate the wash sale rule and your loss will be disallowed.

At the end of each calendar year, stocks that have not done well are often subject to tax-loss selling. Many investors will dump losing stocks for the write-off. Be careful when selling a stock that is down at this time of year. This beaten-down stock may rally sharply in the new year once the tax selling has let up. Your tax saving may pale in comparison to the lost ground that the stock makes up.

When you have a winning stock, but it is time to sell, don't let the thought of paying taxes override a decision based on your new fundamental outlook for the stock. Be glad you made a profit, pay your taxes, and move on.

CONTROLLING COSTS

Like any good manager of a business, you will want to maximize profits in a prudent manner. Besides picking winning stocks, another way to increase your bottom line is to keep costs as low as possible while still getting the services that you need. Cost items would include things such as commissions, investment services, management fees, and taxes.

When you are just starting out and your portfolio is not very big, costs will eat up a greater portion of your profits. For example, let's say you subscribe to a number of investment services at a total annual cost of $500. If your portfolio is only $10,000 to begin with, you are paying 5% of the total value each year for these services. An investor subscribing to the same service with a $200,000 portfolio would be paying only 0.25% of the value of his portfolio. Obviously, the larger your portfolio grows, the more cost effective the services become.

If you are just a beginner at investing but have made a serious long-term commitment to stocks, look at above-average expenses as part of your tuition for learning about investing. As your skills rise and your portfolio grows, these cost items will pay for themselves. Striking a balance between what you spend on investment services and what these items give you back in return is crucial. Don't skim on services that you really need. At the same time, don't become an information junkie either. Learn what is important for your investment decision making and forget the rest. A number of the key sources of information covered in Chapter 6 are available at little or no cost. These include company literature, which may be some of the most valuable information of all. You may find many of the sources you need at your local library. You might also want to share the costs of various subscriptions with a friend or coworker.

You should also look at your time as a cost of investing. Plan to spend a reasonable amount of time on your investments without going overboard. In the early years, when you are just learning about investing and your portfolio is small, equate the time you spend as you would if you were taking night classes. Plan to make it pay big dividends for you in the long run.

The discussion on taxes compared buying and selling annually versus the buy and hold approach. The example excluded commission costs. Below are the results you would achieve with a return of 20% annually. This time, however, a rather modest commission cost of 1% is added each time you buy and sell. As you can see, the long-term approach to investing increases your returns dramatically when factoring in reduced commission costs and taxes.

$10,000 Initial Investment
20% Annual Return / 35% Taxes / 1% Commissions

Buy/Sell Annually	*Buy and Hold/Selling Once*
Five Years $17,153	$19,317
Ten Years $29,491	$42,910

In the example, the investor who bought and sold annually compounded his money at 11.4% for ten years after commissions and taxes. Meanwhile, the buy and hold investor earned a compound rate of 15.7% after ten years.

Your commission rates may vary from the example, depending on whether you use a discount or full-service broker. Discounted commissions can save you money. However, they could also cost you more if you are tempted to overtrade your account because of the low rates. In sharp contrast, the commissions of a full-service broker may be reasonable if you make full use of their services and invest for the long haul. By investing long-term, the 2%-4% you pay to a full-service broker may turn out to be rather insignificant. Suppose, for example, that you buy a stock and hold it for five years before selling and it appreciates 300%. The services of the broker will make the buy and sell commissions seem very reasonable. In the end, you get what you pay for. If you use a discounter, be prepared to do some extra work yourself. Should you decide on a full-service broker, make sure that you get the services your extra commissions pay for. By learning to control your costs, you may be able to pick up 2%-3% a year on your bottom-line profits. Previous examples have shown that a few extra percentage points earned annually, combined with the power of compounding, will significantly improve your returns in the long run.

SUMMARY

- Manage your portfolio with a businesslike attitude.
- Allocate the proper amount to small growth stocks. Make the commitment.
- The further you are from retirement, the more you should allocate for growth. It's strictly an individual matter.
- Devise a strategy to meet your long-term goals.
- Take a long-term approach.
- Diversify into ten to twelve stocks (at least five to six when starting out).
- Always keep looking for new ideas.
- When you find a company you like and it is priced right, buy!
- Check your turnover ratio to test your stock-picking skills.
- Be sure to put a limit on how much you overweigh your favorite stocks.
- Diversify into different and unrelated industries.
- Resist the temptation of selling for small gains; let your profits run.
- Sell part of big winners to maintain prudent portfolio diversification.
- Prune your portfolio regularly of the dead weight.
- Assess your results periodically. Measure your portfolio against an appropriate index, such as the NASDAQ Composite or the Russell 2000.
- Remember that an index includes all stocks, and it doesn't pay taxes or commissions.
- Beating an index consistently will enable you to meet your goals.
- Maintain reasonable expectations; steadily compounding your money over the long run can produce wondrous results.
- Be aware of how well you are doing on a quarterly or annual basis.
- Don't just follow a stock's price—also monitor fundamental developments at the company.
- Don't be overly concerned if your portfolio is down when a benchmark, such as the Russell 2000, is also off. Performance is relative.

- The long-term approach shields you from current taxation.
- Your investments should beat inflation and taxes by a meaningful amount.
- Make good use of tax-deferred retirement accounts.
- Split assets between taxable and tax-deferred accounts properly to minimize current taxation.
- Tax loss selling, used wisely, can help you reduce the impact of a losing stock.
- Keep your costs at a reasonable level (charts, newsletters, magazines, commissions, etc.) to help improve your bottom line.
- Get the information you need, but don't become an information junkie. The purpose of information is to help you arrive at good investment decisions.
- Consider your time as part of the cost of investing.

QUESTIONS

1. You've just finished investing 100% of the funds you have allocated for a portfolio of small growth stocks. What is one of the things you should now be doing?

2. Eight years ago you invested $10,000 in small growth stocks. During that time the Russell 2000 compounded at 15.3% annually. Your portfolio beat the Russell 2000 by 3.6% annually. How much money do you now have?

3. The NASDAQ Composite declined 22% one year, then gained 31% and 16% in the next two years. Meanwhile, your portfolio outperformed the NASDAQ by 3% in the first and second years, then lagged behind it by 2% in the third year. If you started with $36,500, how much would you have at the end of three years? What would your portfolio's total percentage gain be over three years?

4. At the start of the year you owned twelve stocks. During the next twelve months you had a portfolio turnover ratio of .75. How many stocks would you have sold and replaced?

5. You have just invested $10,000 in each of eight different stocks. Two years later, seven of the stocks gained a total, on average, of 16% while

one superstar stock gained 375%. What is the portfolio's total value? What would be three prudent moves to make now? What's the total percentage gain of the portfolio? What percent of the portfolio is the big gainer after two years?

6. Mr. Jones is in good health, has a secure job, and plans to work another twenty years. His portfolio is allocated as follows: cash equivalents—$22,000; long-term bonds—$17,000; small growth stocks—$6,000. Should he maintain this mix, or should he reallocate his assets?

7. There is a company that you've researched thoroughly and feel has a great future. The stock has recently run from 20 to 28. Despite this, you think it may continue to go higher but know that it is also vulnerable to a pullback. What's a good strategy to follow at this time?

8. Mr. Smith is sixty-five years old and nearing retirement. He's done very well in small growth stocks over the last 30 years. His portfolio mix is currently 65% small growth stocks, 15% blue chips, 10% utilities, and 10% cash. The small growth stocks pay 1%, the blue chips yield 3%, the utilities pay 6.5%, and cash earns 5%. The total value is $2.4 million. He will need to draw income from his portfolio of about 4% annually. In broad terms, what would you recommend? Why? What is the current dollar return on the portfolio? What will it need to be to yield 4%?

9. You're a small investor aged 28, and just getting started. Your portfolio's total value is $8,000. The cost of the investment services you're using is $500 annually (about 6.3% of your portfolio's value). Can this relatively high cost be justified? If so, why?

10. Your small stock portfolio consists of eight stocks that are equally weighted. As a long-term investor, you should be in how many industries? __2 __5 __8

11. The NASDAQ Composite has gone up 34% over the last nine months and a couple of your stocks have doubled. Your portfolio is now worth $30,000. Over the next three years your goal is to have your portfolio grow to $100,000. Is this a reasonable goal?

12. Mr. Jones has a portfolio in small growth stocks of $10,000. Over the next seven years his portfolio gains an average of 15% annually. Because he takes profits each year, he pays 28% of this gain in taxes. How much is his portfolio worth after seven years? Mr. Smith also has a $10,000 portfolio. He also makes 15% on his stocks each year. How-

a $10,000 portfolio. He also makes 15% on his stocks each year. How-
ever, he takes his profit and pays 28% in taxes only after holding his
stocks for seven years. What is the value of his portfolio after seven
years? Why did Mr. Smith have more money in the end?

Chapter 9

HOW TO INVEST IN SMALL GROWTH STOCK MUTUAL FUNDS

Small growth stocks, as shown earlier in the book, experience periodic cycles of above average performance that last for as long as eight to ten years. In October 1990, small stocks reached their lowest relative valuation in 30 years. From the market's bottom in October 1990 through December 31, 1991, small growth stocks went on a tear. During that time, the NASDAQ Composite shot up 80% while the Russell 2000 gained 58%. Should interest rates and inflation remain low, the possibility exists that this rally in growth stocks has kicked off a multiyear trend that could last through the 1990s and beyond. With interest rates now at levels not seen since the early 1960s, many investors will begin to make the switch from income investments to growth. Certainly the money is available to fuel a long-term boom in growth stocks.

As of December 31, 1991, there were only two small-company mutual funds with assets above $1 billion. In sharp contrast there were over 40 taxable bond funds that exceeded $1 billion. If even a small portion of these fundholders made the switch to small growth, the supply/demand equation favoring these small companies could turn decidedly more bullish. Add to these funds the trillions of dollars in low-paying short-term cash equivalents and you have the makings for a true growth stock bonanza.

Throughout this book steps have been given to show you how to proceed with your investment in individual issues. However, for many investors, mutual funds may be an appropriate vehicle for participating in small growth companies. Although you are advised to take a diversified approach to building a portfolio, this may not be practical if you are starting with a small sum. Let's say you have $3,000 to invest in a minimum of six stocks, which works out to $500 each. Because most all brokerages, including discounters, have a minimum transaction cost, commissions could have a serious impact on your performance. In cases like this, you may be better off starting with a mutual fund.

Perhaps you may wish to build your own portfolio and have adequate resources, but don't feel ready to make the plunge. A mutual fund will get your money working harder for you while you hone your skills. When you're ready to pick stocks on your own, simply sell your fund shares and start building your own portfolio. Finally, some investors just like the convenience of the fund approach and don't want to take the time to buy individual issues. For those of you who choose this route, top quality funds can help you meet your goals. Of course, you'll never have a fund go up ten times in value in 12 months, but with the power of compounding at work, small company funds with even an average track record can grow substantially given enough time.

Before getting into the selection process, you will need to keep a few caveats in mind. The philosophy of this book is that good solid stocks you can own for years are your best avenue to stock market profits. And like a good manager of a business, you will want to keep your costs under control without sacrificing performance. Finally, to achieve superior results you will need to do your homework. The pages that follow contain suggestions for picking good funds that incorporate the principles above.

STARTING YOUR SEARCH

The growing popularity of mutual funds has led to increased coverage in a variety of financial publications. As a result, you can start your screening process by acquiring the issues of a number of periodicals, including *Barron's Financial Weekly*, that feature extensive listings of mutual fund facts and figures. The table below lists some of the best compilations and when they come out.

Publication	When Listed
Barron's	About six weeks after the end of each quarter
BusinessWeek	February
Money	February
Kiplinger's	September

Not all of these publications contain the same information, nor is it presented in exactly the same fashion. Therefore, you may want to get a copy of each publication. This will enable you to get all of the information you need to complete your initial screening process.

Once you have a list in hand, your first step will be to segregate all of the funds in the small company growth category. Despite the size of these lists, you can quickly identify all funds in this classification. The total number of small growth funds should, depending on the publication, be about 60 to 100. Don't be intimidated by this many funds. By the time you are through with the initial testing, you'll be down to 10-15 funds. An accent marker applied to each listing will allow you to quickly find the funds once you begin your second screen.

PERFORMANCE

No fund statistic catches an investor's attention more than performance. Indeed, the bottom line is what you are after, so a complete understanding of how to use performance data is crucial to picking potentially rewarding funds. You don't want to simply rush in and buy the hottest fund over the last three months. With this approach you might wind up buying a fund overloaded in an industry that has recently experienced a fantastic surge and that may be ready to head down for the next six months. Successful fund investing (unless you plan to switch to individual stocks soon) is a long-term affair. Therefore, the numbers that really count cover from one to five years. Ten-year performance numbers are also available for some small company growth funds. However, because this category has grown rapidly over the last few years, a lot of good funds with five years under their belt fail to make the ten-year statistics.

The most important performance number is for five-year appreciation. Over five years, a fund has the opportunity to prove its mettle under a variety of market conditions. The ability of a fund manager to weather these storms and profit from the good times is the sign of a manager for all seasons. Just consider the five-year period from 1987 to 1991. During this time fund managers experienced the following:

Time	Event
1987	A strong market for nine months followed by the crash.
1988-1989	An extended rally that took the NASDAQ Composite to new all-time highs.
1989-1990	A persistent decline in small stocks that began in October 1989 and ended in October 1990 and included a recession.
1990-1991	One of the strongest market rallies for small stocks in history.

Three-year figures also give their just due to funds that have done well over a reasonably long period of time. This category will include some fine, up-and-coming funds that don't qualify for the five-year ratings. Remember that, everything else being equal, the longer a fund has been around, the more you have to go on. If you do find a three-year fund that looks promising, you might discover that it goes back 4 3/4 years and barely misses the five-year rankings. By extrapolating their results, you may find a winner that you can compare with the five-year funds that would have slipped through the cracks under tighter screening criteria.

To find out if a fund is in step with current market conditions, you should check the one-year performance data. If small company growth funds were up 51% for the last 12 months (the 1991 average performance) and the fund you are looking at was only up 35%, you'd better forget it, even if its longer-term record is good. Underperformance like this is a sign that the fund manager has lost touch with prevailing trends in individual stocks and the market. Should the fund far outpace the market, that could issue another warning. Perhaps the manager is in overly aggressive stocks or has overconcentrated the fund's holdings in only a couple of industries. Quite often you'll find that funds with spectacular one-year records can get lost in the shuffle for the next several years. So be sure to also check the three- and five-year figures.

Sometimes the rankings will show the best performers to be those funds that have gone down the least over the last 12 months. You need to be really careful here because a fund that's leading in a down market may be heavily in cash. Fund managers as a whole are terrible market timers.

Therefore, there's no assurance that the manager of this cash-rich fund will be in a fully invested position (which is what you want) when the market is heading back up again.

There are a number of methods that gauge performance in the tables of mutual funds. Sometimes you'll find how much $10,000 would have grown to over the last five years. Quite often you'll be given the rate that your investment would have compounded at over the last one, three, and five years. For example, if a fund grew at a compound rate of 15% for five years, that would be the same as $10,000 growing to $20,114. While conducting your performance evaluation, look at how each fund did versus its peers. You may also want to check a fund's record against such small stock barometers as the NASDAQ Composite, or better yet the Russell 2000. Make sure you don't use the S&P 500 or the Dow because they are loaded with big cap stocks that often bear little resemblance to what's going on in the world of small growth stocks.

As you go through the lists, start to check off those funds that stand out over the last three to five years. Write down (or enter on your computer) the names of the top 20 funds. This will give you the superstars as well as the above average funds that may be coming into their own. You might want to start with all funds where $10,000 grew to, let's say $18,000 in five years, which may give you a list of 20 to 25 names to start with.

MANAGEMENT

The next thing you'll want to check out is the management of the fund. In fact, you are really investing in the skills of the manager as much as you are in the fund itself. Ideally, what you are looking for is continuity of management. In *Barron's Financial Weekly*, their quarterly fund review lists the managers of each fund and how long they've been with the fund. The *Barron's* listing will tell you if current management is the one that is responsible for the track record. If present management has been in charge for five years, you can move on to the next criteria for selection. However, if they took over more recently, you will need to dig into their background to find out what their record was like at another fund. In most cases, it will be easier to move on to another fund where management has been around for five years or longer.

LOAD VERSUS NO-LOAD

Investors today have become increasingly cost-conscious. As a result, almost all fund listings include initial sales charges, if any. There's nothing wrong with being cost-conscious as long as it is not carried to an extreme. When it comes to mutual funds, there seems to be no end to the controversy over whether you should invest in a no-load fund versus one that imposes an upfront sales charge. Obviously, everything else being exactly equal, you will be better off in a no-load fund. In reality, when evaluating growth stock funds for possible purchase, you'll discover that the case for no-loads is not exactly cut and dried. Remember, after all fees and expenses, you want performance.

Taking these costs into account, there are some small company growth funds that have been well worth the initial sales charge. Table 9-1 lists the top five small company growth funds according to *Money* magazine from Dec. 31, 1986 to Dec. 31, 1991 (omitted is Janus Venture, which is currently closed to new investors). The figures show how much money you would have as of December 31, 1991, based on an initial investment of $10,000. With the load funds, the maximum initial sales charge was deducted at the outset. All returns are net of fees and expenses and assume reinvestment of capital gains and dividends. Massachusetts Financial and the Alger Small Capitalization Fund do not levy an initial sales charge. However, they do deduct 12b-1 fees annually, which act as an ongoing sales charge. Clearly, Table 9-1 demonstrates that, including sales charges, load funds do not need to take a back seat to the no-loads.

When it comes down to choosing between a no-load and a load, you need to determine how long you plan to be in a fund and how much

Table 9-1
Top Five Small Company Growth Funds
(Dec. 31, 1986 - Dec. 31, 1991)

Fund	$10,000 Grows to . .	Sales Charge
Alger Small Cap. Fund	$31,627	Backend
Hartwell Emerging Growth	$28,897	4.75%*
Mass. Financial Lifetime— Emerging Growth	$26,246	Backend
Sit New Beginnings	$25,192	NL
Oppenheimer Discovery	$25,156	5.75%*

*Maximum sales charge.

you're going to invest. At the beginning of the chapter, I suggested that some of you will use funds for a relatively short period of time, until your skills are developed and/or your capital is sufficient to buy individual issues. With this in mind, you probably would be best off in a no-load if your time horizon is less than two years.

Let's suppose you are planning to hold a fund for one year. Your choices are between a no-load fund and a load fund that charges an up-front fee of 5%. Over the course of your 12-month holding period, the load fund's manager would have to give you a 5% better return just to put you even with the no-load fund. On the other hand, if you do plan to own a fund for several years, the impact of the initial sales charge diminishes over time. In fact, the percentage return that the load fund needs to deliver to equal or come out ahead of the no-load may be negligible providing the load fund is a winner. Table 9-2 illustrates this point.

In Table 9-2, Funds A and B both compounded at 15% for 1, 3, 5, and 10 years. Fund B trailed behind Fund A from the start despite their equal growth rate of 15% because of the sales charge. If you invested in Fund B for only one year, you would need a return of 21.1% on the net dollars invested to put you even with the no-load. For Fund B to stay even with Fund A over five years, it would have to compound at 16.2% annually (only 1.2% above Fund A). The real life examples demonstrate that several load funds have indeed paid for themselves, and then some, from 1987 to 1991. Over the long haul, up-front sales charges become relatively insignificant if you are getting superior performance.

Table 9-2
Effects of a Load on Performance
(\$10,000 Initial Investment)

		Years			
Fund	1	3	5	10	Comment
A	\$11,500	\$15,209	\$20,114	\$40,456	15% no-load compounded return—no-load
B	\$10,925	\$14,448	\$19,108	\$38,433	15% compounded return—5% load deducted initially
C	21.1%	17.0%	16.2%	15.6%	Rate for B to catch up to A

Investors who choose load funds need not be too concerned with initial sales charges in the long run. Similarly, those who plan to make a substantial investment in small company growth funds also need not be too concerned about sales charges. The results of fund performance always assume that the maximum sales charge is deducted from the initial investment. This calculation fails to recognize that load funds offer significant reductions in sales charges as the size of the investment increases.

12b-1 FUNDS

In addition to considering loads versus no-loads, you should also be aware of the cost involved with investing in a fund with 12b-1 charges. 12b-1 funds, as they are commonly referred to, do not charge you an up-front commission at the start. However, when you sell your fund shares, you could pay a hefty charge at the time of redemption. Typically, 12b-1 funds charge you a declining percentage each year until the fee for selling disappears altogether. The downward progression in backend sales charges may go from 4%-6% down to 0% after four to six years. The fund's prospectus will give you the details on how this works. Even if you don't sell your fund, you will still be subject to an ongoing annual expense that ranges up to a maximum of 1.25%. The fund deducts this expense from your net asset value to help pay the commissions of the brokers that sell the fund. If you hold a 12b-1 fund long enough, a 1.25% annual charge can make an up-front loaded fund's initial sales charge look cheap in comparison. And remember that 12b-1 charge continues to go up in dollar terms as your fund's value increases in size. On a $10,000 investment your first year's 12b-1 fee would be $125 (assuming a 12b-1 charge of 1.25%). At 1.25%, after five years of 15% annual compound growth, your yearly bill for the 12b-1 fee would now be up to $251!

Whether a fund is a load, no-load, or 12b-1, keep in mind that sales charges are only part of the overall equation. Don't ignore any expense involved with a fund you are considering, but do keep sales charges in perspective. There are several fine funds in all of the above classifications that may merit your attention. Keep both your immediate and long-term goals and plans in mind, and put the load versus no-load controversy to rest.

SIZE OF THE FUND

The purpose of small company growth funds is to invest in young and rapidly growing businesses with outstanding potential for appreciation. Some of the biggest possible winners are stocks with relatively small market capitalizations (shares outstanding times current market price). As of June 1991, the market caps of the stocks in the Russell 2000 ranged from about $15 million to $300+ million. Buying large blocks of stocks, as the fund managers must do, is not always easy when you're investing millions of dollars. For example, a manager with a $100-million fund may wish to take 2% of the fund's assets and buy a particularly promising stock. That represents a $2-million buy order. An order of this size may take days to execute if the manager wishes to avoid upsetting the price of the stock. As you can see, even the managers of relatively small funds have their work cut out for them when they go to buy (or sell) a small growth stock.

A fund's liquidity problem is only compounded when a fund grows in size. As you might expect in the fund business, success begets success. Small funds with outstanding track records start to gain attention. Their name begins to appear in recaps of the top-performing funds. In addition, they begin to heavily promote their status. Don't forget that funds make money by having dollars under management; in their eyes the more the better.

In sharp contrast, you should be less than excited if a fund grows rapidly because investors begin to flock to it. As the money comes in, the manager will be under pressure to employ it quickly into additional shares of stock. Should he sit too long with a sizeable cash position, his fund may start to lag behind other similar funds, especially in a sharply rising market. On top of this, the additional dollars mean he will have to, at some point in time, start focusing on stocks with larger capitalizations or increase the number of stocks in the portfolio to an unwieldy number. In either case, the growth of the fund could start to undermine its basic purpose. Interestingly enough, a comparison of the largest small growth funds versus the top five for 1987-1991 bears this out (Table 9-3). In addition, Table 9-4 lists the sizes of these funds as well as their five-year track records. The five largest funds all were well in excess of $780 million, with the average being $996 million. Their five-year compound growth rate averaged 15.5%. The size of the five top-performing funds was $150 million. Their smaller size helped them post a 22.9% growth rate from 1987 to

Table 9-3
Large Funds in Small Stocks

*Five Largest Funds	Size (000,000) 12/31/91	Compound Growth Rate
T. Rowe Price New Horizon	$1,470.4	12.9%
Fidelity OTC	$1,045.8	18.3%
Scudder Development	$ 892.8	18.7%
Pennsylvania Mutual	$ 789.1	11.4%
Keystone S-4	$ 783.2	16.2%
Average	$ 996.3	+15.5%

*Excludes Janus Venture because it is currently closed to new investors. Janus, with over $1.3 billion under management, would have made both lists for size and performance.

1991. The above data supports the conclusion that the smaller funds offer better appreciation potential. That doesn't mean the sizeable funds listed above are bad investments. Each of their records would suggest otherwise. It just means that their size may have an impact on their growth potential. Because of their size, these funds may offer less risk because of additional diversification as well as the presence of some larger, more well-established companies.

Table 9-4
Top Five Small Stock Funds
(12/31/86–12/31/91)

*Five Best Performance Funds (By Size)	Size (000,000) 12/31/91	Compound Rate
Alger Small Capitalization Portfolio	$ 80.9	25.9%
Hartwell Emerging Growth	$107.7	24.9%
Oppenheimer New Discovery	$166.7	21.7%
MFS Lifetime Emerging Growth	$189.4	21.3%
Sit New Beginnings	$204.8	20.5%
Averages	$149.9	+22.9%

*Excludes Janus Venture because it is currently closed to new investors. Janus, with over $1.3 billion under management, would have made both lists for size and performance.

Small funds with big numbers attract new money. There's an easy way to find out how big a fund would be if new money was not added throughout the year. By doing a simple calculation you can determine how large a fund would be based on share appreciation only.

At the end of 1990, the Alger Small Capitalization Portfolio's net assets stood at $30 million. If you tack on a gain of 55.3% in 1991 to the fund's net asset value, NAV, that would compute to an asset size of $46.6 million on December 31, 1991. However, the combination of new money and capital gains on the additional funds swelled the fund to $81 million by the end of 1991. Certainly, you want your fund's assets to grow because its portfolio is doing well. What you don't want is for new money to flood into your favorite fund at a rate that hampers performance and puts pressure on the fund manager. So if you discover that the fund you are considering is growing at an alarming rate in excess of its NAV, consider that as a yellow flag.

Perhaps a useful way to conceptualize small company growth funds is to look at their life cycle as you would that of an individual company. When a company is small, its percentage gains can be rather large. As it reaches maturity, the growth rates inevitably will slow. That doesn't mean its a lousy company, rather that it fits into a different category. The same thing is true with small company growth funds as they increase in size over the years.

FUND LITERATURE

The initial screening process discussed in this book covered performance, management's length of service, sales charges, and size of the fund. By now your list of potential purchases should be whittled down to 10-15 funds. Your next step will be to call each fund's toll-free 800 number and ask for the prospectus, annual and semiannual reports, and any other literature they may have regarding the fund. These materials will help you to arrive at a decision on which fund or funds to invest in.

When you receive your fund information, take some time to investigate the listing of the fund's investments in their periodic reports (not the prospectus). First of all, you may wish to determine their cash position. An especially high level is a warning that the fund manager is a market timer or that the fund has been attracting large amounts of money that it has been unable to put to work quickly. Mutual fund managers do best when they invest in stocks and not cash, which has been the worst performer. In addition, the record has shown that those who do time the market often are heaviest in cash at market lows when they should be fully invested.

Small funds that have been attracting large amounts of new money may grow to a size where it is difficult for them to match previous performance numbers. In either case, if the fund you're examining has a cash balance above 7%-10%, call the fund and try to find out why it is this large. If you find that they are heavily in cash for either of the reasons above, consider that as a strike against them.

SIZING UP THE FUND PORTFOLIO

When constructing your personal portfolio of stocks, the emphasis is on individual stock selection. Along with this, you will also seek to establish diversification among different industries. A fund manager, because of the amount of money he is responsible for, must consider industry diversification first. For example, if the manager is particularly fond is of medical service stocks, he may place 15%-20% of the fund's assets there. The fund may then, in order to achieve proper diversification, invest in as many as 10-20 stocks within this group. This is a common procedure with funds. In essence, they are investing in industries they like more than they are in individual issues. You may also wish to observe which high-growth industries are conspicuous by their absence.

As you study the industry breakdown, take notice of the groups where the bulk of the fund's money is invested. You may discover that 80% of the fund's assets are in four or five pet industries. If so, make sure these industries have particularly exceptional promise and are in tune with the accepted macrotrends in the economy. If the fund turns out to be too heavily concentrated in one or two areas, you may be buying the equivalent of a sector fund. There's nothing necessarily wrong with this in the short run when a particular sector is hot. However, one purpose of a fund is to lower your risk through industry diversification. Therefore, if you find a fund is heavily specialized in a couple of promising industries, and you do decide to buy it, try to balance this selection with another fund emphasizing other industry groups.

After sizing up the industries, it is time to move on to the stocks themselves. The periodic reports will list the market values of the fund's stocks as of the date of the report. Within a few minutes, you can quickly decipher the fund's most heavily weighted issues. How do the names of the fund's biggest holdings grab you? Are the companies virtually unknown to you, or do some of the names ring a bell? Are there major holdings in companies that you recognize as up-and-coming stars, the possible blue chips of tomorrow? You may wish to further check out a fund's top holdings by reading S&P reports on them.

PORTFOLIO TURNOVER

Within the prospectus, you will find a fund's annual turnover ratio, dating back several years. This figure tells how frequently the managers buy and sell securities within the portfolio. A ratio of 100% would indicate that on average, the whole portfolio is turned over once a year. A ratio of 300% would indicate that the portfolio is turned over three times annually. Obviously, this figure doesn't necessarily mean that all of the stocks are traded with that frequency.

Even in portfolios with a high turnover rate, some stocks may be held for years while others may only last for weeks. But generally speaking, the higher the turnover ratio, the more the fund manager is oriented toward trading in and out of stocks. Conversely, a low turnover ratio would demonstrate that the fund manager is an advocate of the buy and hold approach. Small company turnover ratios range from a low of about 75% to around 300%.

Keep this ratio in mind when you're studying a fund's holdings. By the time you receive the reports, it's possible that several big holdings have been replaced. To update a fund's portfolio, call the fund and ask a representative for the fund's current top-ten holdings. For those of you who wish to learn about growth stock investing by investing in and following a fund's portfolio, you will probably be best served by buying those funds with the lowest turnover ratios. That way, there's less of a chance that a position you are following will disappear from the portfolio. A low portfolio turnover can also help keep your taxes down, as stock profits on long-term holdings can appreciate tax-deferred. Funds with a higher turnover ratio may result in more realized gains, which in turn could increase your taxes.

FUND OBJECTIVES

The prospectus always contains a statement of the fund's objectives. Look in this section for confirmation that the fund invests primarily in small company growth stocks. What you don't want is a fund that is overly involved in a host of offbeat strategies such as selling short, option buying, restricted securities, or leveraging the portfolio (borrowing to buy more stock). If you're investing in a fund for small company stock profits, then leave it at that.

LETTER TO SHAREHOLDERS

The periodic reports will usually contain a letter to shareholders written by the manager of the fund. This letter will give you some thoughts on their philosophy of investing and their strategy for profiting from current economic and market trends. The letter may also summarize briefly the fund's performance as well as their most heavily concentrated areas of investment. Make sure that the manager's investment principles are in concert with the philosophy of investing covered earlier in this book.

TRACKING YOUR FUND

Once you invest, it's easy to track the fund's progress. A call to the fund's 800 number leads to a recorded message which will give you the fund's net asset value (NAV). Your daily newspaper may also list your fund. If not, you can most likely find it in *Barron's*, *Investors Business Daily*, or *The Wall Street Journal*. Simply look at the movements in a fund's NAV as you would the fluctuations of a share of stock. If your fund's NAV has rallied from $10 to $12 over the last six months, it has gained 20% in value. Be on the lookout for splits in the fund's NAV. This will increase the number of shares you own but decrease the value of each share. The total dollar value of your investment following a split remains unchanged. Dividends and capital gains distributions (which are issued once annually) can also affect the NAV. So when tracking your fund's value, take into account all of the possible events that could alter its NAV overnight.

SELLING YOUR FUND

Mutual funds are normally considered a long-term investment. The longer you can hold them, the better your chances become for meaningful stock market profits, providing you've done your homework well and have selected a top performing fund. However, there may come a time when you will need to consider switching from one fund to another for any number of reasons.

The fund could become a victim of its own success, growing so large that it can no longer buy in size the kind of small company stocks that led to its early success. Perhaps the portfolio manager responsible for the fund's outstanding track record may leave the fund. The objectives of the fund might change, or the fund's performance may lag too far behind its peers for an unacceptably long period of time. Whatever the case may be, when it's time to sell, sell. Don't let the initial sales charge, redemption charge, or back-end sales cost keep you from moving your funds to a more productive investment. Most importantly, remember that the best thing you can do to avoid incurring excessive sales costs (assuming a load fund) is to make sure your selections are sound in the first place.

SUMMARY

- Low interest rates and low inflation could help fuel a long-term bull market in small growth stocks. Plenty of money in cash equivalents is available to fuel the boom.

- Mutual funds may be appropriate for small or beginning investors who wish to learn about the market while controlling their risk.

- With the power of compounding at work, small company funds can produce some substantial returns over the long haul.

- To get the best results from your funds, do your homework; don't just buy performance.

- You can start your search for the best funds by using the lists compiled by a number of top financial publications.

- Small growth stocks are usually listed under "Small Company Growth."

- Five-year performance is the most important length of time for evaluating a fund.

- One-year performance will tell you if a fund is in step with the current market.

- Compare your fund against the NASDAQ Composite and Russell 2000, as well as other funds within the category.

- Make sure current management is responsible for the company's track record.

- Keep the load versus no-load controversy in perspective—either kind can be useful in meeting your goals.
- If your time frame is short term, go with a no-load.
- Be aware of the cost of investing in 12b-1 funds.
- For the most part, confine your investment in small company funds to those that are also small in size.
- Large funds that invest in small companies may have less upside potential but also may have less risk and, thus, may be suitable for some investors.
- Successful small company funds may become the victims of their own success.
- After your initial screening, call the fund's 800 number for the prospectus, annual and semiannual reports, and anything else they may have.
- Look at the fund's cash position. Be wary if it is too high (7%-10%). Remember: Look for fund managers who are good stock selectors, not market timers.
- Examine the industries that are emphasized in the fund. Does it give sufficient weight to those that are in the megatrends of the economy (i.e., medical services, environment, etc.)?
- Check out the stocks that represent the fund's largest holdings. Do you recognize some of the names?
- Try to stick to funds with a relatively low turnover ratio.
- Read the fund's statement of objectives. Avoid funds that can and do use offbeat strategies.
- You can monitor a fund by calling their 800 number or checking the fund's listings in the paper.
- For any of a number of reasons, when it's time to sell, don't hesitate to sell your shares and move on.

QUESTIONS

1. Your choice is between two small company growth funds. The no-load has compounded at 16.2% annually over the last five years. The up-front load fund charge is 4 1/2% based on the amount you are going

to invest. Its performance over the same time is 18.5% annually. Based on this information, which is the best fund if you plan to hold for one year and for four years? Why?

2. What do you need to know about management's length of service at a fund?

3. You've been in a highly successful small company fund for four years now. Your original investment of $15,000 has grown to $37,807 (26% compounded with reinvestment of all capital gains and dividends). During this time, the assets of the fund have grown from $122 million to $525 million. The fund has lagged behind the average small company fund (which was up 17%) by 5% over the last year. What can you conclude from this? Should you continue to hold or should you sell your fund?

4. A fund you're evaluating has a portfolio turnover ratio of 325%. Is the fund manager a trader or a buy and hold investor?

5. Upon studying a fund's holdings, you find that you like everything about the fund except that 85% of the assets are concentrated in three industries. Should you drop this fund because of its lack of diversity, or is there a strategy that you can adopt that would make investing in this fund prudent?

6. Funds can produce some impressive long-term results given the power of compounding. You've just put $28,000 in your 401(k) in a fund that has registered an annual compound return of 18.2% over the last five years. If the fund can match this performance over the next 15 years, how much will you have in your 401(k)?

7. Why is five-year performance possibly the most important criterion in evaluating a fund? What is the value of the one-year figures?

8. Give three good reasons why an investor should consider a mutual fund over buying individual issues.

9. Upon reading the fund's portfolio holding, you find that the fund is 15% in cash or cash equivalents. The market has been going down for the last 12 months and the Dow Industrials are 24% below their previous peak. Based on the information, should you invest in this fund or look for another?

10. A fund you are considering has no upfront charges but does have what are called 12b-1 charges. What are two key fees that you should

know about before investing? Which of these would especially influence your decision if you don't plan to be in the fund more than 12-18 months?

Chapter 10

PUTTING IT ALL TOGETHER

Now that you have read the book and tested your understanding of the material, you should be ready to begin your search for the next winners on Wall Street. However, before you begin your search, take a few moments to read this brief chapter. Investing your money properly to achieve your goals is serious business. To maximize your long-term returns, you will need to skillfully manage all parts of the investment process. Using an analogy from the world of sports to explain this further, assume that you aspire to become a top professional golfer. You have perfected all of the skills necessary, such as driving and iron play, with one exception: You can't make a putt over two feet long. This one deficiency alone will keep you from competing at the top level of the game. Similarly, the success of your investments depends on your ability to play all parts of the "game" at an acceptable level of skill.

Over the next few pages we will review some of the basic components of a winning game so that you can proceed with your investments with complete confidence. By keeping these points in mind, you should have the fundamental basis for a successful investment program. Make sure that you establish a relationship with a broker (either full-service or discount) that is right for you. Determine the level of service that you need to invest successfully. Be aware of the various kinds of orders and be sure to use the one that is appropriate for the specific transaction.

When you begin your analysis of a stock, be sure that it meets the definition of a small company growth stock. Avoid the highly speculative penny stocks and confine your buying of large capitalization stocks to the more conservative portion of your overall portfolio. Be very selective in your purchases; remember to run a stock through the fundamental criteria presented. First and foremost, invest only in businesses that make sense to you and that feel like something you'd like to be involved in. You will want to be in companies with rising sales, expanding profit margins, and they should have management motivated by its ownership in company stock. Of course, you'll also want stocks that are capable of turning a triple play: rising sales, expanding margins, and an expanding P/E multiple.

Small growth stocks have more risk than bigger, more well-established companies. So be sure to check out the financial condition of your purchase candidates from both the short-term and long-term perspectives.

An investment approach that stresses long-term results and fundamentals necessitates that you be willing to buy into good companies whenever the opportunities become available. You must, therefore, learn to buy stocks when it is the hardest thing to do, when the country is mired in a recession and your friends and associates are urging you to stay put in T-Bills. The proper use of individual stock charts can help you to buy fundamentally solid companies at reasonable price levels.

Information is the lifeblood of your decision-making process. Carefully examine company literature, including annual reports, quarterly reports, press releases, and brokerage reports. Call the company and ask questions, and plan to visit the company if possible. Make use of all of the various sources of information that you feel are necessary to arrive at an intelligent decision on a stock, but don't become an information junkie. Study what you need to, but don't suffer from paralysis by analysis.

Once you buy a stock, immediately assume responsibility for the ownership of a valuable asset. Although it is not necessary to follow all of your stocks like a hawk, you will still want to make sure that each purchase gets off to a good start. Establish a discipline that will cause you to recheck a company's fundamentals, should it decline anywhere from 15%-25% from your initial purchase price. Selling a winning stock at the right time may be just as important as your decision to buy. Evaluate the company's fundamentals, including financial strength, insider selling, institutional activity, EPS growth, and sales growth. If the fundamentals turn for the worse and the chart pattern looks bad, don't hesitate to sell.

You should adapt a businesslike attitude toward the management of your portfolio. Take great care in allocating the right amount to your small growth stock portfolio. How much you invest is an individual matter related to your assets, risk tolerance, and financial objectives. Learn to achieve proper portfolio diversification by investing in a number of different stocks in unrelated industries. Even when you are fully invested, always be on the lookout for new ideas. Be sure to occasionally prune your portfolio of the deadwood and to periodically reduce your position in your big winners. It's fun to compete for stock market profits and to beat the averages. Good performance from your portfolio will also enable you to meet your goals. Therefore, you will want to monitor your results by comparing them to an appropriate market barometer such as the NASDAQ Composite or Russell 2000. Try to control your costs, and make sure to use available tax strategies to boost your profits.

In the long run, small company growth stocks have proven to be America's top-performing investment. Learn to be patient as the market fluctuates through its normal series of ups and downs. Remain confident that good solid companies with growing profits and sales will, in the long run, earn an above-average rate of return for you.

Investing for your financial future is serious business, but you should also have fun running your portfolio. View investing as a game that you are going to win. Keep the points covered in this chapter in mind so that your game will remain strong in all the key areas necessary for top performance. When necessary, be sure to refer to the book as a refresher course from time to time as needed.

I hope that this book has been of value to you. I wish you the best of luck with your investments in the years ahead.

ANSWERS TO CHAPTER QUESTIONS

CHAPTER 2

1. Establish the parameters for the relationship so that you can work as a team to meet your goals.

2. Stock reports, charts, opinions on securities, updates on the status of orders, and phone calls when important developments occur in one of your holdings are among the most important services.

3. Don't let him talk you out of a stock you've done your homework on and know better than he does.

4. To maintain an orderly market in the stocks that he specializes in.

5. 16 7/8.

6. The stock has a very wide percentage spread between the bid and ask. Only long-term investors should purchase a stock like this.

7. Average daily volume, shares in the float, and the bid-ask spread.

8. Shares outstanding is, as the name implies, all stock that has been authorized and issued. This includes stock of officers and directors of the company that might not be readily available for sale. By subtracting their shares and other closely held stock, you arrive at the float.

9. The bid would have to increase to double the size of the ask. For example, to sell at a 100% profit, the stock would need to be quoted at

15 1/2 bid - ask (a price above 15 1/2). In percentages the bid would have to go up 121% (7 to 15 1/2) for you to get a double. To break even the bid would need to go from 7 to 7 3/4 (or up 10.7%).

10. The stock was bought at 9 5/8 and sold at 6 7/8. The difference of 9 5/8 – 6 7/8 is 2 3/4. 500 shares x 2 3/4 = a dollar loss of $1375. The percentage loss was 2 3/4 divided by 9 5/8 = 28.6%

11. It's probably time to change brokers.

12. If you are unable to monitor your stocks throughout the day perhaps you need a full-service broker who can alert you to important developments such as this.

CHAPTER 3

1. Very selective.

2.
*1st Quarter Earnings = $\dfrac{\$360,000}{\$4,500,000} = .08$

*2nd Quarter Earnings = $\dfrac{\$403,200}{\$6,500,000} = .06$

*Earnings per share declined 25% (from .08 to .06) because of the dilution.

3.

	Three Years Ago	Current	% Gain
International Sales (000)	$1,442	$7,084	391%
Domestic Sales (000)	$8,858	$18,216	106%
Total	$10,300	$25,300	

Judging by these results management should definitely consider raising funds to finance its high-growth international operations.

4. $\dfrac{\$1.4 \text{ million}}{\$6.7 \text{ million}} = 20.9\%$

5. Call the company - investor relations
   Suppliers
   Customers
   Trade Journals
   Have you tried their product or service?

6. Wall Street tends to reward consistent growth companies with EPS growth way above the norm. This is demonstrated by a steadily expanding multiple.

7. The stock has definite seasonal tendencies. Quarterly comparisons are favorable in all cases versus the same quarter of a year ago. Annual EPS growth is impressive. Based on this information alone, the stock is quite possibly a buy. June third quarter EPS is up 24% compared to the third quarter of a year ago.

8. Earnings per share.

9. Profit margins peaked in the third year and have declined steadily the last couple of years (in order, they are 14.3%, 16.4%, 17.1%, 15.6%, 14.2%). Sales are growing at a rapid rate, but the slippage in margins is worrisome. You should probably avoid this one unless other factors are compelling.

10. Second, third, fourth year EPS growth rates are, respectively 50%, 73%, 54%. The P/E ratio is 11.3. Despite its fine performance, the company appears to have gone relatively unnoticed, as evidenced by the low percentage of institutional ownership.

11. Proprietary.

12. After approximately five years and nine months the plant will be running at full capacity with 20% unit sales growth.

13. Summary of positive financial results.
Statements regarding company's success.
Plans for continued growth of the business.
A definition of the company's mission.

14. Don't be concerned about their increase in ownership as it is low, still just 8.0% versus 3.7% six months ago for ABC. What you want is low but growing institutional ownership. The big boys are just starting to jump on the bandwagon. XYZ is currently 40% owned by the institutions. Because they have already bought a lot of XYZ (about 20%), ABC looks like the better bet.

15. Institutional investors and brokerage coverage.

16. EPS in two years will be 1.47 at 40% compounded growth. XYZ's P/E based on future earnings is $\dfrac{18}{1.47} = 12.2$

17. Industry sales will total $234 million in three years. ABC's share will be $105 million. In a high-tech industry, ABC is planning for the future with its sizeable research and development budget.

18. No. Investors understand that small companies can't double sales annually for more than a short time. 50% growth is an excellent rate.

19.

	Beginning	*Five Years Later*
Revenue	$7,600,000	$22,280,350
Profit Margin	8.2%	14.6%
Shares Outstanding	1.1 million	1.4 million
P/E	10	22

Revenues grew to $22 million + at 24%

Net Income:
1st year   .082 x 7,600,000 = $623,200
Five Years Later   .146 x 22,280,350 = $3,252,931

EPS:

1st Year $\dfrac{\$623,200}{1,100,000} = .57$

Five Years Later $\dfrac{\$3,252,931}{1,400,000} = 2.32$

Stock Price:
1st Year   10 P/E x .57 EPS = 5 3/4
After Five Years   22 P/E x 2.32 EPS = 51

Stock Gain: $\dfrac{45.25}{5.75} \dfrac{\text{(Stock Gain)}}{\text{(Starting Price)}} = 787\%$

ABC Corporation benefitted from the triple play of growing revenues, expanding margins, and an expanding P/E. The increase in shares outstanding slightly diluted this performance.

20. XYZ should be rated a buy. The CEO wisely sold some stock, which will enable him to prudently diversify his assets. He still owns 24% of the company. If XYZ appreciates 20% in the next 12 months, the CEO's

remaining stock would go up $1.2 million in value. By comparison, his salary is relatively modest.

21. From 1985 to 1990, sales grew from $2 million to $37 million! Even though percentage growth was its lowest in years, they still grew impressively from 25.2 million to 37 million (47%). This slowdown in percentage growth is no cause for alarm as they were growing at a high and unsustainable rate.

22. Patience.

23. 2.38 EPS in five years at 25% growth
    2.89 EPS in five years at 30% growth
    Stock in five years: 16 P/E x 2.89 EPS = 46 1/4
    Stock percent gain: $\dfrac{35\ 1/4}{11}$ = 320%

24. Annual report, quarterly report, press releases.

25. Total sales should be $25,200,000.

26. In ten years the dividend would be $1,164.
    The dividend as a percent of original investment $\dfrac{1{,}164}{15{,}000}$ = 7.8%

27. The company's ROE for 1990 and 1991 was 32.2% and 32.3%, respectively. This return is more than enough to provide the company with the funds needed to allow them to grow at 25%. If the company wanted additional capital, two possible choices would be a stock offering or long-term debt. The company can afford to pay a dividend and still meet its growth objectives.

28. Book value per share is 3.29.

CHAPTER 4

1. Businesses with a higher debt load than average should be highly predictable in their performance.

2. Assets = Liabilities + Stockholders' Equity.

3. An increase in inventories above the company's normal growth in sales may be alright if they are preparing to introduce a new product.

4. Company 3 is strongest from the long-term perspective as it has no debt. Company 2 is the weakest with a debt to equity ratio of .45, well above the industry average of .23. Company 1 looked to be the best overall as it has an acceptable amount of coverage of its short-term liabilities and has a below-average amount of debt.

5.

	1991	1990
Current Ratio	2.7	2.3
Quick Ratio	1.3	1.1

The company is in a very good position to meet its short term obligations. Their cash and cash equivalents alone are well in excess of their current liabilities. The quick ratio is above 1 at 1.3. Inventories were up 25% in 1991, which is exactly in line with the company's growth in sales. ABC's capital structure is fairly conservative as it has a debt to equity ratio of .16 for the year ending in 1991.

This is an improvement on the debt to equity ratio of .28 at the end of 1990. Notice that the company has paid down a big part of its bonds payable. ABC appears to be a financially sound company that's growing even stronger. Based on this information, ABC appears to be a buy.

CHAPTER 5

1. The Dow is down 23% $\left(\dfrac{718}{3,122} = 23\% \right)$

Because the Dow is down over 20% from its previous peak, the chances are you are getting close to an important bottom. Rather than trying to call the bottom, you should be putting idle funds to work. Don't engage in panic selling. Given the magnitude of the decline, the economy is most likely in a recession.

2. Knowing when to change timers, when the timer's hot hand cools off.

3. 20%

4. Prime rate and the discount rate. For a positive signal, watch for two successive cuts in each rate.

5. 10%, 39-week moving.

6. • Investment advisors turn increasingly bullish.

   • The Dow Industrials rally above their 39-week moving average.

   • Interest rates are stable or still declining.

   • GNP turns positive following successive negative quarters.

7. The Dow Industrials have dropped 25% from their previous peak, indicating the presence of a bear market and possibly a recession. The Fed is trying to stimulate the economy, evidenced by the three successive cuts in the discount rate. Rather than wait for a 60% reading on the I.I. index, you should be buying now. A reading of 58.4% is close enough, especially given the other bullish indicators.

8. Examine your own opinion on investing in stocks. Are you positive or negative toward equities? Why do you feel that way? Emphasize information on individual companies that can help you make wise investment decisions.

9. Decline in the stock market; a new bull market.

10. Re-examine the indicators for signs that the market may be at or near an important low. Put idle funds to work in stocks.

11. Great buying opportunity.

12. Use charts as a tool, as a guide to help you in fine-tuning your stock investments.

13. Over- and undervaluation.

14. Re-check the fundamentals to make sure you didn't overlook a big negative or find out if any new developments have occurred that may change the outlook for the company.

CHAPTER 7

1. The company apparently depends on new products and product improvements to help keep sales growing. The combination of slowing sales growth and a decline in research and development spending indicates that they are not making an effort to stay competitive. Based solely on this information, the stock should be sold.

2. Recheck the fundamentals to make sure there's nothing you've overlooked. If you find a glaring negative that you passed over in your

initial analysis, then you should probably sell and cut your losses. On the other hand, if the stock passes your complete inspection, then continue to hold.

3. An acquisition in an unrelated business is definitely a red flag. This successful company would probably be better off sticking to its own business. You'll more than likely want to sell this stock.

4.

	1991	1990
Current Ratio	2.2	2.9
Quick Ratio	.4	1.2

The current ratio is still above the 2:1 minimum standard at the end of 1991. That's a small plus. The decline to 2:2 from 1990's reading of 2.9 is worrisome, indicating a negative trend. Worse yet is the quick ratio which, at .4, is well below the acceptable minimum of 1:1. Finally, inventories have grown 39% over last year's while sales are up only 18%. This company is heading toward trouble. You should probably sell your shares.

5. The company has turned in another outstanding performance. All of these results are positive. Looking ahead, the one thing you should be concerned with is the amount of stock owned by institutions. It has grown to a large and troublesome figure. Should the company stumble and the institutions then begin to sell, the stock could drop like a rock. You should continue to hold the stock, but watch for any developments that could change the fundamental outlook of the company.

6. Try to learn from the mistake. It can help you in becoming a better investor.

7. Learn to deal with the fear of losing money as well as the greed that can keep you in a stock too long.

8. When the company went public, Mr. Jones owned company stock valued at $10 million and had a very modest salary. Eight years later his salary had swelled to $675,000 while his ownership of stock had shrunk to $2.2 million. Mr. Jones has obviously diversified the majority of his company holdings into other investments. His motivational level may be suspect as he apparently has it made, financially speaking. The CEO has done some major selling; so should you.

9. Fundamentals.

CHAPTER 8

1. Start looking for new ideas should one of your stocks not work out, or in case other money becomes available.

2. $39,944

3. After three years the portfolio would be worth $45,163. The total percentage gain would be 23.7%

4. Nine.

5.

7 Stocks grew to	$81,200
The Big Gainer to	$47,500
Total Portfolio	$128,700

$$\text{Portfolio \% gain} = \frac{\$48,700}{\$80,000} = 60.9\%$$

Prudent Moves: Sell part of the winner; eliminate the deadwood in the portfolio (with an average gain of 16% in two years there's got to be some subpar stocks); further diversify the portfolio up to 10-12 stocks.

6. Mr. Jones should be taking more risk. His allocation to small growth stock is way too low.

7. A good move may be to average your way in. Establish a pilot position, and then add to it if the stock does pull back.

8. Mr. Smith will need to significantly reduce his exposure to small stock, as they pay little income. In addition, he should reduce his risk at this point in his life. The portfolio breaks down as follows:

	Allocation Percentage	$ Value	Income Percentage	$ Income
Small Stocks	65%	$1,560,000	1%	$15,600
Blue Chips	15%	$360,000	3%	$10,800
Utilities	10%	$240,000	6%	$14,400
Cash	10%	$240,000	5%	$12,000
Total	100%	$2,400,000	2.2%	$52,800

Income needs to be $96,000 (to be at 4%). To provide 4% income, Mr. Jones's portfolio may wind up looking something like this after changing his asset allocation:

	Allocation Percentage	$ Value	Income Percentage	$ Income
Small Stocks	20%	$480,000	1%	$4,800
Blue Chips	31.7%	$760,000	3%	$22,800
Utilities	43.4%	$1,040,000	6%	$62,400
Cash	5%	$120,000	5%	$6,000
Total	100%	$2,400,000	4%	$96,000

With increased income and the more conservative nature of the portfolio, Mr. Smith should reduce the sizeable cash balance. Small stocks still deserve a place in the portfolio as they can help it to continue to grow in real terms.

9. The cost of these services relative to the portfolio's value is rather high. Nevertheless, they can be justified if our young investor views them as part of his tuition for his education in investing.

10. Eight industries are needed to achieve prudent diversification.

11. The portfolio would have to compound at 44% over the next three years to reach $100,000. Despite the recent strength in the market, this appears to be an unrealistic goal given the historical returns in small growth stocks.

12. Mr. Jones has $20,501 while Mr. Smith's portfolio is now valued at $21,952. Mr. Smith benefitted from tax deferral.

CHAPTER 9

1. If you plan to hold for just one year, go with the no load. The expected return should be 16.2% versus 13.2% (the return earned after deducting the initial sales charge) for the load fund. The four-year investor should go with the load as its expected return after the initial charge is 88.3% versus 82.3% for the no-load fund. The long-term investor has time for the superior fund to overcome the sales charge. The one-year investor needs to keep costs down by going with the no-load.

2. Find out if current management has been at the fund for a while. Are they responsible for the five-year track record?

3. The fund may have become a victim of its own success. While your investment has grown by 152%, the fund's net assets have grown by 330%! All this new money has apparently put a drag on the fund's performance as it is up only 12% the last year versus 17% from the average small company fund. More than likely you should sell this fund and buy a smaller one unless you now prefer the decreased risk that a larger fund offers you.

4. A trader. The fund's portfolio is being turned over more than three times annually.

5. If you plan to invest in only one small company fund, you probably will want a more diversified approach. On the other hand, if you plan to invest in two or more funds, you may be able to complement this fund with one or more other funds that emphasize other industries.

6. $343,890

7. Five-year performance tests the skills of a manager over a variety of market conditions. The one-year figure allows you to know if the fund manager is in tune with current market conditions.

8. Funds should be considered if the investor wants to establish a diversified portfolio and has a small amount to work with (under $5,000). Funds can also be appropriate for investors who wish to gain skill before investing in individual stocks. Finally, funds can provide a convenient means of investing for growth for those who don't want to bother picking their own stocks.

9. Chances are the market is near or at a bear market low. If anything, you will want to be fully invested at the lows. This fund manager appears to be a market timer. You should invest with fund managers that are excellent stock pickers. Look for another fund.

10. 12b-1 funds typically levy a redemption charge, which usually declines over time until it disappears in about 4-6 years. Annual 12b-1 charges are also deducted from the fund's net asset value. If the redemption charge is particularly stiff, move on to the next fund, as the fees will hamper 12-18-month results.

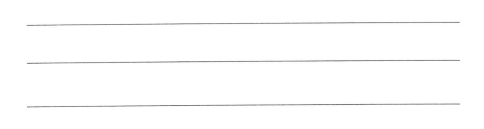

GLOSSARY

Agency Trade. When the broker buys or sells a stock from a specialist or market maker on behalf of the client.

Annual Report. A document issued each year by publicly traded companies that summarizes key financial data and discusses the company's business in detail.

Arithmetic Charts. Charts on stocks and the market that use the same actual distance between price intervals.

Ask Price. The lowest price at which a stock is currently offered for sale.

Asset. Property owned by a company including cash, inventory, plant, and equipment.

Asset Allocation. Diversifying your assets among a variety of different classes of investments according to your financial goals and tolerance for risk.

Balance Sheet. A statement that shows the financial condition of a company at a particular date. It includes a company's assets, liabilities, and stockholders' equity.

Base Building. Sideways movement in a stock following a decline in its value.

Bear Market. A severe decline in the overall stock market which usually takes 20% or more off the popular averages.

Benchmark. Using a market index or group of stocks as a means of measuring portfolio performance.

Bid. Highest price at which buy orders currently ~xist for a stock.

Block. A large buy or sell of stock that is done together at once, usually consisting of 1,000 or more shares.

Blue Chip. Large, well-established companies that are valued for their safety and income.

Bonds. Securities of indebtedness issued by a corporation that have a maturity date of more than a year. Bonds usually pay interest semiannually, and a principal is due on a specific date.

Book Value. Stockholders' equity divided by the total shares outstanding.

Break Out. A move by a stock or market index above or below an established trading range.

Bull Market. A long-term uptrend in the overall stock market that usually lasts several years.

Buy And Hold. An investment approach that emphasizes buying fundamentally sound companies for long-term gains.

Buy Signal. A technical indication that it's time to buy a stock or invest in the stock market in general.

Capital Gains Distribution. A cash payment made annually to the owners of a mutual fund from the profits earned on the sale of stocks.

Capitalization. The sum total of all of the funds that have been invested in a company. This includes retained earnings, equity capital, and long-term debt.

Cash. The amount of funds that are liquid and available at any given time. This would include cash and cash equivalents, such as money markets and short-term T-Bills.

Commission. Amount paid to a broker for executing a transaction.

Comparisons. Quarterly and annual sales and earnings are compared to similar periods of a year ago as part of the analysis of a company's performance.

Compound Returns. The growth of capital over a long time at various rates of gain.

Consolidation. A stock that is undergoing a decline or sideways movement following a significant rise in price.

Constant Dollars. Eliminating the effects of inflation when measuring investment returns or growth in Gross Domestic Product.

Contrary Opinion. The tactic of going against the prevailing sentiment of investors, particularly at important market bottoms.

Correction. A declining trend in stock prices that usually occurs within the context of a long-term bull market. The popular averages will typically lose 7%-15% during a correction.

Current Assets. Cash or other assets of a company that are expected to be converted to cash within the next year.

Current Liabilities. Obligations that will be paid within the next year including notes payable, accounts payable, and that portion of long-term debt coming due within the next twelve months.

Current Ratio. A measurement of a company's short-term financial condition. The ratio is calculated by dividing a company's current assets by their current liabilities.

Cyclical Business. A company whose business tends to be significantly impacted by shifts in the economy.

Debt. The long-term and short-term obligations of a company.

Debt To Equity Ratio. A measurement of the long-term financial strength of a company. It compares a company's equity to its level of long-term indebtedness.

Depression. An extremely severe and prolonged decline in economic activity lasting several years.

Dilution. The impact of an increase in a company's shares outstanding on earnings and earnings per share.

Discount Multiple. A stock with a price/earnings ratio below its industry average and/or the multiple of the market.

Discount Rate. The interest rate that the Federal Reserve charges the banks to borrow money from them.

Distributional Top. A topping formation in a stock that takes a long time in developing as the stock trades in a fairly narrow range.

Diversification. A technique for lowering portfolio risk by buying a number of stocks in a number of unrelated industries.

Dividend. A cash payment made to stockholders of a company on a quarterly basis. It serves for many as an important source of income.

Dollar Cost Averaging. Purchasing stock at differing prices, the technique is often employed by buying stock after it has declined to create a lower average cost than the amount paid on the original purchase.

Double Bottom. A chart pattern that suggests that a stock is ready to reverse a declining trend. It features two low points at approximately the same level that are separated by a few weeks or months.

Double Top. A chart pattern that suggests that a stock is ready to begin declining. It is characterized by two peaks at about the same level that are separated by a few weeks or months.

Downtick. A downward change in a stock's price from the previous trade.

Earnings. The total profit earned by a company after all expenses (also known as net earnings).

Earnings Per Share. The net earnings of a company divided by the total shares outstanding.

Expansion. A period when the economy (as measured by Gross Domestic Product) is growing.

Fairly Valued. A company whose current stock price is closely aligned to the actual value of the company.

Float. The total number of shares outstanding minus those that are owned by insiders and others that are not likely to sell at anytime in the near future.

Floor Broker. Buys and sells stocks while acting as an agent for a brokerage.

Fundamentals. Evaluate a stock by examining a company's fundamentals, which include earnings, sales, return on equity, quality of management, etc.

Good Till Canceled. A type of limit order which remains in effect for up to several months before it needs to be renewed if it hasn't yet been filled.

Gross Domestic Product. A measurement of the total domestic economic output of the nation.

Head And Shoulders Top. A chart pattern formed by a series of three tops that indicate a stock is about to enter into a decline.

Inflation. An economic measurement that gives the rate of increase in the price of all goods and services.

Insiders. Corporate officers and directors who may own a significant number of shares of a company and be privileged to important information on developments at the company.

Institutions. A segment of big money investors that would include banks, insurance companies, pension funds, and mutual funds. They usually buy and sell large blocks of stocks.

Interest Income. The money received periodically from loaning funds to places such as banks, companies, and the government.

Investor Sentiment. A number of indicators are available that measure the prevailing or dominant mood of the majority of investors at any given time.

Investors. Those who buy stocks for long-term profits.

Large Capitalization. Companies that have a substantial amount invested in them, considered as perhaps the nation's five hundred largest publicly traded companies.

Limit Order. An order that specifies a specific price a stock will be bought or sold at. Limit orders to buy are always below the market, limit orders to sell are always above the current price.

Liquidity. Refers to the ease or difficulty with which a stock can be bought or sold at, or reasonably close to, the current quote.

Load Fund. A mutual fund that imposes an upfront sales charge to purchase shares of the fund.

Long-Term Debt. Liabilities of the company that will come due after the next twelve months.

Margin Account. A brokerage account that allows an investor to buy securities without putting up the entire purchase price. Initial margin requirements are 50%.

Markdown. The amount by which a principaled trade is reduced from the actual selling price. It acts, in effect, as a commission for the brokerage that sold the stock.

Market Maker. A trader at a brokerage who stands ready to buy or sell shares of a designated OTC stock.

Market Multiple. The price/earnings multiple of a specific stock market index such as the S&P 500 or Dow Industrials.

Market Order. The most commonly used order that sells or buys a stock as quickly as possible at the best available price.

Market Timing. An investment approach whose success depends on buying stocks near market bottoms and selling stocks near market tops.

Markup. The amount by which a principaled trade is increased from the actual buying price. The markup acts, in effect, as a commission for the brokerage that bought the stock.

Maturity Date. The exact time at which debt issued by a company, or funds that they have borrowed, is due and payable.

Mission Statement. A brief message presented by a company (typically in their annual report) that tells investors what the company's long-term goals are.

Moving Average. The average closing price for a stock or market index over a specific period of time. Each day or week the latest price is figured into the average, while the oldest price is dropped.

Mutual Fund. An open-end investment company that buys and sells securities and manages the investments on behalf of the fund's shareholders.

Net Asset Value. The total value of a mutual fund portfolio divided by the total number of shares outstanding in the fund. Also known as NAV.

No-Load Fund. A mutual fund that does not levy a charge to either buy or sell shares of the fund.

Odd-Lot. An amount of stock to be purchased or sold that totals from 1 to 99 shares.

Overvalued. A stock that, from a fundamental perspective, appears to be selling for more than it's worth.

Overweight. A portfolio strategy that calls for putting significantly more money in a specific stock (or industry) than is invested in the average stock (or industry) in the portfolio.

Payout Ratio. The percentage that a company's dividend represents in relation to its net income.

Penny Stock. A very speculative and risky stock that usually trades for well under $1 per share.

Portfolio. The sum total and listing of an investor's current holdings.

Premium Multiple. A stock that is selling at a P/E in excess of its industry average and/or the market multiple.

Pretax Income. The amount a company earns net of all costs except for taxes.

Pretax Margin. The percentage of profit that a company earns on all revenues before taxes are paid.

Price/Earnings Ratio. Known as the P/E ratio, it measures how much a stock is selling for relative to $1 of earnings. P/E's are calculated by dividing the current price of the stock by the company's earnings over the latest reported twelve month period.

Prime Rate. The rate of interest that the banks charge their most credit-worthy customers.

Principal Trade. A transaction whereby the investor buys stock from the inventory of his firm's market maker, or whereby the market maker purchases the customer's stock for his own inventory.

Profit Margin. The percentage of profit earned by a company on all revenues after taxes have been paid.

Prospectus. A document that is issued by a corporation when it seeks to raise money. The prospectus gives details on the company, including the use of proceeds, the background of management, and the history of the company. Mutual funds also issue a prospectus to potential investors that gives details on the fund's objectives and costs of investing in the fund.

Quarterly Report. A summary of the most recent three months' activity within a company. It covers basic financial data and usually has a letter from the CEO explaining how the company is doing.

Quick Ratio. The most stringent measure of a company's short-term financial condition. The quick ratio is calculated by dividing cash and cash equivalents by current liabilities.

Real Rate Of Return. The net return on investment after subtracting taxes and compensating for inflation.

Recession. A periodic slowing of economic activity, usually thought of as two or more successive quarters of negative growth in the economy.

Recurring Revenue. Sources of income that a company can reasonably rely on year after year. Recurring revenue generally comes from service-oriented businesses.

Resistance. An area where a stock has come under selling pressure, which has acted as a barrier to further upward movement.

Restricted Stock. Shares of a company's stock that can't be immediately sold. Restricted stock may include shares held by officers and directors of the company as well as shares issued in a private placement.

Retained Earnings. The after tax or net income of a company that they retain (as opposed to paying it out as a dividend) for corporate purposes, such as investing to help the company grow.

Return On Equity. The rate of return earned on the stockholders' equity. ROE is calculated by dividing net income by stockholders' equity (or average stockholders' equity).

Round Lot. An order to buy or sell stock in even multiples of 100.

Seasonality. The tendency for a business to be stronger during certain times of the year than others.

Sell Signal. A technical indication that it is time to sell a stock or exit from the market in general.

Semi-Logarithmic Charts. The magnitude of stock or index fluctuations are shown to be equal by percentage movements.

Shares Outstanding. The total number of authorized and issued shares.

Short Sale. Technique for profiting from the decline in a stock's price. Shares are borrowed and then sold. The short seller aims to eventually buy the shares back at a lower price, thus covering his short position at a profit.

Small Capitalization. Companies that have a comparatively small amount invested in them.

Specialist. A member of a listed exchange who buys and sells shares of a designated stock, and whose job it is to maintain a continuous and orderly market in a stock.

Sponsorship. The following that develops for a stock as evidenced by brokerage reports and institutional investors taking a position in the stock.

Spread. The difference between the bid and ask price of a specific stock.

Stair Step. A chart pattern that shows a stock's upward movement in price to be similar in nature to a flight of stairs. Each advance in price tends to be straight up, followed by a sideways correction before the next move to higher highs.

Steady Riser. A chart pattern that demonstrates a stock's steady and persistent advance to new highs.

Stockholders' Equity. The total of the stockholders' net worth, or ownership in a company. Stockholders' equity is calculated by subtracting a company's liabilities from its assets.

Stock Split. The creation of more shares of a company's stock at a lesser price. A stock split does not change the value of an investor's position. (Note: a reverse split results in less shares at a correspondingly higher price).

Stop Orders. An order to sell stock that is placed below the prevailing price. It becomes a market order when the stock trades at the stop price. Stop orders are often used to protect profits or to prevent large losses.

Tax Deferral. An investment strategy that postpones the payment of taxes. Included would be tax-deferred accounts and long-term stock positions.

Tax Loss Selling. Selling losing stocks to take advantage of the tax deduction.

Technical Analysis. The study of chart patterns, a variety of indicators of market direction, and psychology to determine when to enter and exit individual issues and the market.

Technician. One who uses technical analysis as the basis of the investment decision-making process.

10-K. A very detailed description of a company's annual performance. It also contains background information on the company.

10-Q. A detailed discussion of a company's quarterly results.

Trader. Someone who invests primarily for short-term profits.

Turnover Ratio. Measures the amount by which the securities in a portfolio are bought and sold annually. A low ratio indicates a buy and hold approach. A high ratio shows an orientation toward trading.

12b-1 Fund. A mutual fund that charges an annual fee used to pay for the commissions paid to brokers who sell the fund. 12b-1 funds typically levy a declining sales charge to exit the fund.

Undervalued. A stock that, from a fundamental perspective, appears to be selling for less than what it's worth.

Underweight. A portfolio strategy that calls for investing less money in a particular stock (or industry) than is invested in the average stock (or industry) in the portfolio.

Uptick. An upward change in a stock price from the previous trade.

Volume. The amount of trading taking place in a stock.

Wall Street. An actual street in New York City, it refers to the major exchanges where stocks trade.

Warrants. A certificate that gives the owner the right to purchase shares of stock at a specified price, and often within a predetermined time frame.

Wash Sale. The sale and repurchase of a losing stock within thirty days. A wash sale will disallow a loss for tax purposes.

Waterfall Decline. A decline in the market that sends stock prices heading straight downhill. Declines such as this often come at the end of the bear market.

INDEX

Rich Poliquin

ABOUT THE AUTHOR

Philip B. Capelle graduated from the University of California at Berkeley with a B.S. in Business Administration. He has served as the editor of a stock market advisory service. Since 1981, Mr. Capelle has been working with both individual and corporate investors. Mr. Capelle specializes in small company growth stocks with Cruttenden and Company in Irvine, California.

Mr. Capelle has written several publications on investing in the stock market. Included among these are his cassette "Investment Outlook For the 1990's," which outlines his bullish stance for the decade. He is a financial columnist for the *Orange County Business Journal* and has published interviews with a number of corporate executives. He currently resides in Huntington Beach, California.

For further information on the services rendered by Mr. Capelle, he can be reached at:

Cruttenden Company
18301 Von Karmen, Suite 100
Irvine, CA 92715

Phone: (714) 757-5700
Phone: (800) 678-9147

About the Publisher

PROBUS PUBLISHING COMPANY

Probus Publishing Company fills the informational needs of today's business professional by publishing authoritative, quality books on timely and relevant topics, including:

- Investing
- Futures/Options Trading
- Banking
- Finance
- Marketing and Sales
- Manufacturing and Project Management
- Personal Finance, Real Estate, Insurance and Estate Planning
- Entrepreneurship
- Management

Probus books are available at quantity discounts when purchased for business, educational or sales promotional use. For more information, please call the Director, Corporate/Institutional Sales at 1-800-PROBUS-1, or write:

Director, Corporate/Institutional Sales
Probus Publishing Company
1925 N. Clybourn Avenue
Chicago, Illinois 60614
FAX (312) 868-6250

Additional Titles in
The Investor's Self-Teaching Seminars Series
Available from Probus Publishing